365 Ultimate Vegetable Side Dish Recipes

(365 Ultimate Vegetable Side Dish Recipes - Volume 1)

Nina Petty

Content

CHAPTER 1: BRUSSELS SPROUT RECIPES..9

1. BRAISED BRUSSELS SPROUTS WITH PEPPERS Recipe 9
2. Bacon And Brussel Sprout Salad Recipe.....9
3. Bacon Bits Amp Brussels Sprouts Recipe 10
4. Bacon Roasted Brussel Sprouts Recipe.....10
5. Bacon Tossed Brussels Sprouts Recipe.....10
6. Bacon, Brussels Spout And Potato Hash Recipe 11
7. Baked Brussel Sprouts Recipe...................11
8. Baked Brussels Sprouts Recipe 11
9. Balsamic Glazed Brussels Sprouts With Pancetta Recipe 12
10. Balsamic Maple Brussels Sprouts And Cauliflower Recipe 12
11. Balsamic Roaster Brussel Sprouts Recipe . 13
12. Best Brussel Sprouts Ever Recipe 13
13. Best Brussels Sprouts Ever Recipe 14
14. Braised Brussels Sprouts With Bacon And Chestnuts Recipe 14
15. Breaded Brussels Sprouts Recipe 15
16. Broasted Brussels Sprouts Recipe 15
17. Brussel Sprout Goodness Recipe 15
18. Brussel Sprout Hash With Carmelized Shallots Recipe 16
19. Brussel Sprout Casserole For Ragdolly Recipe 16
20. Brussel Sprouts Gratin Recipe 16
21. Brussel Sprouts Hash Recipe 17
22. Brussel Sprouts Hey They Arent So Bad After All Recipe 17
23. Brussel Sprouts Nancys Way Recipe 18
24. Brussel Sprouts Recipe 18
25. Brussel Sprouts Sauteed In Garlic Recipe 18
26. Brussel Sprouts With Bacon Horseradish Cream Recipe 19
27. Brussel Sprouts With Chorizo Recipe 19
28. Brussel Sprouts With Pancetta And Rosemary Recipe 19
29. Brussel Sprouts And Chestnuts Recipe.....20
30. Brussel Sprouts And Tomato Recipe 20
31. Brussel Sprouts With Apricot And Pistachios Recipe 21
32. Brussel Sprouts With Beer Recipe.............21
33. Brussel Sprouts With Garlic Recipe 21
34. Brussel Sprouts With Panchetta Balsamic Recipe................................22
35. Brussel Sprouts With Pecan Butter Recipe 22
36. Brussel Sprouts With Sour CreamHorseradish And Bacon Recipe 22
37. Brussel Sprouts With Bacon Blue Cheese And Spiced Walnuts Recipe 22
38. Brussel Sprouts In Cream Sherry Bacon Sauce Recipe 23
39. Brussels Sprout With Caramelized Onion And Dried Cranberry Recipe 24
40. Brussels Sprouts And Cream Recipe..........24
41. Brussels Sprouts In Garlic Butter Recipe..25
42. Brussels Sprouts In Lemon Cream Recipe25
43. Brussels Sprouts In Lemon Juice Recipe ..26
44. Brussels Sprouts Prince Albert Which Is A La Mornay Recipe 26
45. Brussels Sprouts With A Balsamic And Brown Butter Sauce Recipe 26
46. Brussels Sprouts With Bacon Recipe 27
47. Brussels Sprouts With Caraway Cheese Sauce Recipe 27
48. Brussels Sprouts With Chipotle Butter Recipe................................27
49. Brussels Sprouts With Pancetta Recipe 28
50. Brussels Sprouts With Walnuts Recipe......28
51. Brussels Sprouts Au Gratin Recipe 29
52. Brussels Sprouts With Balsamic Vinegar Recipe................................29
53. Brussels Sprouts With Marjoram And Pine Nuts Recipe................................30
54. Brussels Sprouts With Mustard Viniagrette Recipe................................30
55. Brussels Sprouts With Pancetta Recipe 30
56. Brussels Sprouts With Smoky Onions On Cheddar Toast Recipe................................31
57. Brussels Sprouts With Walnuts Bacon And Blue Cheese Recipe 31
58. Brussels Sprouts With Walnuts And Mandarin Oranges Recipe................................32
59. Buttah And Fried Onions Brussel Sprouts Recipe................................32
60. Caramelized Brussels Sprouts Pearl Onions

Shallots And Bacon Recipe.................................33
61.   Carrots And Brussel Sprouts Recipe 33
62.   Cauliflower And Brussels Sprout Gratin With Pine Nut And Breadcrumb Topping Recipe 33
63.   Cheesey Gratin Of Brussels Sprouts Recipe 34
64.   Cider Roasted Brussels Sprouts And Carrots Recipe 35
65.   Cider Glazed Brussels Sprouts With Bacon & Almonds Recipe 35
66.   Creamy Vegetable Casserole 35
67.   Crispy Brussel Sprouts Recipe 36
68.   Crispy Brussels Sprouts Recipe.................36
69.   Crunchy Brussels Sprouts Recipe.............36
70.   Decadent Cream Braised Brussels Sprouts Recipe 37
71.   Dijon Brussel Sprouts Recipe 37
72.   Dill Marinated Brussels Sprouts Recipe 38
73.   Easy Lime Shredded Brussels Sprouts Recipe 38
74.   Fall Spiced Roasted Brussel Sprouts Recipe 38
75.   Fried Brussel Sprouts Recipe 39
76.   GLAZED BRUSSELS SPROUTS Recipe 39
77.   Garlic Balsamic Roasted Brussel Sprouts Recipe 39
78.   Grilled Brussel Sprouts Recipe 39
79.   Grilled Brussel Sprouts And Potatoes Recipe 40
80.   Holiday Brussel Sprouts And Purple Potatoes Recipe..40
81.   Holiday Sides: Roasted Brussels Sprouts With Dijon Cream Sauce Recipe 40
82.   Jasmines Brussels Sprouts Recipe 41
83.   Jo_jo_ba's Brussells Sprouts Recipe 41
84.   Kielbasa With Brussels Sprouts Recipe.....41
85.   Lemon Parmesan Toasted Almond Brussels Sprouts Recipe 42
86.   Lemony Sprouts And Shoots Recipe.........42
87.   Lemony Sweet Brussels Recipe..................42
88.   Marinated Brussels Sprouts Recipe 43
89.   Miso Roasted Brussels Sprouts Recipe......43
90.   Mrs Claus Brussels Sprouts With Bacon And Onion Recipe 44
91.   Mustard Brussel Sprouts Recipe................44
92.   Orange Kissed Brussels Sprouts Recipe....45
93.   Pan Fried Brussel Sprouts Recipe..............45
94.   Pan Browned Brussel Sprouts Recipe........45
95.   Pasta With Brussel Sprouts Recipe............46
96.   ROASTED BRUSSEL SPROUTS WITH POTATOES BACON Recipe 46
97.   Red Grapes With Brussel Sprouts Recipe.46
98.   Roasted Brussel Sprouts Recipe.................47
99.   Roasted Brussels Sprouts And Sweet Potatoes Recipe 47
100.   Roasted Brussels Sprouts Recipe 48
101.   Roasted Brussels Sprouts With Dijon Cream Sauce Recipe 48
102.   Roasted Brussels Sprouts With Garlic Recipe..48
103.   Roasted Brussels Sprouts With Walnuts Recipe..49
104.   Roasted Brussels Sprouts With Cranberries Recipe..49
105.   Roasted Maple Dijon Brussel Sprouts Recipe..50
106.   Saucy Brussels Sprouts Recipe 50
107.   Sauteed Brussels Sprouts With Onions And Lemon Zest Recipe 50
108.   Sauteed Corn And Brussel Sprouts Recipe 51
109.   Scalloped Brussel Sprouts Recipe 51
110.   Sesame Brussels Sprouts Recipe 52
111.   Shreaded Brussel Sprouts With Bacon Recipe..52
112.   Shredded Brussels Sprouts Recipe 52
113.   Skillet Braised Brussels Sprouts Recipe 53
114.   So Good They Cant Be Brussel Sprouts Recipe..53
115.   Southern Style Brussel Sprouts Recipe......53
116.   Spicy Fried Brussels Sprouts Recipe 54
117.   Sports Illustrated Brussels Sprouts Recipe 54
118.   Surprisingly Delicious Brussel Sprouts Recipe..55
119.   Totally Awesome Brussel Sprouts Recipe.55
120.   Whuebel And ChefMeows Marinated Brussel Sprouts Recipe 55
121.   Brussel Sprouts On A Skewer Recipe........56
122.   Brussels Sprouts With Shallot And Capers Recipe..56
123.   煎烤的球芽甘蓝 Chinese Style Brussel

Sprouts Recipe 57

CHAPTER 2: AWESOME VEGETABLE SIDE DISH RECIPES................................ 57

124. 1015 ONION RINGS Recipe 57
125. African Spinach Recipe 57
126. Amaretto Carrots Recipe 58
127. Artichoke Pilaf Recipe......................... 58
128. Artichoke Tart Recipe 58
129. Asian Cole Slaw Recipe 59
130. Asian Sesame Grilled Asparagus Recipe ... 59
131. Asian Slaw Recipe 60
132. Asparagus And Parmesan Foldovers Recipe 60
133. Asparagus And Toasted Pine Nuts With Lemon Vinaigrette Recipe 60
134. Asparagus Artichoke And Shitake Risotto Recipe 61
135. Asparagus Au Gratin Recipe 62
136. Asparagus Casserole Recipe 62
137. Asparagus On The Grill Recipe 62
138. Asparagus Parmesan Recipe 63
139. Asparagus Squares Recipe 63
140. Asparagus Strudel Recipe...................... 63
141. Asparagus And Irish Cheese Gratin Recipe 64
142. Asparagus With Blue Cheese Recipe 65
143. Asparagus With Lemon Butter Recipe 65
144. Avocado And Corn Salsa Recipe 65
145. BAKED MEDITERRANEAN VEGETABLES Recipe.............................. 65
146. Bacon Wrapped Grilled Corn On The Cob Recipe 66
147. Bacon Wrapped Asparagus Recipe 66
148. Baked Artichokes And Tomatoes Recipe . 67
149. Baked Avocado Vinaigrette Recipe.......... 67
150. Baked Breaded Eggplant Slices Recipe 67
151. Baked Carrot Fries Recipe 68
152. Baked Carrots Recipe 68
153. Baked Spinach Casserole Recipe 68
154. Baked Stuffed Avocado Recipe 69
155. Baked Stuffed Vidalia Onions Recipe 69
156. Baked Tomatoes Stuffed With Cheesy Potatoes Recipe.................................... 69
157. Balsamic Vinegar Glazed Vegetables Recipe 70
158. Barley Mushroom Bake Recipe................. 70

159. Beekeepers Cabbage Recipe 71
160. Beer Braised Cabbage Recipe 71
161. Beet With Orange Puree Recipe 72
162. Beets Roasted In Wine Recipe 72
163. Beets With Maple Syrup Recipe 72
164. Beets With Mushrooms Recipe................... 72
165. Black Bean Salad With Couscous Recipe ..73
166. Black Beans And Rice Recipe................... 73
167. Black Eyed Pea Salad Recipe 73
168. Bok Choy Apple Slaw Recipe 74
169. Bourbon Baked Beans Recipe 74
170. Braised Cauliflower With Anchovies Garlic And White Wine Recipe 74
171. Braised Eggplants Recipe 75
172. Braised Greens And Garlic Recipe.............75
173. Braised Kale Recipe 76
174. Braised Red Cabbage With Apple And Onion Recipe 76
175. Broccoli Rice Casserole Recipe 76
176. Broccoli Cream Cheese Casserole Recipe .76
177. Broccoli Deluxe Recipe 77
178. Broccoli For Garlic And Almond Lovers Recipe 77
179. Broccoli Salad Recipe............................78
180. Buffalo Chili Onions Recipe.....................78
181. Butterbeans Bacon And Tomatoes Recipe 78
182. CABBAGE ON THE GRILL Recipe 79
183. CAMPFIRE POTATOES Recipe 79
184. COLLARD GREENS Recipe 79
185. CREAMED GREEN BEANS Recipe 80
186. Cabbage Smothered And Southern Recipe 80
187. Cabbage Torta Recipe.............................81
188. California Spinach Casserole Recipe 81
189. Candied Carrots Recipe 81
190. Candied Pickled Baby Beets Recipe 82
191. Carrots Souffle Recipe 82
192. Cauliflower With Bacon And Cheese Sauce Recipe..82
193. Charcoal Roasted Beets And Red Onions Recipe...83
194. Cherry Tomato And Zucchini Saute With Basil And Pine Nuts Recipe 83
195. Chinese Restaurant Style Sauteed Green Beans Recipe.......................................84
196. Chipotle Glazed Vegetable Kebabs Recipe

84

197. Cider Glazed Roots With Cinnamon Walnuts Recipe 85
198. Collard Greens Recipe.................................86
199. Colourful Veggies With Serious Kick Recipe 86
200. Corn Pudding 11 Recipe 86
201. Cranberry Coleslaw Anthonys Home Port Seattle Recipe 87
202. Creamed Corn With Bacon And Blue Cheese Recipe 87
203. Creamed Peas Recipe.....................88
204. Crockpot Stewed Tomatoes Recipe...........88
205. Dads Style BBQ Corn Recipe 88
206. Dans Fried Green Tomatoes Recipe 89
207. Delicious Creamed Cabbage With Bacon Recipe 89
208. Delicious Onion Rings Recipe................89
209. Double Broccoli Quinoa Recipe 90
210. Easy Easy Country Corn Casserole Recipe 91
211. Easy Easy Greek Style Green Beans Recipe 91
212. Easy Pesto Cauliflower Recipe 92
213. Easy N Delicious Country Onion Casserole Recipe 92
214. Eggplant Al Fresco Recipe 92
215. Eggplant Deluxe Casserole Recipe 93
216. Eggplant Fans Recipe 93
217. Eggplant Fingers Recipe 94
218. Elaines Pepper Stir Fry Recipe 94
219. Elaines Roasted Onions Recipe................94
220. FRIED GREEN TOMATOES Recipe....95
221. Fiery Hot Green Beans Recipe 95
222. Fontina Aparagus Bake Recipe 95
223. Fresh Sweet Corn Cakes Recipe................96
224. Fried Corn Tennessee Style Recipe...........97
225. GARLICKY BRAISED KALE WITH SUN DRIED TOMATOES Recipe...............97
226. GERMAN SWEET AND SOUR RED CABBAGE Recipe........................98
227. GUACAPICO AKA PICO DE GALLO WITH AVOCADO Recipe.......................98
228. Garden Casserole Recipe 98
229. Garden Zucchini Gratin Recipe 99
230. Garlic Asparagus And Pasta With Lemon Cream Recipe 99

231. Garlic Butter Green Beans Ci Recipe 99
232. Garlic Sesame Kale Recipe 100
233. German Onion Cake Recipe 100
234. German Red Cabbage Recipe 101
235. Ginger Carrots Recipe 101
236. Glazed Carrots Recipe 101
237. Greek Tomatoes Recipe 102
238. Greek Zucchini Patties Recipe 102
239. Green Bean Casserole Recipe...................102
240. Green Bean Salad Recipe 103
241. Green Bean And Mushroom Casserole Recipe 103
242. Green Beans With Red Peppers And Garlic Recipe...............................104
243. Green Tomato Casserole Recipe 104
244. Grilled Cabbage Recipe 104
245. Grilled Corn With Ancho Avocado Butter Recipe 105
246. Grilled Romaine Lettuce Recipe 105
247. Grilled Veggies With Basil Mayonnaise Recipe...............................105
248. Guacamole Full On No Holds Barred Recipe 106
249. Guacamole With Roasted Corn And Chipotle In Adobo Sauce Recipe......................106
250. Guinness Battered Onion Rings Recipe. 107
251. Harvard Beets Recipe 107
252. Hashbrown Casserole Recipe 108
253. Healthy Oven Fried Vegetables Recipe.. 108
254. Heart Healthy N Hearty Layered Broccoli Salad Recipe 109
255. Heart Healthy Pumpkin And Black Bean Soup Recipe 109
256. Herb Stuffed Tomatoes Recipe 109
257. Holiday Vegetable And Hass Avocado Saute Recipe 110
258. Honey Baked Squash Recipe 110
259. Honey Roasted Beets Recipe 111
260. Honey Dijon Glazed Baby Carrots Recipe 111
261. Hop In John Recipe 111
262. Imam Bayildi Recipe 112
263. Italian Kabobs Recipe 112
264. Italian Stuffed Zucchini Recipe...............113
265. Janets Zucchini Surprise Recipe.............113
266. Judys Mediterranean Quinoa Salad Recipe 114

267. Lanas Accidental Healthy Vegan Ginger Stir Fry 114
268. Lanas Southern Style Beer Batter Onion Rings Recipe 115
269. Lemon Glazed Carrots Recipe 115
270. Lovely Black Bean And Corn Salad Recipe 116
271. Mandarin Coleslaw Recipe 116
272. Maple Glazed Baby Carrots Recipe 116
273. Maple Glazed Carrots Recipe 117
274. Marinaded Roasted Asparagus With Garlic Recipe 117
275. Marinated Grilled Corn With Chili Avocado Butter Recipe 117
276. Mexican Coleslaw Recipe..........................118
277. Mushroom Asparagus And Artichoke Salad Recipe 118
278. Mushroom Pancakes In Cheese Sauce Recipe 119
279. My Famous Green Beans Recipe 119
280. New Age Green Bean Casserole Recipe .120
281. ORANGE GLAZED CARROTS WITH CRANBERRYS Recipe 120
282. Oklahoma Joes Smoked Cabbage Recipe 121
283. Oven Fried Zucchini Sticks Recipe 121
284. Oven Fried Zucchini In A Crunchy Parmesan Crust Recipe....................................121
285. Pa Dutch Old Fashioned Green Beans And Bacon Recipe 122
286. Pan Fried Cabbage Recipe 122
287. Paneer Butter Masala Recipe 123
288. Papas Potato Cabbage Casserole Recipe.123
289. Pinto Beans Recipe 123
290. Poached Eggs With Roasted Asparagus And Truffle Oil Recipe.............................124
291. Pumpkin Fritters With Caramel Sauce Recipe 124
292. Quick N Tasty Carrot Casserole Recipe .125
293. Rapini With Garlic N Anchovies Recipe 125
294. Ratatouille My Way Recipe 126
295. Ratatouille Not The Movie Recipe...........127
296. Red Beans And Rice New Orleans Meat And Vegetarian Recipe 127
297. Red Beans And Rice Recipe 128
298. Red Cabbage Recipe 128
299. Red Lentil Patties Vegetarian Meatballs Recipe.. 129
300. Refrigerator Pickled Beets And Onions Recipe.. 129
301. Remys Ratatouille Recipe 130
302. Roasted Asparagus Recipe 131
303. Roasted Asparagus With Balsamic Browned Butter Recipe 131
304. Roasted Beets Recipe 132
305. Roasted Corn Salad Recipe 132
306. Roasted Green Beans Recipe 132
307. Roasted Herb Tomatoes Recipe 133
308. Roasted Root Vegetables Recipe 133
309. Roasted Shallots And Tomatoes Recipe. 133
310. Roasted Vegetables Recipe 134
311. Roasted Winter Vegetables Recipe......... 134
312. Romaine Grilled Avocado And Smoky Corn Salad With Chipotle Caesar Dressing Recipe 135
313. Root Vegetables Casserole Recipe.......... 135
314. Rotkraut Red Cabbage Recipe.................. 136
315. Ruths Chris Sweet Potato Casserole Recipe 136
316. SOUTHERN SPINACH Recipe 136
317. Samhain Mushroom Casserole Recipe.... 137
318. Sauted Green Beans With Smoked Paprika And Almonds Recipe 137
319. Sauteed Asparagus And Mushrooms Recipe 138
320. Sauteed Asparagus And Mushrooms In A Lemon Thyme Butter Recipe 138
321. Savory Cabbage Seasoning Recipe 138
322. Savory Fresh Corn Fritters Recipe 139
323. Scalloped Cauliflower Recipe 139
324. Scalloped Eggplant Recipe....................... 140
325. Sensational Asparagus Roll Ups With Herb Cheese And Sun Dried Tomatoes Recipe 140
326. Skinny Potatoes Recipe 141
327. Smoked Bbq Beans Recipe 141
328. Some Of The Best Green Beans Recipe 142
329. Southern Asparagus Casserole Recipe 142
330. Southern Collard Greens Theyre Not Just For New Years Anymore Recipe 142
331. Southern Collards Recipe.......................... 143
332. Southern Corn Pudding Recipe 143
333. Southern Fried Cream And Butter Corn Recipe.. 143
334. Southern Fried Okra Recipe.................... 144

335. Southern Scalloped Tomatoes Recipe 144
336. Southern Smothered Green Beans Recipe 144
337. Southern Squash Casserole Recipe 145
338. Spicy Eggplant Recipe 145
339. Spiffy Spiced Roasted Carrots Recipe 146
340. Spinach Artichoke Gratin Recipe.............146
341. Spinach And Artichoke Au Gratin Recipe 147
342. Spinach With Chickpeas And Peppers Recipe 147
343. Squash Casserole Country Style Recipe ..147
344. Squash With Dill Tejfeles Tokfozelek Recipe 148
345. Stir Fried Asparagus With Ginger Garlic And Basil Recipe......................................148
346. Stir Fried Cabbage Recipe........................149
347. Stir Fried Eggplant Recipe.......................149
348. Stuffed Artichokes Recipe 150
349. Summer Eggplant Gratin Recipe 150
350. Super Spinach Casserole With Bleu Cheese Recipe 151
351. Thai Coleslaw Claim Jumper Recipe........152
352. Tomato Fritters Recipe 152
353. Vegetable Fried Rice Recipe.....................152
354. Veggie Jack Salad Recipe 153
355. Way Good Pinto Beans With Sausage Recipe 153
356. Wild N Wonderful Wine Poached Beets Recipe 153
357. Zucchini Boats With Corn Stuffing Recipe 154
358. Zucchini Fritters 1 Recipe 154
359. Zucchini Lace Fritters Recipe 155
360. Zucchini Parmesan Recipe 155
361. Zucchini Patties Recipe............................156
362. Zucchini Rice Casserole Recipe...............156
363. Zucchni Patties Recipe.............................157
364. Pan Fried Green Beans Recipe 157
365. South Of The Border Baked Cous Cous Recipe 157

INDEX..158

CONCLUSION...161

Chapter 1: Brussels Sprout Recipes

***

1. BRAISED BRUSSELS SPROUTS WITH PEPPERS Recipe

Serving: 4 | Prep: | Cook: 6mins |Ready in:

Ingredients

- 1 lb Brussels sprouts
- 1 tsp veg. oil
- 1/2 tsp caraway seeds
- 1/2 tsp mustard seeds
- 1 small jalepeno; seeded and minced
- 1/3 cup chicken broth
- 1 jar roasted red peppers; reised and finely chopped
- salt &pepper to taste

Direction

- Trim Brussels sprouts and slice each on in half vertically.
- Carve out the core of each half and slice the sprouts crosswise into shreds.
- In a non-stick skillet, heat oil over medium heat.
- Add caraway and mustard seeds and cook, stirring for 1 minute. Stir in broth.
- Stir in jalepenos and the sprouts and cook.
- Cover pan tightly and reduce heat to low and simmer for 3-5 minutes, or until sprouts are just tender.
- Stir in red peppers and season with salt &pepper.
- Serve immediately

2. Bacon And Brussel Sprout Salad Recipe

Serving: 6 | Prep: | Cook: 30mins |Ready in:

Ingredients

- °1 lemon
- °1 orange
- °1 large shallot, minced
- °1/2 cup olive oil
- °salt and pepper
- °6 slices cooked bacon, crumbled or chopped
- °4 dozen brussel sprouts
- °1 cup almonds
- °1 cup grated Pecorino-romano cheese

Direction

- 1. Cook and crumble the bacon.
- 2. Squeeze the juice of the lemon and orange into a large bowl with the shallots. Pour the oil into the bowl in a steady stream, whisking to form an emulsion (it should appear creamier and less transparent). Season generously with salt and pepper. Refrigerate until ready to use.
- 3. Using a mandoline, shave the Brussels sprouts (not including the stems) into thin slices to make a shredded/slaw texture. I rinsed and dried mine again after shaving them just to be sure they were totally clean.
- 4. Place the almonds in a food processor and pulse until chopped coarsely. Add 3/4 of the almonds, cheese, and bacon to the shredded Brussels sprouts; toss to combine. When ready to serve, toss with the dressing and sprinkle remaining almonds, cheese, and bacon over the top. If needed, add a few more tablespoons of olive oil and toss.
- Serving size: 10 servings Calories: 284 Fat: 22 grams Saturated fat: 4.5 grams Unsaturated fat: 17.5 grams Carbohydrates: 11 grams Sugar: 2 grams Fiber: 5 grams Protein: 11 grams Cholesterol: 11 grams

- Notes
- The serving size depends on how you are eating it. If it's for an entree sized portion, you'll get about 8-10 servings. If it's a side, it could be closer to 14. We served this on Mother's Day with eleven people and we had some left over.
- Keep in the fridge for 1-2 days.

3. Bacon Bits Amp Brussels Sprouts Recipe

Serving: 4 | Prep: | Cook: 30mins | Ready in:

Ingredients

- 1 lbs bag frozen Brussels sprouts
- 5 slices bacon, cooked and crumbled
- 2 tbsp extra-virgin olive oil
- .5 tsp garlic salt
- .25 tsp onion powder
- .25 tsp oregano

Direction

- Cook Brussels sprouts according to the directions on the package.
- Cook bacon and crumble.
- Put Brussels sprouts in serving dish and add all ingredients.
- Toss well and top with bacon crumbles.
- Makes 4 servings.

4. Bacon Roasted Brussel Sprouts Recipe

Serving: 4 | Prep: | Cook: 40mins | Ready in:

Ingredients

- 1 lb brussel sprouts
- 3 slices bacon,cut in 1/2" pieces

- 2 tsp packed brown sugar
- salt and black pepper

Direction

- Preheat oven to 400'. Trim ends from Brussels sprouts. Cut in half lengthwise.
- Combine Brussels sprouts, bacon and brown sugar in glass baking dish. Roast 25 to 30 mins or till golden brown, stirring once. Season with salt and pepper.

5. Bacon Tossed Brussels Sprouts Recipe

Serving: 2 | Prep: | Cook: 22mins | Ready in:

Ingredients

- 1 tablespoon plus 1/2 teaspoon salt
- 3 pints Brussels sprouts, stem ends trimmed
- --each halved lengthwise
- 8 strips thick-sliced bacon
- --cut crosswise into thin strips
- 1/2 cup chopped onion
- 1/2 teaspoon pepper
- 3 tablespoons white-wine vinegar (3 to 4 tbsps)
- 1 tablespoon unsalted butter

Direction

- Fill 6-quart Dutch oven with water; add 1 Tbsp. salt. Bring to a boil; add Brussels sprouts. Reduce heat to medium; cook 12 minutes, until crisp-tender. Drain; rinse under cold water to stop cooking.
- In large non-stick skillet over medium heat, cook bacon 5 minutes until slightly crisp. Pour off fat. Add onion to bacon in skillet; cook 5 minutes, until tender. Add sprouts, remaining salt and the pepper; heat through. Add vinegar and butter; cook, stirring, to melt butter. Serve.

6. Bacon, Brussels Spout And Potato Hash Recipe

Serving: 6 | Prep: | Cook: 40mins | Ready in:

Ingredients

- 2 Tablespoons extra-virgin olive oil
- 4 Slices Thick Cut bacon, chopped cross-wise into pieces
- 4 Sprigs Fresh thyme
- 2 Pints Brussels sprouts, cleaned and cut in 1/2
- 1 Pound fingerling potatoes, halved or quartered
- 1/2 Pound Pearl onions, peeled
- kosher salt and fresh cracked pepper
- 1/2 Cup low sodium chicken broth
- 2 Tablespoons balsamic vinegar
- 1/4 Bunch Flat-Leaf parsley, roughly chopped

Direction

- Chop bacon strips cross-wise into pieces
- Heat large skillet over medium heat with Olive Oil
- Add Bacon and Thyme Sprigs and render bacon until crisp
- Remove Bacon with a slotted spoon to a dish and reserve oil and grease in the skillet
- Toss in Brussels sprouts, Potatoes and Pearl Onions
- Salt and Pepper liberally
- Sauté without disturbing too much (turn once) until Sprouts and Potatoes are browned (about 10 minutes)
- Add Chicken Broth, deglaze pan and allow to steam veggies until most of the broth has evaporated (about 3 to 5 minutes)
- Add the Balsamic Vinegar and stir for a minute
- Toss in bacon and parsley and stir briefly
- Serve immediately

7. Baked Brussel Sprouts Recipe

Serving: 6 | Prep: | Cook: 35mins | Ready in:

Ingredients

- 1 1/2 pounds Brussels sprouts, trimmed and halved
- o 4 small red onions, cut into wedges
- o 2 tablespoons olive oil
- o 2 tablespoons chopped fresh rosemary leaves
- o 1 teaspoon kosher salt
- o 1/2 teaspoon freshly ground black pepper
- o 1 tablespoon apple cider vinegar

Direction

- Preheat oven to 425F.
- Toss Brussels sprouts and onions together with oil, rosemary, salt, and pepper, and arrange in 1 layer on 2 shallow baking sheets.
- Roast in middle of oven, stirring occasionally, until spouts are golden brown, about 20 minutes.
- Toss with cider vinegar and season with additional salt and pepper as desired.

8. Baked Brussels Sprouts Recipe

Serving: 4 | Prep: | Cook: 35mins | Ready in:

Ingredients

- 2 lbs. fresh brussel sprouts
- salt
- 1/2 cup bacon, diced
- 1 onion, chopped
- 1 1/2 cups sour cream
- 4 tps. bread crumbs
- 2 tps. butter

Direction

- Wash and trim Brussels sprouts and drop them into a large pot of boiling salted water. Boil, uncovered, for 10 minutes, then drain and rinse with cold water. Fry the bacon bits in a 3-qoaut saucepan until they render fat. Add the chopped onion and sauté until it turns translucent. Pour in 1/4 cup of warm water, scrape up any bits stuck to the bottom. Season with pepper and 1/4 tsp. of salt, simmer for 1 minute. Remove pan from heat.
- When sauce is cool enough to put a finger in, add the sour cream and blend thoroughly. Add the sprouts and turn carefully to coat every piece. Turn into a greased 3-quatr ovenproof casserole, sprinkle with bread crumbs, and dot with butter.
- Bake in a pre-heated 325F. oven for 20 minutes or until golden brown on top.

9. Balsamic Glazed Brussels Sprouts With Pancetta Recipe

Serving: 4 | Prep: | Cook: 30mins | Ready in:

Ingredients

- 2 oz. pancetta, cut into 1/4-inch dice (about 1/2 cup)
- 1 to 2 Tbs. extra-virgin olive oil
- 10 oz. Brussels sprouts (about 18 medium sprouts), trimmed and halved through the core
- 1/4 cup balsamic vinegar
- Freshly ground black pepper
- 2 Tbs. unsalted butter
- kosher salt

Direction

- In a heavy 10-inch straight-sided sauté pan set over medium- low heat, slowly cook the pancetta in 1 Tbs. of the oil until golden and crisp all over, 10 to 15 minutes.

- With a slotted spoon, transfer the pancetta to a plate lined with paper towels, leaving the fat behind.
- You should have about 2 Tbs. of fat in the pan; if not; add the remaining 1 Tbs. oil.
- Have ready 1/2 cup water.
- Put the pan over medium-high heat and arrange the sprouts cut side down in a single layer.
- Cook undisturbed until nicely browned, 2 to 3 minutes.
- When the sprouts are browned, add the water to the pan, cover immediately, and simmer until the sprouts are tender when poked with a fork or skewer, about 3 minutes.
- (If the water evaporates before the sprouts get tender, add more water, 1/4 cup at a time.) With a slotted spoon, transfer the sprouts to a plate.
- Return the pan to medium-high heat and if any water remains, let it boil off.
- Add the balsamic vinegar and a few grinds of pepper.
- Boil the vinegar until it's reduced to about 2 Tbs. and looks lightly syrupy, about 2 minutes.
- Reduce the heat to low, add the butter, and stir until melted.
- Return the sprouts and pancetta to the pan and swirl and shake the pan to evenly coat the sprouts with the sauce.
- Season to taste with salt and more pepper and serve.
- From Fine Cooking Magazine.

10. Balsamic Maple Brussels Sprouts And Cauliflower Recipe

Serving: 8 | Prep: | Cook: 30mins | Ready in:

Ingredients

- 1 pound Brussels sprouts, washed
- 1 pound cauliflower florets, washed and cut bite-size

- 1 large red onion, thickly sliced
- 2 tablespoons oil
- salt, to taste
- dash of black pepper
- pinch of granulated garlic or garlic salt
- 2 tablespoons balsamic vinegar
- 1/4 cup pure maple syrup

Direction

- 1. Bring a large pot of water to a rolling boil. Add Brussels sprouts to the boiling water, cover, and boil for 6-8 minutes, until Brussels sprouts are hot in the middle (don't overcook).
- 2. Add cauliflower florets to the Brussels sprouts in the pot, and cook for 3-4 minutes, just until cauliflower is starting to get tender. Drain water.
- 3. In a heavy skillet, sauté onions in oil over medium-high heat for about 2 minutes until slightly browned but still crisp.
- 4. Add the still-hot Brussels sprouts and cauliflower to skillet and cook and stir for a couple minutes. Season with salt, pepper, and garlic. Remove skillet from heat.
- 5. Pour vinegar and maple syrup over vegetables, tossing gently to coat. Serve hot in bowls.
- Leftovers are good cold, too!

11. Balsamic Roaster Brussel Sprouts Recipe

Serving: 4 | Prep: | Cook: 35mins | Ready in:

Ingredients

- 1/3 cup of balsamic vinegar
- 1/3 cup of extra virgin olive oil or coconut oil
- 2 garlic cloves, minced
- 1 tsp of oregano
- 1 tsp of basil
- 1 tsp of thyme
- 1 1/2 teaspoon of salt
- 1 teaspoon of pepper

- one bag of trimmed brussel sprouts

Direction

- Preheat the oven to 400 degrees. Cut each of the Brussels sprouts in half.
- In a large mixing bowl combine balsamic vinegar, oil, herbs, salt and pepper and whisk until ingredients are evenly mixed.
- Add Brussels sprouts to the mixing bowl and stir the Brussels into the vinegar/oil mixture until they are evenly coated.
- Spread the coated Brussels sprouts on you a cookie sheet and ensure they are spread out and not laying on top of each other. Bake for 35 minutes and enjoy!

12. Best Brussel Sprouts Ever Recipe

Serving: 6 | Prep: | Cook: 30mins | Ready in:

Ingredients

- 4 slices bacon,cut in small pieces
- 1 lb brussel sprouts
- 3 garlic cloves,sliced
- 3 sage leaves
- 2 bay leaves
- 2 oz. olive oil
- pinch of salt and fresh ground black pepper
- 3 slices lemon
- 1 TB butter
- 1/4 c chicken broth
- 2 TB butter

Direction

- Preheat oven to 350'
- In sauté pan, over med. heat, sauté bacon and cook till fat has been rendered. Remove to drain.
- In large bowl, add all remaining ingredients except chicken broth and butter, and toss until Brussels sprouts are coated with the oil. Lay

out 20" piece of parchment over aluminum foil on a sheet pan and pour Brussels sprout mixture into the middle, then top with bacon and 1 TB butter.

- Fold foil over itself and put in pre-heated oven. Cook 25-30 mins or till they smell done. Remove sprouts.
- Discard the herbs, garlic and lemon and place sprouts in large sauté pan with 2 TB butter, bacon and 1/4 c chicken broth. Cook down till the mixture bubbles and caramelizes.

13. Best Brussels Sprouts Ever Recipe

Serving: 12 | Prep: | Cook: 30mins | Ready in:

Ingredients

- Adapted from a 1997 Sheila Lukins recipe. Thanks to the Washington Post
- Best Brussels sprouts Ever
- □
- size: 8-12
- Ingredients
- •2 1/2 pounds Brussels sprouts
- •1 pound slab bacon (rind removed), cut into 1/4-inch-thick strips
- •2 tablespoons olive oil
- •2 tablespoons unsalted butter
- •6 medium carrots (about 1 pound), peeled and cut into 1/4-inch dice
- •Freshly ground black pepper
- •1 bunch fresh chives, snipped, for garnish

Direction

- Trim the stem ends of the Brussels sprouts and remove any tough outer leaves. Cut the sprouts in half through the stem ends, then cut each half into very thin strips (julienne).
- Cut the fatty strips from the bottom of the bacon slices and reserve. Cut the remaining meaty portions of bacon into 1/4-inch dice.

- Heat the oil and butter in a large, heavy pot over medium heat. When the butter has melted, add the bacon pieces and the reserved strips of bacon fat; cook for 5 to 6 minutes, stirring occasionally, until the meaty bacon pieces turn golden. Add the carrots and cook for about 5 minutes, stirring constantly, until they begin to soften. Remove the strips of bacon fat from the pot and discard.
- Add the sprouts to the pot, toss well to coat, and cook for about 5 minutes, stirring, just until crisp-tender. Taste, and add pepper as needed. Transfer to a serving bowl. Sprinkle with the chives; serve warm.

14. Braised Brussels Sprouts With Bacon And Chestnuts Recipe

Serving: 4 | Prep: | Cook: 15mins | Ready in:

Ingredients

- 1 1/2 pounds Brussels sprouts
- 4 strips bacon, chopped
- 1 shallot, minced
- 1 cup peeled and coarsely chopped chestnuts (about 1/2 pound nuts in their shell)
- 1 cup chicken broth
- 1 1/2 teaspoons sherry vinegar
- salt
- Freshly ground black pepper

Direction

- Cut an X in the stem end of each Brussels sprout and remove any outer leaves that are discolored or loose. In a covered pot, steam the sprouts over rapidly boiling water until they are tender, about 8 to 10 minutes. Cut each sprout into lengthwise quarters and set aside. (The Brussels sprouts can be prepared up to this point 8 hours in advance and refrigerated, tightly covered.)
- Render the bacon in a dry skillet over medium heat until it softens and releases its fat, about 5

minutes. Add the minced shallot and cook just until fragrant, about 1 minute. Add the chestnuts and chicken broth to the pan, cover and simmer until the chestnuts are quite tender and sweet, about 10 minutes.

- Add the vinegar and Brussels sprouts and cook, letting the flavors marry, about 5 minutes. Season to taste with salt and pepper and add a little more vinegar, if necessary, to brighten the flavors.

15. Breaded Brussels Sprouts Recipe

Serving: 10 | Prep: | Cook: 12mins | Ready in:

Ingredients

- 1 1/2 pounds Brussels sprouts
- 1 teaspoon salt
- 4 tablespoons butter melted and divided
- 4 tablespoons freshly grated parmesan cheese
- 4 tablespoons dried fine bread crumbs
- 1/4 teaspoon granulated garlic powder
- 1/4 teaspoon freshly ground black pepper or regular black pepper
- 1/4 teaspoon seasoning salt

Direction

- Wash and trim Brussels sprouts. Cut an "X" about 1/4-inch deep in the stem of the sprouts, this helps cook the sprouts more evenly and quicker.
- In a medium size cooking pot or saucepan, add Brussels sprouts, cover with water and add 1 teaspoon salt and bring to boil. Reduce heat, cover and simmer for 6 minutes or until just tender, do not overcook; drain.
- Place sprouts in a six-cup casserole oven-proof dish. Sprinkle 2 tablespoons butter over the sprouts and mix well to coat.
- Combine Parmesan cheese, dried bread crumbs, garlic powder, black pepper, seasoning salt and remaining butter and mix

well. Sprinkle mixture over sprouts. Heat sprouts under broiler, about 3 inches away from element until crumb mixture is lightly browned; about 5 minutes. Serve immediately.

16. Broasted Brussels Sprouts Recipe

Serving: 4 | Prep: | Cook: 30mins | Ready in:

Ingredients

- 1 1/2 lbs fresh Brussels sprouts
- 3 tablespoons extra virgin olive oil
- 1/2 teaspoon garlic powder
- 1/2 teaspoon ground black pepper
- 1/2 teaspoon salt
- 1/2 teaspoon dried sage

Direction

- Preheat oven to 400 degrees F.
- Cut the bottom of each Brussels sprout off (about 1/4" or less) and then slice in half lengthwise.
- Toss all ingredients and place in a single layer on a baking dish.
- Roast for 25 minutes or until Brussels sprouts are slightly browned and tender throughout.
- Serve hot or cold.
- Great served with my Shallot, Yogurt & Parsley Dip, Golden Pheasant Cocktail, Olive Cake...etc. :)

17. Brussel Sprout Goodness Recipe

Serving: 6 | Prep: | Cook: 25mins | Ready in:

Ingredients

- 2 bags brussel sprouts, fresh or frozen(thawed)
- Parmesan cheese
- 3 cloves garlic, minced

- 1 large onion, diced
- bread crumbs
- salt and pepper to taste
- butter

Direction

- Quarter Brussels sprouts.
- Heat butter in a large sauté pan on medium heat.
- Stir in onions and garlic, let them cook until they start sweating.
- Place Brussels sprouts in the pan, let sauté for 15 - 20 minutes.
- Sprinkle cheese and bread crumbs on the top, stir and serve.

18. Brussel Sprout Hash With Carmelized Shallots Recipe

Serving: 4 | Prep: | Cook: 18mins | Ready in:

Ingredients

- 6 tablespoons butter, divided
- ½ pound shallots, thinly sliced
- Coarse kosher salt
- 4 teaspoons sugar
- 2 tablespoons apple cider vinegar
- 1 ½ pounds Brussels sprouts, trimmed
- 3 tablespoons olive oil
- 1 cup water
- pepper

Direction

- Melt 3 tablespoons butter in medium skillet over medium heat. Add shallots; sprinkle with kosher salt and pepper. Sauté until soft and golden about 10 minutes. Add vinegar and sugar. Stir until brown and glazed, about 3 minutes. Halve Brussels sprouts lengthwise and then into thin ½ inch slices lengthwise. Heat oil in large skillet over medium high heat. Add sprouts; sprinkle with salt and

pepper. Sauté until brown at edges, about 6 minutes. Add 1 cup water and 3 tablespoons butter. Sauté until most of water evaporates, and sprouts are tender but still bright green, about 3 minutes. Add shallots, season with salt and pepper.

19. Brussel Sprout Casserole For Ragdolly Recipe

Serving: 6 | Prep: | Cook: 35mins | Ready in:

Ingredients

- 1/2 C. chopped hazelnuts
- 1 lge. pkg. frozen brussel sprouts OR 15 fresh brussel sprouts, cleaned and halved
- cooking spray
- 1 can cream of celery soup
- 1/2 can milk (or 1/2 and 1/2 if not dieting)
- 1/2 tsp. granulated garlic

Direction

- Roast chopped hazelnuts in a 350 degree oven for 15-20 min. or until brown.
- Defrost frozen sprouts in the microwave or steam fresh 1/2's until just tender
- Spray a non-stick casserole or large sauce pan with spray
- Mix soup and your choice of milk or 1/2 and 1/2 together well with garlic
- Pour into casserole and fold in sprouts and 3/4 of the toasted nuts.
- Top with remaining nuts and bake uncovered for 20 minutes.
- Serve

20. Brussel Sprouts Gratin Recipe

Serving: 6 | Prep: | Cook: 45mins | Ready in:

Ingredients

- 2 hickory-smoked bacon slices
- 4 large shallots, thin sliced
- 2lbs brussel sprouts, trimmed and halved
- 1 c water
- 1/2 tsp kosher salt, divided
- 1/4 tsp black pepper
- cooking spray
- French bread baguette
- 3 TB butter

Direction

- Preheat broiler.
- Cook bacon in lg. skillet over med. heat until crisp. Remove bacon from pan; reserving drippings; crumble.
- Increase heat to med-high. Add shallots to drippings in pan; sauté 2 mins or till tender, stirring occasionally.
- Add Brussels sprouts and 1 c water; bring to boil. Cover pan loosely with foil; cook 6 mins or until Brussels sprouts are almost tender.
- Uncover and remove from heat. Sprinkle with 1/4 tsp. salt and pepper; toss to combine.
- Spoon Brussels sprouts into 2qt. broiler-safe glass or ceramic baking dish, coated with spray.
- Place bread in food processor and process till finely ground. Melt butter in skillet over med-high heat. Add breadcrumbs and remaining 1/4 tsp. salt to pan; sauté for 2 mins or till toasted, stirring frequently. Sprinkle breadcrumbs mixture over Brussels sprouts mixture.
- Broil 3 mins or till golden and thoroughly heated.

21. Brussel Sprouts Hash Recipe

Serving: 4 | Prep: | Cook: 20mins | Ready in:

Ingredients

- 2 lbs fresh Brussels sprouts
- 1 TBL. olive oil
- 5 strips bacon, finely chopped
- 2 apples, cored and diced
- 1 onion, finely chopped
- salt and pepper

Direction

- Boil sprouts for 15 minutes. Drain, rinse with cold water. Cut into quarters.
- Heat sauté pan, add olive oil and bacon cook until crisp. Add onions and apples, sauté for a few minutes, then add the quartered sprouts. Season with salt and pepper, and serve.

22. Brussel Sprouts Hey They Arent So Bad After All Recipe

Serving: 4 | Prep: | Cook: 15mins | Ready in:

Ingredients

- 1T oil
- 300g brussels, shredded
- 1 red pepper, thinly sliced
- 1 carrot, thinly sliced
- 1 garlic clove, crushed
- 227g can, water chestnuts, drained
- 410g can baby corn, drained(I use frozen corn kernals
- 1/4c kecap manis(sweet soy sauce)
- 1T sweet chilli sauce
- toasted sesame seeds

Direction

- Heat oil in wok. Stir fry sprouts, carrot and pepper until just tender.
- Add crushed garlic, water chestnuts, corn, kecap manis and sweet chilli sauce.
- Stir fry until hot.
- Garnish with toasted sesame seeds

23. Brussel Sprouts Nancys Way Recipe

Serving: 4 | Prep: | Cook: 10mins | Ready in:

Ingredients

- 1 box of brussel sprouts cleaned and stems removed
- some olive oil
- salt and pepper
- fresh squeezed lime juice to taste

Direction

- Clean and remove stems from Brussels sprouts
- Cut each sprout in half and then then thinly slice each half as you were preparing cabbage for coleslaw
- Sauté them in some olive oil until tender but not over cooked
- Add salt and fresh grated black pepper to taste.
- Then squeeze on some fresh lime juice
- If you want some extra zing, add some grated lime zest
- I personally would sauté in some finely chopped shallots

24. Brussel Sprouts Recipe

Serving: 4 | Prep: | Cook: 6mins | Ready in:

Ingredients

- 1 lb brussel sprouts, cleaned and with an x cut in the bottoms
- 1/4 cup creme fraiche
- 4 slices bacon, finely diced
- 1/4 cup pecans, finely chopped
- 1 Tbsp onion, finely chopped
- salt and pepper to taste

Direction

- Put a pot of salted water on the stove and bring to boil. Add the Brussels sprouts and boil for 6 minutes, drain and set aside.
- Heat a pan on medium-high heat while the sprouts are cooking. When warm add the pecan pieces to roast. About 2 minutes. Remove and set aside. Keep your eye on them or they will burn!
- In the same pan, add the bacon, cook until brown and crispy. Add onions and cook until tender.
- Add the cooked Brussels sprouts to the pan and mix thoroughly. Then add the crème fraiche and mix until warm. Then add the roasted pecans and salt and pepper. Serve.

25. Brussel Sprouts Sauteed In Garlic Recipe

Serving: 8 | Prep: | Cook: 15mins | Ready in:

Ingredients

- 2 lbs brussel sprouts
- 1 tbsp chopped garlic
- 1/4 cup extra virgin olive oil
- salt & pepper to taste

Direction

- Boil Brussels sprouts for 10-15 minutes depending on desired crunchiness.
- While boiling, chop garlic
- Put olive oil and chopped garlic into a large sauté pan
- Remove sprouts and put into large bowl, cover with cool water
- On a large cutting board, cut sprouts in half once cool
- Sauté garlic over medium heat until it is golden brown (~1 min)

- Put sprouts in pan and sauté approximately 2 min, then turn sides and sauté for another 2 min
- Add salt and pepper to taste and serve.
- Add grated parmesan cheese if desired.

26. Brussel Sprouts With Bacon Horseradish Cream Recipe

Serving: 6 | Prep: | Cook: 20mins |Ready in:

Ingredients

- 11/2lbs brussel sprouts,trimmed and halved
- 4 strips crisp cooked bacon,fine chopped
- 1/4c sour cream
- 2tsp prepared horseradish
- 1/4tsp salt
- 1/8tsp pepper

Direction

- Place steamer basket in large saucepan, add 1" water and bring to boil. Put Brussels sprouts in the basket and steam till tender, 6 to 8 minutes.
- Mix bacon, horseradish, sour cream, salt and pepper in a medium bowl. Add the Brussels sprouts and toss to coat.

27. Brussel Sprouts With Chorizo Recipe

Serving: 4 | Prep: | Cook: 30mins |Ready in:

Ingredients

- kosher salt to taste
- 1 lb. brussel sprouts,trimmed and halved lengthwise
- 2 tsp extra-virgin olive oil

- 6 oz cured Spanish chorizo,quartered lengthwise and cut crosswise into 1/4" slices
- 1/2 small yellow onion,roughly chopped
- 2 cloves garlic,finely chopped
- fresh ground black pepper

Direction

- Heat a 6 qt. pot of salted water to boiling. Add Brussels sprouts and cook till just tender, 6 mins
- Using slotted spoon, transfer Brussels sprouts to bowl of ice water, let sit 5 mins.
- Drain Brussels sprouts and pat dry with paper toolset aside.
- Heat 1 Tbsp. of oil in a 12" cast iron skillet over med-high heat. Add chorizo and cook, stirring occasionally till browned, about 5 mins. Add onions and cook, stirring occasionally until golden brown and soft, about 8 mins. Add the garlic and cook till soft, about 2 mins more. Transfer chorizo mixture to a bowl. Increase heat to high and add remaining oil and the reserved Brussels sprouts; cook, flipping once or twice, until the Brussels sprouts are browned and tender, about 8 mins. Stir in the reserved chorizo mixture and season with salt and pepper.

28. Brussel Sprouts With Pancetta And Rosemary Recipe

Serving: 8 | Prep: | Cook: 20mins |Ready in:

Ingredients

- salt and pepper
- 3 containers (10 oz. each) brussel sprouts
- 1 Tablespoon olive oil
- 2 oz. pancetta, chopped (1/2 cup)
- 1 teaspoon chopped fresh rosemary
- 1/4 cup pine nuts (pignoli), toasted

Direction

- In covered 5 to 6 quart saucepot, heat 3 quarts water and 1 teaspoon salt to boiling on high.
- Meanwhile, pull off any yellow or wilted leaves from Brussels; trim stem ends.
- Cut each sprout in half.
- Add Brussels to boiling water and cook, uncovered, 5 minutes.
- Drain.
- Plunge Brussels into large bowl filled with ice water to chill quickly; drain well.
- In 12 inch skillet, add Brussels and 1/2 teaspoon each salt and freshly ground black pepper, and cook on medium-high heat 5 minutes or until heated through, stirring frequently.
- Add pine nuts; toss to combine.

29. Brussel Sprouts And Chestnuts Recipe

Serving: 6 | Prep: | Cook: 20mins | Ready in:

Ingredients

- 1 1/2 lb brussel sprouts
- 1/2 lb chestnuts
- 1/2 ts rosemary
- 1/2 ts tarragon
- 1/2 ts cumin
- 1 c chicken broth
- 1 ts cornstarch

Direction

- Blanche Brussels sprouts in boiling water 5 - 10 minutes. Run cold water over them.
- Take chestnuts, with a sharp knife, make an "X" on the top of each one. Brush each chestnut with oil. Bake for 20 minutes at 400F. Then shell the chestnuts.
- Mix sprouts, chestnuts and seasoning. Season with salt and pepper. Pour over broth.
- Bake at 350F for 20 minutes
- Remove from oven.

- Pour liquid into pan and mix with cornstarch and water. Cook over medium heat till thickened. Pour over vegetables.

30. Brussel Sprouts And Tomato Recipe

Serving: 2 | Prep: | Cook: 25mins | Ready in:

Ingredients

- 1 lb (500 g) frozen Brussels sprouts
- 4 fl oz (125 ml) chicken stock
- 10 oz (300 g) tomatoes
- salt
- pepper
- 1/4 tsp dried oregano
- freshly grated nutmeg
- butter to grease the oven proof dish
- 5 oz (150 g) Parma ham
- 3 1/2 oz (100 g) grated mild Cheddar

Direction

- 1. Blanch the Brussels sprouts in the chicken stock for approximately 3 minutes. Pop the tomatoes into boiling water, hold under running cold water and skin them. Slice the tomatoes and add to the chicken stock.
- 2. Season well with salt, pepper, oregano and the freshly grated nutmeg. Crease an oven proof dish with the butter. Preheat the oven to gas mark 6 (400° F or 200° C). Transfer the mixture into the casserole.
- 3. Cut the Parma ham into thin strips and spread together with the cheese over the casserole. Put in the centre of the oven and bake for approximately 20 minutes.

31. Brussel Sprouts With Apricot And Pistachios Recipe

Serving: 8 | Prep: | Cook: 7mins | Ready in:

Ingredients

- 1-1/2 lbs brussel sprouts,stems trimmed
- 2 Tbs. olive oil
- 1/2 tsp kosher salt
- 1/3 c shelled pistachios,coarsely chopped
- 1/4 c dried apricots,finely diced

Direction

- Bring large pot of lightly salted water to boil. Remove ant damaged outer leaves from Brussels sprouts and slice sprouts in half through the stem. Add to boiling water and cook till just tender,3 mins; drain (If making ahead, cool sprouts in ice water, drain and store, wrapped, in the fridge until ready to use.)
- Heat olive oil in large non-stick skillet over med-high heat. Add sprouts and salt; cook, turning occasionally, until sprouts are golden around the edges and heated through, 5 to 6 mins (7 min if you blanched earlier). Transfer to a serving dish and garnish with apricots and pistachios.

32. Brussel Sprouts With Beer Recipe

Serving: 2 | Prep: | Cook: 14mins | Ready in:

Ingredients

- 2 lbs brussel sprouts
- 4 oz bacon
- 2 garlic cloves, chopped
- 1/2 cup beer

Direction

- Trim Brussels sprouts of limp leaves, then cut an "x" in the base of each stalk.
- Bring a large pan of water to a boil, add sprouts and back to a boil.
- Boil 1 minute, then drain and run cold water over until cool.
- Cut sprouts in half.
- In separate skillet, sauté Bacon 3 minutes.
- Add garlic and sauté till Bacon is crisp.
- Add sprouts and sauté till warmed through.
- Pour in beer and bring to a boil.
- Simmer till sprouts are crisp-tender, about 3 minutes.
- Season with salt and pepper.
- Place in gratin dish and reheat, covered at 350f for 10 minutes or till hot.
- Or leave in skillet and reheat in it.

33. Brussel Sprouts With Garlic Recipe

Serving: 6 | Prep: | Cook: 25mins | Ready in:

Ingredients

- 1lb. brussel sprouts,halved
- 3 cloves garlic,thinly sliced
- 1Tbs plus 1tsp. extra virgin olive oil
- 1/4tsp salt
- 1/2c water

Direction

- Heat oven to 425
- Place Brussels sprouts, garlic, oil, salt and pinch of fresh ground pepper in 13 x9 baking dish. Toss to coat. Spread out in single layer
- Pour water into dish and roast until Brussels sprouts are lightly browned and pierced easily with a paring knife, about 25 mins.
- Serve warm

34. Brussel Sprouts With Panchetta Balsamic Recipe

Serving: 6 | Prep: | Cook: 12mins | Ready in:

Ingredients

- 6 slices pancetta, chopped
- 1 large onion, chopped
- salt and pepper
- 3 pints Brussels sprouts, large ones cut in half, small ones left whole
- 1 cup chicken stock
- 1/2 cup aged balsamic vinegar (eyeball it)

Direction

- Heat a large skillet over medium-high heat with about 2 tablespoons EVOO.
- Add pancetta and cook until crisp, about 4 minutes.
- Add the onion, and season with salt and pepper.
- Cook, stirring occasionally, for 2-3 minutes. Add the sprouts along with the chicken stock and the balsamic vinegar.
- Stir to combine and continue to cook for 10-12 minutes or until the Brussels sprouts are tender.

35. Brussel Sprouts With Pecan Butter Recipe

Serving: 6 | Prep: | Cook: 30mins | Ready in:

Ingredients

- 1 lb. brussel sprouts, trimmed and an x cut into the base of each sprout
- 2Tbs. extra virgin olive oil
- 1Tbs unsalted butter
- 1/4c chopped pecans
- salt and fresh ground pepper
- pinch of brown sugar

Direction

- In a steamer set over boiling water, stream Brussels sprouts, covered 7-8 mins, until just tender. Drain under cold running water to stop them from cooking. (You can do this step 1 day in advance)
- In large skillet, heat oil and butter. Add nuts; cook over medium heat until golden brown. Add sprouts, salt, pepper and sugar. Sauté 1 to 2 minutes, until heated through!

36. Brussel Sprouts With Sour CreamHorseradish And Bacon Recipe

Serving: 4 | Prep: | Cook: 40mins | Ready in:

Ingredients

- 11/2lbs brussel sprouts
- 3Tbs olive oil
- 1/2tsp pepper
- sour cream,to taste
- horseradish to taste
- bacon,to taste

Direction

- Cut ends away from Brussels sprouts and remove any yellow leaves.
- Toss with oil. Salt and pepper and roast on baking sheet for 35 to 40 mins. When don roasting, toss with mixture of sour cream, horseradish and bacon. Serve hot

37. Brussel Sprouts With Bacon Blue Cheese And Spiced Walnuts Recipe

Serving: 6 | Prep: | Cook: 30mins | Ready in:

Ingredients

- for spiced walnuts
- 2/3 walnuts
- For sprouts:
- 1 tbsp molasses
- 1 1/2 lbs Brussels sprouts, trimmed and halved
- 2-3 oz bleu cheese, crumbled
- 4 thick slices bacon
- 2/3 cup spiced nuts, hand crumbled (recipe follows)
- 1 tbsp peanut oil (or other mild flavored vegetable oils)
- 1 1/2 tbsp red wine vinegar
- kosher salt and fresh cracked black pepper

Direction

- For nuts--Preheat oven to 325 degrees.
- In a small mixing bowl, stir together all the dry spices.
- Stir in molasses, then add walnuts. Toss the mixture to coat the nuts.
- Spread the walnuts out in a single layer on a baking sheet.
- Bake at 325 for 10 to 15 minutes until the nuts have toasted and the seasonings have caramelized.
- Halfway through baking stir the nuts for more even coloring.
- Remove from oven and allow nuts to cool before using.
- For sprouts--Heat a large skillet over medium heat. Once the skillet is hot, add the bacon and cook until most of the fat has rendered out and the bacon is crispy.
- Remove the bacon and allow the bacon to drain on paper towels, set aside for later, and crumble once cool.
- Drain off all but one tablespoon of bacon fat from the skillet, then add the peanut oil to the remaining bacon fat and turn the heat to medium/med-high.
- Once the skillet has had time to reheat, add the Brussels sprouts and toss to coat with oil, then season with salt and pepper. Sauté the

Brussels sprouts for about 10-15 minutes or until the sprouts are tender and caramelized, stirring occasionally.

- Deglaze the pan with the red wine vinegar, stirring and scrapping the bottom of the pan with a wooden spoon to get up all those yummy caramelized bits on the bottom of the pan. Can add a Tbsp. of water if necessary to deglaze.
- Taste one of the sprouts to check the seasoning level, then adjust as necessary with salt and pepper - although remember you will be adding bacon and bleu cheese and thus more sodium.
- Add the crumbled bacon and spiced nuts to the pan and stir. Add the bleu cheese, then immediately remove the sprouts from the pan. Serve hot or at room temperature. Enjoy!

38. Brussel Sprouts In Cream Sherry Bacon Sauce Recipe

Serving: 4 | Prep: | Cook: 15mins | Ready in:

Ingredients

- about 1 lb of brussel sprouts, trimmed and halved
- 4 strips of uncooked bacon, diced
- half a medium onion, diced
- 1 clove garlic, minced
- 1/4 cup sherry (not cooking sherry)
- 1/2 cup cream (not half&half)
- 2 Tbsp olive oil
- salt and pepper to taste

Direction

- Preheat oven to 475
- In bowl, toss halved Brussels sprouts in olive oil
- Place halves sliced side down in a 9x13 baking pan (I used a glass one, cooking times may vary for dark or non-stick pans) This will

- brown the sliced parts, and a little of the tops. I think it makes them very pretty. :)
- Place in hot oven for 15 minutes
- Place diced bacon in cold medium skillet, and sauté over medium heat until starting to brown a little on the edges
- Add onions to bacon and grease and sauté until onion starts to become translucent
- Add garlic, stirring well for about one minute
- Add sherry, stir, then add cream and stir well
- Bring to a boil over medium heat stirring constantly, and as soon as you see it bubbling, reduce heat to low (or med-low, depending on your stove) and simmer until it's reduced by about half, stirring occasionally.
- (Once it's reduced, it will thicken up so that it coats your spoon well, but won't be thick like a white cream sauce)
- Salt and pepper to taste, toss roasted Brussels sprouts in sauce
- Serve and indulge!

39. Brussels Sprout With Caramelized Onion And Dried Cranberry Recipe

Serving: 8 | Prep: | Cook: 10mins | Ready in:

Ingredients

- 2/3 cups of olive oil
- 1 med onion, thinly sliced
- sea salt – I use Baleine
- 1 1/2 pounds brussels sprout, trimmed, wash and slice to about ¼ inch
- 1 cup water
- 4 tbsp white balsamic vinegar or more to taste
- 2 tbsp sugar
- ¾ cups dried cranberry
- salt and pepper to taste

Direction

- In a medium pan, sauté onion over medium heat, sprinkle with salt and pepper. Sauté until caramelized, about 10 minutes. Set aside
- Heat oil in large skillet over medium-high heat. Add sprouts; sprinkle with salt and pepper. Sauté until brown at edges, 6 minutes.
- Add 1 cup water, balsamic vinegar and sugar. Sauté until most of water evaporates and sprouts are tender but still bright green, 3 minutes.
- Add sautéed onion, add more balsamic vinegar to taste if necessary, last add dried Cranberry
- Note:
- I like the somewhat tangy taste, so I add more than 4 tbsp. of White Balsamic Vinegar.
- I think the tanginess of balsamic vinegar and sweetness of dried Cranberry complement the bitterness of Brussels Sprout. DELISH!

40. Brussels Sprouts And Cream Recipe

Serving: 6 | Prep: | Cook: 15mins | Ready in:

Ingredients

- 1 pound bag frozen Brussels sprouts
- 2 Tbsp flour
- 3/4 cup water
- 3/4 cup cream
- 1 tspsalt
- 1/2 tsp ground thyme
- 1/4 cup bread crumbs

Direction

- Cook Brussels sprouts according to package directions or your preferred method, then drain if you added water. (I like to cook mine in the microwave in a shallow dish for about 12 minutes on high, turning the dish twice).
- While the Brussels sprouts are cooking, stir together flour and water in a heavy saucepan until smooth.

- Add cream, salt and thyme and bring to a boil, stirring constantly so it does not burn or stick!
- Turn down heat and simmer gently until it thickens slightly.
- Mix in the cooked Brussels sprouts.
- Top with bread crumbs and serve at once.

41. Brussels Sprouts In Garlic Butter Recipe

Serving: 4 | Prep: | Cook: 20mins | Ready in:

Ingredients

- 15 fresh Brussels sprouts, halved lengthwise (do not use frozen ones)
- 1-1/2 Tbsp butter
- 1-1/2 Tbsp olive oil
- 3 cloves garlic, smashed with the flat of a knife
- parmesan cheese, freshly grated
- salt and pepper, to taste

Direction

- Melt butter and olive oil in a medium skillet (over medium-high heat) until butter is foamy.
- Reduce heat to medium, add smashed garlic and cook until lightly browned.
- Remove garlic and discard. (Note, I usually use 5-6 cloves, mince them, and cook till translucent, and I don't discard them).
- Add sprouts cut side down, cover, and cook without stirring on medium-low heat 10-15 minutes or until tender when pierced with a knife.
- The cut side of the sprouts should get nice and browned, with a nutty, buttery flavor enhanced by garlic.
- Top with freshly grated parmesan and salt & pepper to taste.

42. Brussels Sprouts In Lemon Cream Recipe

Serving: 6 | Prep: | Cook: 45mins | Ready in:

Ingredients

- 1 lb package Brussels Spouts cut in half and trimmed
- 2 tablespoon butter
- 8 ounce package cream cheese softened
- 1/4 cup half-and-half cream
- 1 packet Bouillon powder (can substitute with 1/2 to 1 tsp powder)
- juice of 1 lemon
- 1/4 cup parmesan cheese grated
- grated rind of 1 lemon

Direction

- Bring 5 Quarts of salted water to a boil in a 12 qt. pot.
- Place trimmed Brussels sprouts in a basket and steam, 3 to 5 minutes until crisp tender. Rinse and drain under cold water. Let stand to drain thoroughly (Note: may need to towel off to remove excess moisture).
- Place sprouts in a shallow casserole dish, set aside.
- Preheat oven to 350 F.
- In a med. sauce pan at medium low heat, melt butter, then add cream cheese and whisk until smooth.
- Add bouillon powder and lemon juice and whisk until incorporated.
- Pour over sprouts in casserole dish.
- Dust with Parmesan cheese, fresh ground pepper, and lemon rind.
- Place in oven and bake until bubbly and lightly brown on top, ~ 25 minutes.
- Remove from oven, allow to settle. Serve as a side dish.

43. Brussels Sprouts In Lemon Juice Recipe

Serving: 6 | Prep: | Cook: 20mins | Ready in:

Ingredients

- 20 ounce frozen Brussels sprouts
- 1/4 cup butter
- 2/3 cup mayonnaise
- 2 tablespoons lemon juice
- 1/2 teaspoon celery salt
- 2 tablespoons grated parmesan cheese
- 1/4 cup sliced almonds toasted

Direction

- Cook sprouts according to package directions omitting salt then drain.
- Place sprouts in a shallow casserole and keep warm.
- Melt butter in saucepan then add mayonnaise, lemon juice and celery salt.
- Beat with a wire whisk until smooth then cook over medium heat until hot stirring constantly.
- Pour sauce over sprouts then sprinkle with cheese and almonds.

44. Brussels Sprouts Prince Albert Which Is A La Mornay Recipe

Serving: 4 | Prep: | Cook: 30mins | Ready in:

Ingredients

- 2 lbs. of young tender Brussels sprouts
- 1 large white onion
- 2 cups of double cream
- 3 cups of whole milk
- 2 cups of shredded aged swiss cheese
- ¼ lb. of butter
- Half a cup of flour
- salt, coarse cracked black pepper

Direction

- Clean the sprouts and par-boil them ¾ of the way. Cool them in an ice bath and drain well. Cut them in half lengthwise. Cut the onion into quarters and then into thin slices.
- Heat the butter in a sauce pan and when melted, mix in the flour and cook 2-3 minutes stirring constantly.
- Pour in the cream and milk. Whisk it well to dissolve the roux and then cook until it slowly, until it thickens. Add the onion at this time as well.
- Reduce the heat to almost nothing. A little at a time, fold in the cheese, again stirring continuously until all of it has been incorporated and the sauce is smooth. Season with the salt and pepper.
- Place the Brussels sprouts into a bowl and give them another bath, this time with the sauce. Mix well to coat them thoroughly. Set them into some gratin dishes or in a casserole and bake until the top has browned a little.
- Garnish the top with some very thin fried onion rings and give them a kiss with some fresh chopped parsley.

45. Brussels Sprouts With A Balsamic And Brown Butter Sauce Recipe

Serving: 2 | Prep: | Cook: 7mins | Ready in:

Ingredients

- A handful or two of Brussels sprouts
- 1/4 stick of butter
- splash of balsamic vinegar
- a squeeze of honey
- salt pepper

Direction

- Melt a small part of the butter, (just enough to lightly coat the pan) over medium high heat and lay the sprouts, flat side down for about 4 minutes (check as little as possible, you want some browning)

- When browned slightly, flip them over and splash the vinegar onto the cut sides and toss.
- Let cook for another 2 minutes.
- Remove sprouts from the pan, add the rest of the butter and a bit of honey, salt and pepper. As soon as the butter has stopped bubbling, it will brown very quickly but since your pan is full of vinegar and you can't see the butter, I just counted to 4and added the sprouts back to the pan.
- Toss and enjoy!

46. Brussels Sprouts With Bacon Recipe

Serving: 6 | Prep: | Cook: 20mins | Ready in:

Ingredients

- 24 ounces fresh Brussels sprouts trimmed and halved lengthwise
- 8 ounces bacon diced
- 1 granny smith apple diced
- 1/2 teaspoon coarse salt
- 1/2 teaspoon freshly ground black pepper
- 1/4 teaspoon fresh thyme leaves

Direction

- Bring a large pot of salted water to a boil.
- Prepare an ice water bath and set aside.
- Add Brussels sprouts to boiling water and cook until color sets about six minutes.
- Transfer to ice bath until cool then drain well and set aside.
- Place bacon in a large skillet over medium heat and cook until fat renders and bacon is crisp.
- Add apples and cook stirring occasionally until apples are browned.
- Add Brussels sprouts and thyme then toss to combine.

- Season with salt and pepper and serve immediately.

47. Brussels Sprouts With Caraway Cheese Sauce Recipe

Serving: 4 | Prep: | Cook: 30mins | Ready in:

Ingredients

- 2 cups Brussels sprouts trimmed
- 1 teaspoon chicken stock base
- 1 tablespoon kosher salt
- 1 cup shredded cheddar cheese
- 1 teaspoon caraway seeds
- 1/2 teaspoon dry mustard
- 1/2 teaspoon worcestershire sauce
- 1/2 teaspoon hot sauce
- 1 cup milk

Direction

- Cut cross marks in base of sprouts then cook in salted water 8 minutes then drain.
- Combine cheese, caraway, mustard, Worcestershire, hot sauce and milk.
- Heat until cheese melts stirring often.

48. Brussels Sprouts With Chipotle Butter Recipe

Serving: 6 | Prep: | Cook: 20mins | Ready in:

Ingredients

- 2lbs Brussels sprouts, cleaned and outer leaves removed
- 5-6 green onions, chopped
- 6T butter
- 1T adobo sauce from chipotle peppers
- 1 large, or 2 small chipotle peppers, diced
- 3 cloves garlic, minced

- 1t ground coriander
- about 1tsp fresh lemon juice
- salt and pepper

Direction

- Slice Brussels sprouts thinly
- Melt butter in microwave.
- Whisk in adobo sauce, coriander and salt and pepper
- In medium skillet or sauce pan (I used cast iron), add Brussels sprouts and pour butter mixture over them.
- Add garlic, green onions and diced chipotles.
- Sauté over medium heat until tender, about 10-15 minutes.
- Add lemon juice and toss before serving.

49. Brussels Sprouts With Pancetta Recipe

Serving: 4 | Prep: | Cook: 45mins | Ready in:

Ingredients

- ¾ pound Brussels sprouts
- 2 slices pancetta or nitrite-free bacon, cut crosswise into ¼-inch pieces
- I small yellow onion, finely chopped
- 1 tablespoon finely chopped fresh thyme
- kosher salt
- Freshly ground pepper
- ⅛ teaspoon freshly utmeg

Direction

- 1. Bring a saucepan of salted water to a boil and prepare a large bowl of ice water. Halve and core the Brussels sprouts. Add the sprouts to the boiling water and cook until the color brightens and the sprouts are just beginning to soften, about 3 minutes. Drain the sprouts and plunge into the ice water to stop the cooking. Drain well. Separate as many of the large,

outer leaves from each sprout as will come off easily.
- Leave the smaller, inner leaves attached to each other.
- 2. In a large skillet over medium heat, cook the pancetta until soft but not yet crisp, about 2 minutes. Add the onion and cook, stirring constantly, until softened, about 5 minutes. Add the thyme, Brussels sprouts and leaves, and salt and pepper to taste.
- Stir and toss until heated through, about 1 minute. Add the nutmeg and toss well. Remove to a warmed serving dish and serve.

50. Brussels Sprouts With Walnuts Recipe

Serving: 8 | Prep: | Cook: 15mins | Ready in:

Ingredients

- 2 pounds baby Brussels sprouts, trimmed (try to find the smallest Brussels sprouts you can)
- 1/2 cup toasted walnut pieces
- 1 tablespoon extra virgin olive oil
- 1 tablespoon unsalted butter
- 1 tablespoon balsamic vinegar, or to taste
- salt and freshly ground pepper to taste

Direction

- Trim the Brussels sprouts by taking off the outer leaves and cut in half. Soak in salted ice water for 1 hour in the refrigerator. (This is the secret trick to removing the "smell" associated with Brussels sprouts, it also works for cauliflower). Drain and rinse.
- Bring a pot of water to a boil and add the sprouts (or steamer); cook or steam until tender, about 5 minutes. Remove and transfer to a bowl of ice to stop the cooking (can be prepared 1 day ahead to this point, store in an airtight container that is lined with paper towels to absorb the excess moisture).

- In a sauté pan, heat the olive oil and butter together, when hot, add the Brussels sprouts and cook over moderately high heat until browned in places and hot.
- Add the balsamic, salt and pepper and toss until well combined, remove from heat and toss with the walnut pieces.

51. Brussels Sprouts Au Gratin Recipe

Serving: 6 | Prep: | Cook: 30mins | Ready in:

Ingredients

- For the Brussels Sprouts:
- 1 lb. Brussels sprouts, trimmed and quartered
- 3 strips bacon, diced
- 1 cup leeks, slices thinly
- 1 Tbsp. AP flour
- 2 tsp. minced garlic
- ½ cup heavy cream
- ½ cup low-sodium chicken broth
- 1 Tbsp. fresh lemon juice
- ½ cup grated Gruyère or swiss cheese (I like aged)
- For the Crumb Topping:
- 1 Tbsp. EVOO
- 1 cup dry bread crumbs (I use panko)
- ¼ cup (or more) chopped walnuts
- ½ cup grated Gruyère or swiss cheese
- 2 tsp. mince lemon zest
- ¼ cup (optional) minced craisins (dried cranberries)
- Kosher salt and black pepper to taste

Direction

- Preheat oven to 350®. Coat a 2 quart casserole dish with non-stick spray (or butter)
- Trim off the tough leaves and woody stems of the Brussels sprouts, and then quarter them. Blanch sprouts in a pot of boiling water for 5 minutes; drain and set aside.

- Sauté bacon in a skillet over medium heat until crisp. Using a slotted spoon, remove bacon to a paper-towel-lined plate. Add leeks to skillet; cook over medium heat until softened. Stir in flour and garlic; cook ~ 1 minute.
- Stir in broth, cream, and lemon juice; bring to a simmer and cook until thickened, about 2 minutes. Remove the mixture from heat; stir in sprouts, bacon, and ½ cup Gruyere. Transfer mixture to a prepared dish.
- Heat oil for the crumb topping in a non-stick skillet over medium heat. Stir in crumbs and walnuts; cook until crumbs begin to brown. Remove mixture from heat to a bowl; let cool 5 minutes.
- Stir in ½ cup Gruyere, zest, salt and pepper into the casserole dish (add the craisins here if you like). Top Brussels sprouts with bread crumb mixture and bake until crumbs are brown, 25-30 minutes.

52. Brussels Sprouts With Balsamic Vinegar Recipe

Serving: 6 | Prep: | Cook: 10mins | Ready in:

Ingredients

- 1-1/2 pounds fresh Brussels sprouts
- 2 cloves garlic peeled and sliced
- 1/4 cup balsamic vinegar
- 1 teaspoon salt
- 1 teaspoon freshly ground black pepper
- 2 tablespoons olive oil
- 1 medium yellow onion peeled
- 2 tablespoons butter

Direction

- Trim off the stems and remove any limp leaves from the sprouts.
- Blanch sprouts in boiling water to cover for 5 minutes.

- Drain and rinse under cold water to stop cooking.
- Heat a large frying pan and add the olive oil, garlic and onion.
- Sauté a few minutes until the onion just becomes tender.
- Add the blanched drained sprouts.
- Sauté a few minutes until the sprouts are cooked to your liking.
- Add the vinegar and toss so that all the sprouts are coated with the vinegar.
- Add the butter, salt and pepper and toss together again.

53. Brussels Sprouts With Marjoram And Pine Nuts Recipe

Serving: 8 | Prep: | Cook: 20mins | Ready in:

Ingredients

- 3 tablespoons butter
- 1/2 cup pine nuts
- 1 1/2 pounds fresh Brussels sprouts, halved, or 1 1/2 pounds frozen brussels sprouts, thawed, halved
- 1 cup canned low-salt chicken broth
- 2 shallots, minced
- 1 tablespoon chopped fresh marjoram
- 1/3 cup whipping cream or half and half

Direction

- Melt 1 tablespoon butter in heavy large skillet over medium heat. Add nuts and stir until golden, about 3 minutes. Transfer nuts to small bowl. Melt 1 tablespoon butter in same skillet over medium heat. Add sprouts; stir 1 minute. Add broth; cover and simmer until sprouts are almost tender, about 6 minutes. Uncover and simmer until broth evaporates, about 5 minutes. Using wooden spoon, push sprouts to sides of skillet. Melt 1 tablespoon butter in center of same skillet. Add shallots; sauté until tender, about 2 minutes. Stir in

marjoram, then cream. Simmer until sprouts are coated with cream, stirring frequently, about 4 minutes. Season with salt and pepper. (Can be made 4 hours ahead. Cover and chill. Stir over medium heat to rewarm.)
- Transfer Brussels sprouts to serving platter. Mix in half of pine nuts. Sprinkle with remaining pine nuts.

54. Brussels Sprouts With Mustard Viniagrette Recipe

Serving: 6 | Prep: | Cook: 20mins | Ready in:

Ingredients

- 1 pound Brussels sprouts
- 2 tablespoons coarse grained mustard
- 2 tablespoons vegetable oil
- 1 green onion thinly sliced
- 1 clove garlic finely chopped
- 1/4 teaspoon salt

Direction

- Prepare and cook sprouts.
- Shake remaining ingredients in tightly covered container then toss with sprouts and serve immediately.

55. Brussels Sprouts With Pancetta Recipe

Serving: 4 | Prep: | Cook: 20mins | Ready in:

Ingredients

- 1 pound fresh Brussels sprouts, trimmed
- 2 tablespoons olive oil
- 3 ounces paper-thin slices pancetta, coarsely chopped
- 2 garlic cloves, minced

- salt and freshly ground black pepper
- 3/4 cup low-salt chicken broth

Direction

- Partially cook the Brussels sprouts in a large pot of boiling salted water, about 4 minutes. Drain.
- Meanwhile, heat the oil in a heavy large skillet over medium heat. Add the pancetta and sauté until beginning to crisp, about 3 minutes. Add the garlic and sauté until pale golden, about 2 minutes. Add the Brussels sprouts to the same skillet and sauté until heated through and beginning to brown, about 5 minutes. Season with salt and pepper, to taste. Add the broth and simmer until the broth reduces just enough to coat the Brussels sprouts, about 3 minutes. Serve.

56. Brussels Sprouts With Smoky Onions On Cheddar Toast Recipe

Serving: 2 | Prep: | Cook: 20mins | Ready in:

Ingredients

- pound Brussels sprouts, thinly sliced lengthwise
- 2 tablespoons extra virgin olive oil
- 1 large onion, finely diced
- salt and freshly ground black pepper
- 1 1/2 teaspoons sweet smoked paprika
- 4 slices of multi-grain bread, toasted
- 4 ounces extra-sharp cheddar cheese, thinly sliced
- Preheat oven to 350F.

Direction

- In a pot of boiling, salted water, cook Brussels sprout leaves until they are just tender, about 5 minutes. Drain and pat dry.

- Meanwhile, heat the olive oil in a large skillet. Add the onion, season with salt and pepper, and cook over moderate heat, stirring occasionally, until just softened, about 5 minutes. Add the paprika, cover and cook on low heat, stirring frequently, until the onion is just tender, about 10 minutes; add a little water if it dries out.
- Add the Brussels sprouts to the skillet and cook until tender throughout, about 5 minutes. Season with salt and pepper.
- Arrange the toasts on a baking sheet, top with cheddar. Bake for 2 minutes, until the cheese is melted; mound the Brussels sprouts and onions on top and serve.

57. Brussels Sprouts With Walnuts Bacon And Blue Cheese Recipe

Serving: 6 | Prep: | Cook: 35mins | Ready in:

Ingredients

- 1-1/2 pounds Brussels sprouts trimmed and halved
- 3 ounces crumbled blue cheese
- 4 thick slices bacon
- 2/3 cup spiced walnuts crumbled
- 1 tablespoon peanut oil
- 1-1/2 tablespoons red wine vinegar
- 1 teaspoon kosher salt
- 1 teaspoon fresh cracked black pepper
- spiced Walnuts:
- 2/3 cup walnuts
- 1 tablespoon molasses
- 1/2 teaspoon granulated sugar
- 1/4 teaspoon ground cardamom
- 1/4 teaspoon ground cumin
- 1/4 teaspoon cayenne
- 1/2 teaspoon kosher salt
- 1/8 teaspoon fresh cracked black pepper
- 1 tablespoon peanut oil
- 1-1/2 tablespoons red wine vinegar
- 1 teaspoon kosher salt

- 1 teaspoon fresh cracked black pepper

Direction

- Heat a large skillet over medium heat.
- When hot add bacon and cook until most of the fat has rendered out and is crispy.
- Remove bacon and drain on paper towels
- Crumble once cooled.
- Drain off all but one tablespoon of bacon fat from the skillet then add the peanut oil to the remaining bacon fat and turn the heat to medium then add Brussels sprouts and toss to coat with oil then season with salt and pepper.
- Sauté Brussels sprouts for 15 minutes or until the sprouts are tender and caramelized stirring occasionally.
- Deglaze pan with the red wine vinegar stirring and scrapping the bottom of the pan with a wooden spoon to get up all those yummy caramelized bits on the bottom of the pan.
- Add the crumbled bacon and spiced nuts to the pan and stir.
- Add the bleu cheese then immediately remove the sprouts from the pan.
- Serve hot or at room temperature.
- To make the spiced nuts preheat oven to 325.
- In a small mixing bowl stir together all the dry spices then stir in molasses then add walnuts.
- Toss mixture to coat the nuts.
- Spread walnuts out in a single layer on a baking sheet and bake for 15 minutes.
- Stir the nuts half way through cooking.
- Remove from oven and allow nuts to cool.

58. Brussels Sprouts With Walnuts And Mandarin Oranges Recipe

Serving: 6 | Prep: | Cook: 20mins | Ready in:

Ingredients

- 1 1/2 lb. fresh Brussels sprouts (I've used frozen)
- 1/2 cup olive oil

- 3 tbls. red wine vinegar
- 2 tbls. white wine
- Splash of worcestershire sauce
- 1 tbls. Dijon mustard
- 2 tsp. sugar
- 1/2 tsp. each of salt and pepper
- 2/3 cup walnuts, chopped and toasted
- 1/2 cup mandarin orange segments

Direction

- Wash Brussels sprouts and remove discolored leaves
- Cut off stem ends and cut a shallow x on bottom of sprout
- Add water and Brussels sprouts to saucepan
- Cover and bring to boil
- Cover and reduce heat and simmer for 8-10 minutes or until tender
- (For frozen sprouts, cook according to package directions)
- Drain, put in serving dish and keep warm
- In saucepan, combine oil and next 6 ingredients
- Cook over medium heat until heated through
- Pour over Brussels sprouts
- Sprinkle with walnuts and mandarin oranges
- Gently toss to combine

59. Buttah And Fried Onions Brussel Sprouts Recipe

Serving: 2 | Prep: | Cook: 30mins | Ready in:

Ingredients

- 1 bag frozen/fresh brussel sprouts
- 2-3 tbsp. unsalted butter
- 3 gloves of garlic (slivered)
- fried red onions (you can get this at at the asian supermarket)
- salt + pepper to taste
- 1-2 tsp. olive oil

Direction

- Heat oil and butter in sauté pan and let it butter turn slight brown, put in the slivered garlics for just a minute
- Put in the Brussels sprouts, salt, pepper to taste
- Cook for about 15-20 minutes when the butter has been reduced and the sprouts are caramelized.
- Dish it and garnish with fried red onions

60. Caramelized Brussels Sprouts Pearl Onions Shallots And Bacon Recipe

Serving: 12 | Prep: | Cook: 30mins | Ready in:

Ingredients

- 4 pints Brussels sprouts cleaned
- 1 pint pearl onions cleaned
- 4 shallots peeled and sliced thin
- 6 ounces bacon strips julienned
- 2 tablespoons softened butter
- 1 teaspoon salt
- 1 teaspoon freshly ground black pepper

Direction

- Preheat oven to 375.
- In a 2 quart pot of boiling salted water blanch sprouts for 2 minutes then strain and immediately shock in a bowl of ice water.
- Drain well and cut in half then set aside.
- Repeat this procedure for the pearl onions except blanch for about 1 minute then strain and shock in ice water.
- Drain well and set aside keeping whole.
- In a mixing bowl toss all ingredients together with softened butter then season with salt and pepper.
- Transfer to a small roasting pan in a single layer.
- Place in a preheated oven uncovered and roast for 30 minutes stirring every 10 minutes.

- Serve hot.

61. Carrots And Brussel Sprouts Recipe

Serving: 6 | Prep: | Cook: 15mins | Ready in:

Ingredients

- 2Tbs.chopped shallot(from 1 med)
- 3Tbs. unsalted butter ,divided
- 1lb.carrots,cut diagonally into 1/2" thick pieces
- 1lb. brussel sprouts,halved lengthwise
- 1/3c. water
- 1Tbs.cider vinegar

Direction

- Cook shallot in 2 Tbs. butter in a 12" heavy skillet over med-high heat, stir occasionally until softened 1-2 mins. Add carrots, Brussels sprouts, 3/4tsp salt and 1/2 tsp pepper and cook, stir occasionally until vegetables begin to brown, 3-4 mins.
- Add water and cover skillet, then cook over med-high heat until vegetables are tender, 5-8 mins. Stir in vinegar, remaining tbsp. of butter and salt and pepper to taste.

62. Cauliflower And Brussels Sprout Gratin With Pine Nut And Breadcrumb Topping Recipe

Serving: 8 | Prep: | Cook: 60mins | Ready in:

Ingredients

- 1½ pounds Brussels sprouts, trimmed, quartered lengthwise through core
- 1 1½- to-1¾-pound head of cauliflower, trimmed, cut into small florets

- 2¾ cups heavy whipping cream
- ½ cup chopped shallots
- 1 tablespoon chopped fresh sage
- 1½ tablespoons olive oil
- ½ cup plain dry breadcrumbs
- ½ cup pine nuts
- 2 tablespoons chopped fresh Italian parsley
- 3 cups grated parmesan cheese, divided

Direction

- Cook Brussels sprouts in large pot of generously salted boiling water 2 minutes. Add cauliflower to same pot; cook until vegetables are crisp-tender, about 3 minutes longer. Drain.
- Transfer vegetables to a large bowl of ice water to cool. Drain well.
- Combine cream, shallots, and sage in large saucepan. Bring to boil. Reduce heat; simmer until mixture is reduced to 2½ cups or less, about 10 minutes. Season with salt. Remove from heat. Cool slightly.
- Place the pine nuts in a dry skillet and heat, tossing gently, until the pine nuts are toasted. Be careful not to let them burn. Remove from heat and set aside.
- Heat oil in large non-stick skillet over medium heat. Add breadcrumbs; stir until beginning to brown, about 2 minutes. Transfer to bowl; cool. Stir in toasted pine nuts and chopped parsley. Season with salt and pepper.
- Butter 13x9x2-inch glass baking dish; arrange half of vegetables in dish. Sprinkle with salt and pepper, then 1½ cups Parmesan. Arrange remaining vegetables evenly over, then sprinkle with remaining 1½ cups Parmesan. Pour cream mixture evenly over.
- NOTE: Breadcrumb topping and gratin can be made 1 day ahead. Cover separately and chill. Bring to room temperature before continuing.
- Preheat oven to 375°F. Cover gratin with foil. Bake covered 40 minutes. Uncover; sprinkle breadcrumb topping over and bake uncovered 15 minutes longer.

63. Cheesey Gratin Of Brussels Sprouts Recipe

Serving: 10 | Prep: | Cook: 30mins | Ready in:

Ingredients

- 4 slices of bacon chopped and cooked crisp ....set aside and reserve the grease
- 1 lg. onion fine chopped
- 1 clove garlic minced
- 2 lbs. fresh brussel sprouts halved
- 1 1/2 c. milk
- 1 c. chicken broth
- 1/4 c. butter
- 5 tblspn. flour
- 3/4 c. grated parm cheese
- 1 tblspn. Dijon mustard
- 1/2 tsp. salt
- 1/4 tsp. dried thyme
- fresh cracked pepper to taste
- 1 1/2 c. grated sharp white cheddar
- paprika for garnish (optional)

Direction

- In 2 tbsps. of the bacon grease, cook onion for 6-7 minutes.
- Add garlic.
- Remove from skillet and set aside.
- Trim and half the sprouts and cook in boiling water for about 5 minutes.
- Drain and place in a 2 qt. casserole dish.
- Top sprouts with the cooked onions and garlic.
- Heat oven to 375 degrees.
- Combine milk and chicken broth in a small saucepan.
- Bring to a simmer then remove from heat.
- Melt butter in a large saucepan, add flour and cook stirring over medium heat for about 1 minute until flour is light golden brown.
- Whisk in half of the hot milk/broth mixture.

- Heat and whisk until thick. Add remaining liquid and cook for about 5 minutes whisking frequently.
- Whisk in parmesan cheese, mustard, salt, thyme, and pepper.
- Pour this sauce evenly over the sprouts, onions and garlic.
- Sprinkle evenly with the chopped cooked bacon and shredded cheddar and dust lightly with the paprika.
- Place casserole in oven and bake for 30 minutes until bubbly.
- Cool about 5 minutes before serving.
- Enjoy!

64. Cider Roasted Brussels Sprouts And Carrots Recipe

Serving: 4 | Prep: | Cook: 35mins | Ready in:

Ingredients

- 1/2 cup apple cider
- 1 tsp Dijon mustard
- 2 tbsp finely minced shallots
- 1 tbsp. olive oil
- Salt & pepper
- 1/2 tsp thyme
- 3 cups Brussels sprouts, halved
- 1 1/2 cups sliced carrots
- 1/4 cup chopped walnuts (toasted, if desired)

Direction

- Preheat oven to 350 degrees F.
- Combine cider, mustard, shallots, olive oil, salt and pepper and thyme.
- Pour over sprouts and carrots, tossing to coat. Arrange in a single layer in baking dish.
- Bake for 15 to 20 minutes, stirring occasionally, until tender.
- Sprinkle with walnuts and serve.

65. Cider Glazed Brussels Sprouts With Bacon & Almonds Recipe

Serving: 0 | Prep: | Cook: 27mins | Ready in:

Ingredients

- 4 slices OSCAR MAYER bacon, chopped
- 1 Tbsp. butter
- 1 small red onion, thinly sliced
- 2 lb. Brussels sprouts, trimmed, halved
- 3/4 cup apple cider
- 1/4 cup sugar
- 1/2 tsp. salt
- 1/4 tsp. ground nutmeg
- 1/4 tsp. freshly ground black pepper
- 1/4 cup PLANTERS sliced almonds, toasted

Direction

- Cook bacon in large skillet until crisp. Remove bacon from skillet with slotted spoon; drain on paper towels. Discard all but 1 Tbsp. drippings from skillet.
- Add butter, onions and Brussels sprouts to drippings in skillet; cook and stir on medium-high heat 1 to 2 min. or until Brussels sprouts are lightly browned.
- Mix next 5 ingredients; pour over sprouts. Cook 5 min. or until liquid is evaporated and sprouts are evenly glazed, stirring occasionally. Stir in bacon.
- Spoon sprouts into bowl. Top with nuts.

66. Creamy Vegetable Casserole

Serving: 0 | Prep: | Cook: | Ready in:

Ingredients

- 1 package (16 ounces) frozen broccoli, carrots and cauliflower
- 1 can (10-3/4 ounces) condensed cream of mushroom soup, undiluted

- 1 carton (8 ounces) spreadable garden vegetable cream cheese
- 1/2 to 1 cup seasoned croutons

Direction

- Prepare vegetables according to package directions; drain and place in a large bowl. Stir in soup and cream cheese.
- Transfer to a greased 1-qt. baking dish. Sprinkle with croutons. Bake, uncovered, at 375° for 25 minutes or until bubbly.
- Nutrition Facts
- 1 cup: 212 calories, 16g fat (9g saturated fat), 38mg cholesterol, 650mg sodium, 11g carbohydrate (3g sugars, 2g fiber), 4g protein.

67. Crispy Brussel Sprouts Recipe

Serving: 4 | Prep: | Cook: 10mins | Ready in:

Ingredients

- 1 lb brussel sprouts (I use frozen baby sprouts)
- 3 cloves garlic, thinly sliced
- olive oil
- salt and pepper to taste
- 2 tbls. butter

Direction

- If frozen, thaw Brussels sprouts
- Cut in half
- Cut into thin strips
- Heat oil in sauté pan to medium heat
- Add garlic and sauté for a minute
- Turn heat up to medium high
- Add Brussels sprouts
- Add salt and pepper
- Cook until caramelized
- Add butter

68. Crispy Brussels Sprouts Recipe

Serving: 2 | Prep: | Cook: 10mins | Ready in:

Ingredients

- 1 lb. Brussels sprouts, trimmed and quartered
- 2 tbsp. walnut oil
- 1 tbsp. minced shallot
- 1/4 tsp. freshly grated lemon zest
- 1 tbsp. lemon juice
- 1 tsp. whole-grain or Dijon mustard
- 1/4 tsp. salt
- Freshly ground pepper to taste

Direction

- Place Brussels sprouts in a steamer basket and steam in a large saucepan over 1 inch of boiling water until tender, 7 to 8 minutes. Meanwhile, whisk oil, shallot, lemon zest, lemon juice, mustard, salt and pepper in a medium bowl. Add the sprouts to the dressing and toss to coat.

69. Crunchy Brussels Sprouts Recipe

Serving: 4 | Prep: | Cook: 20mins | Ready in:

Ingredients

- 3 cups Brussels sprouts
- 3 tablespoons sour cream
- 3 tablespoons chopped almonds
- 3 tablespoons parmesan cheese
- 1 tablespoon vermouth
- 1/4 teaspoon nutmeg
- 1/4 teaspoon dried tarragon
- 1/4 teaspoon celery salt - I use regular salt

Direction

- In a med Sauce pan, steam Brussels sprouts till tender, drain.

- While the Brussels sprouts are cooking - Mix remaining ingredients in a skillet and heat through.
- Add Sprouts to the skillet and stir till well coated, serve.

70. Decadent Cream Braised Brussels Sprouts Recipe

Serving: 5 | Prep: | Cook: 45mins | Ready in:

Ingredients

- 1 ¼ lb. Brussels sprouts
- 3 Tbs unsalted butter
- ¼ tsp coarse sea salt, plus more to taste
- 1 cup heavy cream
- 1 Tbs fresh lemon juice, or more to taste

Direction

- First things first: buy good sprouts. They should feel firm and have tight, shiny-edged leaves. I like to buy medium-size ones, with heads that measure, say, 1 to 1 ¼ inches in diameter. You could buy littler ones, if you like, but don't buy them any bigger. I find that the larger they are, the stronger – i.e. more bitter – their flavor.
- First, prep the Brussels sprouts. Trim the stem end of each sprout and pull off any ragged or nasty outer leaves. Cut the sprouts in half from stem end to tip, and then cut each half in half again. Ultimately, you want little wedges.
- In a large (12-inch) skillet, melt the butter over medium-high heat. Add the Brussels sprouts and salt. Cook, stirring occasionally, until the sprouts are nicely browned in spots, about 5 minutes or so. I like mine to get some good color here, so that they have a sweetly caramelized flavor.
- Pour in the cream, stir to mix, and then cover the pot. Reduce the heat to low or medium low: you want to keep the pan at a slow simmer. Braise until the sprouts are tender

enough to be pierced easily with the tip of a paring knife, about 30-35 minutes. The cream will have reduced some and will have taken on a creamy tan color.
- Remove the lid, and stir in the lemon juice. Taste for seasoning, and adjust as necessary. Let the pan simmer, uncovered, for a minute or two to thicken the cream to a glaze that loosely coats the sprouts. Serve immediately.

71. Dijon Brussel Sprouts Recipe

Serving: 4 | Prep: | Cook: 8mins | Ready in:

Ingredients

- 1 lb. brussel sprouts
- 1 TB melted butter
- 1 TB honey
- 2 tsp Dijon mustard
- 1 medium sweet onion, peeled and chopped or sliced
- 1/2 c. water
- 2 TB of olive oil

Direction

- Trim Brussels sprouts. And cut a small X in the stem end, so they cook evenly.
- Place sprouts, chopped onion and the 1/2 cup water in a medium pan. Drizzle olive oil on top of all. Cover and cook on medium-high heat for approx. 8 or so minutes, or until tender. Pour any excess water out when done. Keep sprouts in pan.
- Add the honey, butter and Dijon mustard on top of the cooked sprouts and onions. Stir gently and reheat to blend. If needed, add more water.
- Sprinkle with salt or pepper, if desired.

72. Dill Marinated Brussels Sprouts Recipe

Serving: 8 | Prep: | Cook: 20mins | Ready in:

Ingredients

- 1/2 cup white wine
- 1/2 cup red wine vinegar
- 1-1/2 teaspoons brown sugar
- 2 cloves garlic crushed
- 1-1/2 pounds Brussels sprouts trimmed and cut in half
- 3 tablespoons chopped green onion
- 3 tablespoons chopped dill pickle

Direction

- Combine wine, vinegar, sugar and garlic in sauce pan then bring to boil and add sprouts.
- Reduce heat then cover and simmer 10 minutes.
- Transfer sprouts and liquid to a serving bowl.
- Add green onion and dill pickle then serve at room temperature.

73. Easy Lime Shredded Brussels Sprouts Recipe

Serving: 3 | Prep: | Cook: 8mins | Ready in:

Ingredients

- 1 pound Brussels sprouts
- 1/4 cup butter or olive oil
- juice from 1-2 limes (however limey you want it)
- salt and pepper (I use kosher salt on EVERYTHING)

Direction

- Cut sprouts in half then julienne.

- Heat skillet over medium high. Melt butter then add sprouts and cook till tender, about 6-8 minutes.
- Season with lime juice, salt & pepper.
- Easy huh! Enjoy!

74. Fall Spiced Roasted Brussel Sprouts Recipe

Serving: 4 | Prep: | Cook: 50mins | Ready in:

Ingredients

- fresh brussel sprouts
- oil
- apple cider
- ground cinnamon
- salt
- pepper

Direction

- Remove any imperfect leaves from the Brussels sprouts and wash thoroughly. Cut off any excess stems. Cut the Brussels sprouts in half, then take each half and cut each into thin slices. Put into a roasting pan.
- Drizzle Brussels sprout slices with oil, add a splash of apple cider, and sprinkle with ground cinnamon, salt and pepper. Mix to coat.
- Put into a 350 degree oven and roast for approximately 50 minutes, stirring occasionally. Apple cider will evaporate quickly.
- This length of time and temperature will yield veggies that are still crisp, not soggy. If you increase the oven temp, be sure to stir more frequently - you don't want the apple cider sugars to burn.

75. Fried Brussel Sprouts Recipe

Serving: 4 | Prep: | Cook: 10mins | Ready in:

Ingredients

- 1 package fresh brussel sprouts
- 4 Tbs extra virgin olive oil
- 1/2 Diced onion
- 1 Cup chicken broth

Direction

- Wash and cut Brussels in half
- Place extra virgin olive oil in medium skillet
- Add onion sauté until almost done
- Add Brussels make sure and add them to the pan flat side down
- Once the Brussels start to brown add about 1/2-1 cup chicken broth
- Flip the Brussels a couple of times once they are soft remove from heat and serve.
- ENJOY!!

76. GLAZED BRUSSELS SPROUTS Recipe

Serving: 8 | Prep: | Cook: 20mins | Ready in:

Ingredients

- 4 cups fresh brussel sprouts
- 3 Tbs butter
- 3 Tbs white wine worcestershire sauce
- 2 tsp granulated sugar
- ¼ tsp salt

Direction

- 1. Heat oven to 450 degrees.
- 2. Cut sprouts in half. Toss with melted butter, Worcestershire sauce, sugar and salt in 13×9" baking pan. Roast 20 minutes, shaking pan occasionally.

77. Garlic Balsamic Roasted Brussel Sprouts Recipe

Serving: 2 | Prep: | Cook: 30mins | Ready in:

Ingredients

- 1 frozen packed brussel sprouts, thawed and halved through the core
- 2 cloves garlic, sliced
- 4 tbsp balsamic vinegar
- 2 tbsp extra virgin olive oil
- 2 tbsp honey
- salt and pepper to taste
- 2 tsp Dijon mustard

Direction

- Once thawed, slice Brussels sprouts along the core.
- Preheat oven to 375. Spray a cookie sheet with non-stick cooking spray and in a single layer spread Brussels sprouts and garlic.
- Whisk balsamic, olive oil, honey, salt, pepper, and Dijon mustard and pour over Brussels sprouts and garlic. Ensure everything is covered in the dressing and roast for 25-30 minutes until all Brussels sprouts have turned brown on the edges. Turn every 10 - 15 minutes to make sure none of them burn.
- Easy. Quick. Delicious.
- What do you think?

78. Grilled Brussel Sprouts Recipe

Serving: 4 | Prep: | Cook: 20mins | Ready in:

Ingredients

- 2 pounds brussel sprouts
- 1/4 cup butter
- 1/2 teaspoon garlic salt

Direction

- Trim and clean Brussels sprouts.
- Mix butter and garlic salt together in a small bowl.
- Place Brussels sprouts on the grill and cook until they start to soften.
- Brush with butter every few minutes

79. Grilled Brussel Sprouts And Potatoes Recipe

Serving: 2 | Prep: | Cook: 20mins | Ready in:

Ingredients

- 10-15 brussel sprouts halved outer leaves removed
- 5 small red potatoes halved
- 1/2 a medium vidalia onion or other sweet onion chopped
- 4 garlic cloves minced
- 3 Tablespoons chicken broth
- salt and pepper to taste

Direction

- Combine all above ingredients in a large piece of foil.
- Grill foil pack for 20 minutes shaking occasionally
- If you time it well this recipe is awesome paired with whatever meat you're grilling!!

80. Holiday Brussel Sprouts And Purple Potatoes Recipe

Serving: 6 | Prep: | Cook: 20mins | Ready in:

Ingredients

- 1 1/4 lb fresh brussel sprouts, cleaned and stems removed

- 1 1/2 lb small purple or pink potatoes
- olive oil or butter to taste
- kosher salt and fresh ground black pepper
- garnish if desired such as: fresh chopped parley or lemon wedges
- or a squeeze of fresh lime juice

Direction

- Cook potatoes until tender but not soft or mushy
- Cook Brussels sprouts until fork tender but not overly soft (or they will lose their nice green color
- Drain potatoes, and while warm, peel off the skin
- Cut potatoes in half
- Cut the Brussels sprouts in half, vertically
- Combine both in a serving dish, now either drizzle with extra virgin olive oil OR melted butter
- Sprinkle with salt and pepper
- Lightly toss
- Serve or place back in a warm oven to reheat if desired

81. Holiday Sides: Roasted Brussels Sprouts With Dijon Cream Sauce Recipe

Serving: 6 | Prep: | Cook: 30mins | Ready in:

Ingredients

- Toss:
- 1   lb. Brussels sprouts -- halved lengthwise
- 2   cups red onions -- cut into wedges
- 8   oz. kielbasa -- 1/2 inch thick slices (subbed mini meatballs from home made bulk sausage)
- 2   T. olive oil
- Salt and pepper
- Simmer:

- 1/2   cup heavy cream (subbed canned milk-no heavy cream)
- 1/4   cup Dijon mustard
- 1   T. honey
- 1   teaspoon apple cider vinegar

Direction

- Preheat oven to 450°.
- Toss sprouts, onions, and kielbasa in a bowl with the oil, salt, and pepper. Spread in a single layer on a baking sheet and roast 20 minutes (30 minutes was perfect), or until sprouts are tender, yet still crisp.
- Simmer cream, mustard, honey, and vinegar in a saucepan over low heat for 10 minutes, or until slightly thickened. To serve, spoon sauce over roasted sprouts.

82. Jasmines Brussels Sprouts Recipe

Serving: 4 | Prep: | Cook: 20mins | Ready in:

Ingredients

- 3 c water
- 1 lb Brussels sprouts, trimmed (I use 2 boxes of frozen)
- 2 T olive oil
- 2 cloves garlic, minced
- 8 oz pancetta bacon, diced (8 oz. is too much...use to tast and it's great. I use a small amount or it's over powering for this recipe.)
- 1 t salt
- 1 t ground black pepper

Direction

- Bring the water to a boil in a large saucepan.
- Add Brussels sprouts, and cook for 5 to 7 minutes.
- They should still be slightly firm.
- Drain, and rinse with cold water.
- Slice the sprouts in half, and set aside.

- Heat one tablespoon of olive oil in a large skillet over medium-high heat.
- Add the garlic and pancetta; cook and stir for about 5 minutes, until garlic is lightly browned.
- Add the remaining olive oil and Brussels sprouts.
- Reduce the heat to medium and cook, stirring until the sprouts are well coated with the flavor.
- Season with salt and pepper, and cook for 5 more minutes before serving.

83. Jo_jo_ba's Brussells Sprouts Recipe

Serving: 2 | Prep: | Cook: 30mins | Ready in:

Ingredients

- 1 10.oz. box frozen baby brussells sprouts (fresh would be better but couldn't find any)
- 2 medium onions, thinly sliced
- Small handful dried cranberries
- olive oil to saute
- salt and pepper to taste

Direction

- Thaw Brussels sprouts and halve lengthwise
- Caramelize onions....Caramelized Onions
- Remove from pan
- Add Brussels sprouts, salt and pepper; sauté until golden
- Add onions back to pan and sprinkle with cranberries
- Mix to combine

84. Kielbasa With Brussels Sprouts Recipe

Serving: 4 | Prep: | Cook: 33mins | Ready in:

Ingredients

- 1 tablespoon canola oil
- 1 (16 ounce) package kielbasa sausage, sliced into 1/2 inch pieces
- 1 red onion, chopped
- 14 ounces baby Brussels sprouts, trimmed and cut in half
- salt and ground black pepper to taste

Direction

- Heat the oil in a large skillet over medium-high heat. Add the sausage and onion. Cook and stir until onion is translucent, 8 to 10 minutes. Add the Brussels sprouts, and cook 10 minutes more. Season with salt and pepper to taste.

85. Lemon Parmesan Toasted Almond Brussels Sprouts Recipe

Serving: 6 | Prep: | Cook: 20mins | Ready in:

Ingredients

- 2 (10-ounce) packages frozen Brussels sprouts
- 1/4 cup unsalted butter
- 2/3 cup mayonnaise
- 2 tablespoons fresh lemon juice
- 1/2 teaspoon celery salt
- 2 tablespoons grated parmesan cheese
- 1/4 cup sliced almonds, toasted

Direction

- Cook Brussels sprouts according to directions, omitting salt, drain
- Place Brussels sprouts in shallow 2 quart casserole, keep warm
- Melt butter
- Add mayonnaise, lemon juice, celery salt
- Whisk until smooth
- Cook over medium heat until hot, stirring constantly (do not boil)

- Pour sauce over sprouts
- Sprinkle with cheese and almonds

86. Lemony Sprouts And Shoots Recipe

Serving: 4 | Prep: | Cook: 25mins | Ready in:

Ingredients

- 1 lb. brussel sprouts, trimmed and halved
- 2 oz. pea shoots
- 2 tsp. olive oil
- 1/4 to 1/2 tsp cayenne (depending on your taste)
- 1/2 lemon
- salt to taste (if you have a specialty salt, use that in this recipe, I used a Mediterranean one that was delicious)
- pepper to taste

Direction

- Heat the oil in a large skillet on medium heat. Add the Brussels sprouts and cook for about 10 to 12 minutes. Add the pea shoots, juice of the half lemon, cayenne, S&P. If you need to add a little more oil move everything to the side and add about a tsp. and let it heat up before mixing in. Cook about 3 to 5 more minutes until the pea shoots are wilted and the Brussels sprouts are crunchy, but done. Hope you like this as much as we did :)

87. Lemony Sweet Brussels Recipe

Serving: 0 | Prep: | Cook: 15mins | Ready in:

Ingredients

- Everybody on here already knows I eyeball everything, so these measurements are approximate.

- 1 - 1/2 Cups fresh Brussels sprouts, rinsed well
- 1/2 Cup sliced onions
- 1/2 tsp minced garlic
- 1/4 cup fresh cilantro, rinsed and chopped
- 1 tsp grapeseed oil, for the pan
- juice from 1/2 lemon, divided
- 1/4 cup white cooking wine
- 1/4 tsp cayenne powder

Direction

- Boil the Brussels in water for a few minutes first. I mean, you don't have to, but I did because I like them soft. Screw you, it's been a long day.
- Pour in the oil, onions and now softened (if desired) sprouts. Sauté on medium-high flame, stirring occasionally for a few minutes before you add the garlic. That will burn if you cook it for too long.
- Allow the onions to caramelize and the sprouts to blacken a bit. That's good, it adds flavor for when you dump the wine and 1/2 the lemon juice into it, stir it up and get all that yummy caramel up off the pan and coating your veggies.
- Toss in the cayenne pepper and stir vigorously for an additional 3-5 minutes until blended and cooked evenly. Toss in the cilantro about a minute or two before you're done, while still stirring.
- When it's done, remove from heat into a bowl and sprinkle the remaining lemon juice over the dish. Garnish with more cilantro and a lemon wedge if you want to be all fancy pants.
- This will be sweet enough to convert any Brussels sprout hater. Maybe not kids though... I wouldn't try it with kids unless you dump lots of parmesan cheese-- oh wait, that's not a half bad idea... *Wanders off mumbling to myself*

88. Marinated Brussels Sprouts Recipe

Serving: 6 | Prep: | Cook: 10mins | Ready in:

Ingredients

- 1/2 cup white wine
- 1/2 cup red wine vinegar
- 1-1/2 teaspoons brown sugar
- 2 cloves garlic crushed
- 1-1/2 pounds Brussels sprouts trimmed and cut in half
- 3 tablespoons chopped green onion
- 3 tablespoons chopped dill pickle

Direction

- Combine wine, vinegar, sugar and garlic in a heavy sauce pan.
- Bring to boil.
- Add sprouts.
- Reduce heat then over and simmer 10 minutes.
- Transfer sprouts and liquid to a serving bowl.
- Add green onion and dill pickle.
- Serve at room temperature.

89. Miso Roasted Brussels Sprouts Recipe

Serving: 4 | Prep: | Cook: 45mins | Ready in:

Ingredients

- 1 lb. Brussels sprouts
- ¼ C shiro (white) miso paste
- 1 oz. warm water
- 1 Tbsp. olive oil
- 1 garlic clove
- ¼ tsp. kosher salt

Direction

- Preheat oven to 375 degrees F.

- Cut off the brown ends of the Brussels sprouts and pull off any yellow outer leaves. Mix them in a bowl with the olive oil, garlic, and salt. Spread them on a sheet pan and roast for 15 minutes.
- While the Brussels sprouts are roasting, mix together the miso paste and water. Put half of the miso/water mixture into the bowl you used to toss the sprouts, and set the other half aside.
- After 15 minutes, toss the sprouts in the bowl with the miso paste and return them to the pan. Roast another 15 minutes, then remove and toss with the rest of the miso paste. Roast another 10-15 minutes, until tender on the inside. Serve immediately.

90. Mrs Claus Brussels Sprouts With Bacon And Onion Recipe

Serving: 8 | Prep: | Cook: 15mins | Ready in:

Ingredients

- 2 pounds fresh Brussels sprouts, trimmed*
- salt
- 6 ounces bacon, diced
- 1 medium onions, diced
- 6 tablespoon unsalted butter, divided
- Freshly ground black pepper
- 2 tablespoons cider vinegar

Direction

- Heat large pot of water to boiling. Salt water, add Brussels sprouts and cook just until tender, about 8 minutes or follow directions on package for frozen sprouts.
- Drain and cool sprouts under running water. Cut each in half through the stem end.
- Heat large heavy skillet over medium high heat. Add bacon and fry until golden brown. Transfer to paper towels to drain. Pour off all but 3 tablespoons fat.

- Add onions and 1 tablespoon butter to skillet; cook over medium heat until softened, about five minutes. Remove onions with slotted spoon. Pour off fat and wipe out skillet.
- Add remaining 5 tablespoons butter to skillet and heat over medium heat. Add sprouts and cook until lightly browned, about ten minutes. Add bacon and onions. Season to taste with salt and pepper. Sprinkle with vinegar and heat through. Serve hot.

91. Mustard Brussel Sprouts Recipe

Serving: 6 | Prep: | Cook: 15mins | Ready in:

Ingredients

- 1 1/2 lbs fresh brussel sprouts(all close in size)
- 1 Tbl butter
- 1/2 C chopped shallots (about 2 Lrg) or 1/2 C chopped onion
- 1/3 C half and half
- 1 Tbl plus 1 1/2 tsp Dijon mustard
- 1/4 tsp salt
- 1/8 tsp pepper
- Freshly grated parmesan cheese
- 6-8 servings

Direction

- Cut stem from each sprout and trim.
- Cut an X into stem end of sprout to speed cooking
- Place sprouts in a saucepan in a single layer and cover with water
- Bring to a boil; cook uncovered until almost tender when pierced, about 7 to 10 minutes
- Drain in colander
- Rinse under cold water, drain again
- Melt butter in same saucepan over medium heat
- Add shallots; cook for 3 minutes, stirring occasionally
- Add half and half, mustard, salt and pepper

- Simmer until sauce is thickened, about 1 minute
- Add sprouts; heat until heated through, tossing gently with sauce, about 1 minute
- Sprinkle with grated Parmesan before serving

92. Orange Kissed Brussels Sprouts Recipe

Serving: 6 | Prep: | Cook: 20mins | Ready in:

Ingredients

- 1 1/2 lbs Brussels sprouts, trimmed and halved
- 2 tsp grated orange rind
- 1/2 cup fresh orange juice
- salt and pepper to taste

Direction

- Steam the Brussels sprouts, covered, for 15 minutes or until tender.
- Drain sprouts and return to pan, adding orange rind, orange juice, salt and pepper.
- Cook over medium heat for a minute longer, stirring constantly. Serve immediately.

93. Pan Fried Brussel Sprouts Recipe

Serving: 4 | Prep: | Cook: 10mins | Ready in:

Ingredients

- 1 box or container of fresh brussel sprouts
- 1 small onion thin sliced
- olive oil to stir fry
- 1 clove of garlic minced
- salt and pepper to taste
- Options: juice from a fresh squeezed lemon or a lime

Direction

- The most important part of the recipe is to properly cut the Brussels sprouts
- So cut each spout in half like a cabbage
- Then slice each half as one would do for coleslaw (slice in shreds)
- Heat oil in a pan over medium high heat, I used less than 1/4 cup
- First add the sliced onion and then the sprouts
- Toss vegetables to coat with oil
- Continue to cook and stir to get the texture you want- I like tender and slightly crunchy
- Careful not to overcook or let get too soft or soggy
- Add the minced garlic and toss and cook briefly
- Season with salt and pepper to taste
- Now if you wish, add juice from lemon or lime to kick up the flavor if you wish

94. Pan Browned Brussel Sprouts Recipe

Serving: 4 | Prep: | Cook: 25mins | Ready in:

Ingredients

- 1 lb Brussels sprouts
- 4 large garlic cloves, thinly sliced
- 3 or 4 Tbsp unsalted butter
- 2 Tbsp EVOO
- 3 or 4 Tbsp pine nuts

Direction

- Trim Brussels sprouts and halve lengthwise.
- In a large cast iron skillet, melt 2-1/2 Tbsp. butter over moderate heat and cook the garlic until golden brown. Transfer garlic to a small bowl with a slotted spoon.
- Reduce heat to low, arrange sprout in skillet cut side down in one layer.
- Sprinkle sprouts with the pine nuts and salt to taste.

- Cook sprouts until crisp-tender and undersides are golden brown, without turning, ~ 15 minutes.
- Transfer sprouts to a plate, with tongs, browned side up.
- Add garlic and 1 Tbsp. of butter to skillet and cook over moderate heat, stirring, until pine nuts are an even pale gold, ~ 1 minute.
- Spoon mixture over sprouts and sprinkle with freshly ground pepper.
- Serve as a side dish. We will number these for you! Just hit 'enter' after every step.

95. Pasta With Brussel Sprouts Recipe

Serving: 4 | Prep: | Cook: 10mins | Ready in:

Ingredients

- 6 cup water
- 1/2 teaspoon salt
- 10 0z pack frozen brussel sprouts
- 1 cup uncooked spiral pasta
- 1/4 cup butter melted
- 2 tablespoons whipping cream
- 2 tablespoons grated onion
- 1/4 teaspoon black pepper
- 1/4 teaspoon ground nutmeg

Direction

- In large saucepan: bring water and salt to a boil
- Add Brussels sprouts and pasta
- Return to a boil: then reduce heat and simmer uncovered for 6- 8 minutes or until pasta and Brussels sprouts are tender
- Drain
- Combine the remaining ingredients: pour over pasta mixture and toss to coat
- ENJOY!!!!

96. ROASTED BRUSSEL SPROUTS WITH POTATOES BACON Recipe

Serving: 6 | Prep: | Cook: 35mins | Ready in:

Ingredients

- 1 ½ lbs. baby yukon gold potatoes, Quartered or halved if very small
- 1 lb. brussel sprouts, trimmed and halved
- 6 medium shallots, quartered
- 3 slices thick-cut bacon, cut crosswise into 1/2 inch strips
- 3 Tablespoon olive oil
- 2 teaspoons kosher salt
- ½ teaspoon freshly ground black pepper
- 2 Tablespoons butter, melted
- 1 Tablespoon fresh lemon juice

Direction

- Heat oven to 450 deg. Combine the potatoes, Brussels sprouts, shallots and bacon in large bowl; toss with the oil. Sprinkle with the salt and pepper and toss again. Transfer to a 10 x 15 Pyrex dish and roast (I used my non-stick roasting pan), stirring every 15 min. until the veggies are tender and well browned (35 to 40 min.).
- Combine melted butter and lemon juice in a small bowl and pour over veggies and toss to coat. Serve immediately.

97. Red Grapes With Brussel Sprouts Recipe

Serving: 4 | Prep: | Cook: 10mins | Ready in:

Ingredients

- 3 dozen medium brussel sprouts
- 2 tbs olive oil
- 2 tbs butter
- 1 cup whole seedles sweet red grapes

Direction

- Clean and half the sprouts
- Steam sprouts crisp tender
- Heat olive oil and butter in a large skillet
- Add sprouts cook over med-hi heat till almost tender soft but not mushy and still nice and green
- Lower heat, add grapes
- Stir and simmer till grapes heated through

98. Roasted Brussel Sprouts Recipe

Serving: 4 | Prep: | Cook: 45mins | Ready in:

Ingredients

- 2 pounds brussel sprouts
- 1 tbsp chopped fresh thyme or 1 tsp dried
- 1 tbsp chopped fresh oregano leaves or 1 tsp dried
- 1 tsp garlic powder
- 1/2 tsp kosher salt
- 1/4 tsp fresh ground black pepper
- 1/4 cup extra virgin olive oil
- 1/2 cup balsamic vinegar

Direction

- Preheat oven to 425 degrees F.
- Cut the bottoms off the Brussels sprouts and trim off any damaged outer leaves. Soak them in a bowl of cold water for a few minutes and drain them well.
- Cut them in half and put them into a roasting pan. Add the thyme, oregano, garlic powder, salt and pepper. Add the olive oil and vinegar and toss everything well to coat.
- Put the roasting pan into the oven and cook for 20 minutes. Give everything a good stir and cook for 25 minutes more, or until the Brussels sprouts are nicely browned and caramelized.

99. Roasted Brussels Sprouts And Sweet Potatoes Recipe

Serving: 4 | Prep: | Cook: 1hours | Ready in:

Ingredients

- Roasted Sweet Potatoes and Brussels sprouts
- Yield: Serves 6-8
- Recipe by The Food Charlatan
- Ingredients
- 1 pound Brussels sprouts, trimmed
- 1 large sweet potato (1 pound)
- 2 cloves garlic, smashed
- 1/3 cup olive oil
- 1 teaspoon cumin
- 1/4 or 1/2 teaspoon garlic salt
- 1 teaspoon salt
- pepper to taste
- 1 tablespoon red wine vinegar
- fresh thyme, to garnish

Direction

- Preheat your oven to 400 degrees F.
- Trim your Brussels by cutting off the little brown end. If there are any yellow leaves, pull them off. Cut any large ones in half. Add to a large bowl.
- Peel your sweet potato and chop into 1-2 inch pieces. Add to the large bowl.
- Smash 2 cloves of garlic and add it to the bowl.
- Pour 1/3 cup olive oil over the vegetables.
- Add cumin, garlic salt, salt, and pepper to taste. Stir to coat.
- (Line a large sheet pan with foil if you want super easy clean-up)
- Drizzle a little olive oil onto the sheet pan and rub it all over the pan (or foil) with your hand. Or you could spray it really well with non-stick spray.
- Pour the veggies onto the pan.
- Roast at 400 for about 40-45 minutes. The veggies are done when they are brown and a fork slides into them easily.

- Place the veggies in a serving bowl and toss with 1-2 tablespoons red wine vinegar to taste. Garnish with fresh thyme if you want. Eat hot!
- Notes
- The garlic is there to add flavor, not necessarily to be eaten, although I do think it's quite tasty.
- If you want to reheat these, take them out of the oven and let cool. (Skip adding the red wine vinegar.) Store in a Tupperware in the fridge for up to 2 days. When you are ready to eat, spread the veggies on a greased pan and roast at 400 for about 5-10 minutes until you can hear them sizzling and they are hot. Remove from the oven, add a little red wine vinegar, and serve!

100.   Roasted Brussels Sprouts Recipe

Serving: 4 | Prep: | Cook: 40mins | Ready in:

Ingredients

- 1 Lb. Brussels sprouts
- 1/4 cup olive oil
- 1 lemon, juiced
- salt
- black pepper

Direction

- Preheat oven to 400 degrees
- Trim and clean Brussels sprouts.
- In a large roasting pan, combine Brussels sprouts and olive oil.
- Cook for 30 minutes, stirring occasionally, until cooked through and browned.
- Remove from oven and stir in lemon juice and season with salt and pepper.

101.   Roasted Brussels Sprouts With Dijon Cream Sauce Recipe

Serving: 0 | Prep: | Cook: 30mins | Ready in:

Ingredients

- 1 lb. Brussels sprouts, halved lengthwise
- 2 cups red onions, cut into wedges
- 8 oz. kielbasa, 1/2"-thick slices
- 2 T. olive oil
- salt and pepper
- 1/2 cup heavy cream
- 1/4 cup Dijon mustard
- 1 T. honey
- 1 t. apple cider vinegar

Direction

- Preheat oven to 450°.
- Toss sprouts, onions, and kielbasa in a bowl with the oil, salt, and pepper. Spread in a single layer on a baking sheet and roast 20 minutes, or until sprouts are tender, yet still crisp.
- Simmer cream, mustard, honey, and vinegar in a saucepan over low heat for 10 minutes, or until slightly thickened. To serve, spoon sauce over roasted sprouts.
- Per 1/2 cup: 155 calories; 66% calories from fat; 11g total fat; 10g carb.; 285mg sodium; 2g fiber; 5g protein
- C@H Note: To clean sprouts, remove damaged or yellow leaves and trim the stem.

102.   Roasted Brussels Sprouts With Garlic Recipe

Serving: 0 | Prep: | Cook: 45mins | Ready in:

Ingredients

- http://cooking.nytimes.com/recipes/1890-roasted-brussels-sprouts-with-garlic
- Roasted Brussels sprouts With Garlic

- Ingredients
- 1 pint Brussels sprouts (about a pound)
- 4 to 6 tablespoons extra virgin olive oil, to coat bottom of pan
- 5 cloves garlic, peeled
- Salt and pepper to taste
- 1 tablespoon balsamic vinegar

Direction

- Preparation
- Step 1 Heat oven to 400 degrees. Trim bottom of Brussels sprouts, and slice each in half top to bottom. Heat oil in cast-iron pan over medium-high heat until it shimmers; put sprouts cut side down in one layer in pan. Put in garlic, and sprinkle with salt and pepper.
- Step 2 Cook, undisturbed, until sprouts begin to brown on bottom, and transfer to oven. Roast, shaking pan every 5 minutes, until sprouts are quite brown and tender, about 10 to 20 minutes.
- Step 3 Taste, and add more salt and pepper if necessary. Stir in balsamic vinegar, and serve hot or warm.

103. Roasted Brussels Sprouts With Walnuts Recipe

Serving: 6 | Prep: | Cook: 45mins | Ready in:

Ingredients

- 2 lbs. Brussels sprouts
- 1 t. dried thyme
- 1 t. dried oregano or marjoram
- 1 c. walnuts
- 2 t. garlic powder
- 1/2 t. salt
- 1/4 t. ground black pepper
- 1/4 c. extra-virgin olive oil
- 1/2 c. balsamic vinegar

Direction

- Preheat oven to 425 degrees.
- Cut bottoms off Brussels sprouts and trim any damaged outer leaves. Soak in a bowl of cold water for about 5 minutes, then drain well. Cut in halves and place in roasting pan. Add thyme, oregano or marjoram, walnuts, garlic powder, salt, and pepper. Add olive oil and balsamic vinegar; toss well to coat.
- Cook for 20 minutes. Remove from oven, stir well; cook for about 25 minutes more, or until browned and caramelized.

104. Roasted Brussels Sprouts With Cranberries Recipe

Serving: 4 | Prep: | Cook: 35mins | Ready in:

Ingredients

- 2 tablespoons extra-virgin olive oil
- 1 tablespoon balsamic vinegar (or other sweet vinegar like rice
- vinegar or a reisling vinegar)
- 1 1 1/2 pounds Brussels sprouts (4 cups or so)
- 1/2 cup dried cranberries
- 1 cup pecan halves
- Course sea salt or kosher salt
- .

Direction

- Preheat the oven to 425F.
- Lightly grease a baking pan with olive oil.
- Drizzle the oil and vinegar over the Brussels sprouts in a large bowl and toss gently to coat.
- Arrange the sprouts in a single, uncrowded layer on the prepared pan.
- Roast for about 35 minutes, tossing in pecans and cranberries halfway through.
- Shake the pan occasionally for even cooking.
- Transfer the sprouts to a serving bowl, stir in cranberries and pecans, and sprinkle with salt.
- Serve immediately.
- Variation: Add chunks of butternut squash to Brussels sprouts before roasting

105.   Roasted Maple Dijon Brussel Sprouts Recipe

Serving: 2 | Prep: | Cook: 20mins | Ready in:

Ingredients

- 2 servings of brussel sprouts
- 1 1/2 tsp Dijon mustard
- 1 tbs maple syrup
- 1 tbs aged balsamic vinegar
- 1 tbs olive oil
- salt / pepper

Direction

- Set oven to 400.
- Trim sprouts and cut the larger ones in half.
- Stir together the mustard, syrup, vinegar, oil salt and pepper in a bowl. Toss sprouts with glaze and coat well. Spray or oil baking sheet and roast for 20 minutes, or until done, tossing once.

106.   Saucy Brussels Sprouts Recipe

Serving: 8 | Prep: | Cook: 55mins | Ready in:

Ingredients

- 3 pounds Brussels sprouts
- 1/4 cup butter
- 2 white onions chopped
- 1/4 cup flour
- 2 cups warm milk
- 1-1/2 cups shredded white cheddar cheese
- 3/4 teaspoon ground nutmeg
- 1 teaspoon salt
- 2 teaspoons freshly ground black pepper

Direction

- Trim sprouts and cut x in base of each.
- In large pan of boiling water cook sprouts 10 minutes.
- Drain and chill under cold water and press out excess water with towel.
- Cut in half and place in shallow greased casserole dish.
- Melt butter in saucepan over medium heat and cook onions stirring often for 10 minutes.
- Stir in flour and cook stirring constantly 1 minute.
- Add milk and cook stirring 5 minutes or until thickened.
- Remove from heat and stir in half of the cheese, nutmeg, salt and pepper.
- Pour over sprouts then cover and bake at 375 for 40 minutes.
- Sprinkle with remaining cheese and broil uncovered for 2 minutes.

107.   Sauteed Brussels Sprouts With Onions And Lemon Zest Recipe

Serving: 6 | Prep: | Cook: 15mins | Ready in:

Ingredients

- About 2 lbs Brussels sprouts, washed, brown spots removed, cut in halves
- 1 large onion, thinly sliced
- 1 tbsp butter
- 1 tbsp olive oil
- juice of 1 lemon
- zest of 1 lemon
- 1 tsp herbs de Provence (The mixture typically contains rosemary, marjoram, basil, bay leaf, thyme, and sometimes lavender flowers and other herbs.)
- salt & pepper to taste

Direction

- In a non-stick skillet over medium heat, melt the butter and olive oil and add herbs de Provence and a minute later, the onions. Sauté the onions until they are golden-brown salting them lightly in the end.
- Add the Brussels sprouts and the lemon juice and sauté for about 7-8 minutes until the green color becomes brighter and more intense. Add the lemon zest and mix well in the pan reducing the heat to low. Cook for 1 more minute and remove from heat.
- Season with salt and pepper to taste and serve immediately.

108.   Sauteed Corn And Brussel Sprouts Recipe

Serving: 2 | Prep: | Cook: 20mins |Ready in:

Ingredients

- 1 1/2 cup fresh corn kernals or frozen (I recommend getting the white kernals)
- 1/2 cup chopped/julienned brussel sprouts
- 3-4 slices of turkey or regular bacon roughly snipped (using scissors because i'm lazy)
- 1 scallion chopped (use the white part for cooking and the green for garnish later)
- 1 1/2 tbsp. butter
- 2-3 cloves garlic minced
- 2-3 drizzle of olive oil
- salt + pepper to taste
- the asian fried red onions

Direction

- Heat your wok to medium high and put in the oil, butter, garlic, bacon and the white part of the scallion (if you use regular bacon, you don't need so much butter and oil)
- Sautéed until aromatic and the bacon is fairly crisp
- Put in the corn and Brussels sprouts and sautéed for about 15min. I like to leave mine a bit longer until the corn start browning a bit.

- Make sure you season with salt and pepper to taste
- When done, put in dish and garnish with the green scallions and fried scallions

109.   Scalloped Brussel Sprouts Recipe

Serving: 8 | Prep: | Cook: 45mins |Ready in:

Ingredients

- 2 lb. brussel sprouts
- 2 tbsp. butter
- 1 onion, chopped
- 1/4 tsp. Dried thyme
- 1/4 cup flour
- 2 cups milk, warmed
- 1 ½ cups shredded gruyere cheese
- 3/4 tsp. salt
- 1/4 tsp. pepper
- TOPPING:
- 1 ½ cups bread crumbs
- ½ cup shredded gruyere, cheddar or gouda cheese
- 2 tbsp. butter, melted

Direction

- Trim Brussels sprouts; cut X in base of each. In saucepan of boiling salted water, cover and cook Brussels sprouts until tender-crisp, 7 to 9 minutes. Drain and chill under cold water; press out excess water with towel. Cut in half if large; place in greased shallow 8-cup casserole dish.
- In saucepan, melt butter over medium heat; cook onion and thyme, stirring occasionally, until onion is softened, about 5 minutes. Sprinkle with flour, cook, stirring, for 1 minute. Add milk; cook, stirring, until thickened, 6 to 8 minutes. Remove from heat; stir in cheese, salt and pepper. Pour over Brussels sprouts.

- TOPPING: In bowl, stir together bread crumbs, cheese and melted butter (Make ahead and cover and refrigerate Brussels sprouts mixture and topping separately for up to 24 hours.)
- Cover and bake Brussels sprouts mixture in 375 F oven for 30 minutes. Uncover and sprinkle with topping; bake until golden and bubbling, about 20 minutes. Serves 8

110. Sesame Brussels Sprouts Recipe

Serving: 4 | Prep: | Cook: 10mins | Ready in:

Ingredients

- 1 pound fresh Brussels sprouts
- 2 Tbsp sesame seeds (Can use toasted)
- 1/4 Cup soy sauce (I used reduce sodium)
- 1 Tbsp EVOO (extra virgin olive oil)
- 2 Tbsp sugar
- Dash of salt

Direction

- Wash Brussels sprout thoroughly, remove discolored leaves.
- Cut off stem ends and slash the bottom end with a shallow X.
- Place sprouts in a small amount of boiling water, cover, reduce heat, and simmer for ~ 8 minutes, or until tender.
- Drain sprouts, set aside.
- Brown sesame seeds in hot oil. Remove from heat; add soy sauce, sugar, salt (optional), stirring will.
- Pour over warm Brussels sprouts, tossing gently.
- Serve immediately.

111. Shreaded Brussel Sprouts With Bacon Recipe

Serving: 8 | Prep: | Cook: 20mins | Ready in:

Ingredients

- 11/2 lbs. brussel sprouts
- 4 slices bacon,chopped
- 1 lg. onion,chopped
- 1/2 tsp dried thyme
- 1 14 1/2 oz. can chicken broth
- salt and pepper,to taste

Direction

- Cut and discard the stem ends of Brussels sprouts, pull off and discard any discolored outer leaves. Halve each sprout lengthwise, then slice halves thinly crosswise to make shreds.
- In lg. non-stick skillet over med-high heat, cook bacon till it begins to brown, about 4 mins. Add the onions and thyme and sauté till onions are tender, about 4 mins.
- Add Brussels sprouts and broth. Cover the pan, adjusting the heat to maintain a simmer. Cook, stirring occasionally, until tender, about 10 mins. Season with salt and pepper.

112. Shredded Brussels Sprouts Recipe

Serving: 8 | Prep: | Cook: 20mins | Ready in:

Ingredients

- 1-1/2 pounds Brussels sprouts
- 4 tablespoons unsalted butter
- 1/2 teaspoon salt
- 1/4 teaspoon white pepper
- 2 teaspoons water
- juice of 1/2 lime

Direction

- Soak whole sprouts in a large bowl of cold salted water to clean then trim and discard ends and any bitter outer leaves.
- Cut each in half lengthwise then slice thinly across width.
- Melt butter in a large skillet over medium high heat.
- Sauté sprouts with salt and pepper until they start to brown.
- Add water and cook until barely limp.
- Stir in lime juice and serve immediately.

113. Skillet Braised Brussels Sprouts Recipe

Serving: 4 | Prep: | Cook: 15mins | Ready in:

Ingredients

- 4 slices bacon, chopped fine
- 2 shallots, thinly sliced
- 1 lb. Brussels sprouts, stem ends trimmed, halved through the stems
- 1/2 C. water
- salt
- 1 Tbsp. butter
- 1 Tbsp. red wine vinegar
- pepper

Direction

- Cook the bacon and shallots in a 12 inch skillet over medium heat until bacon is crisp and the shallots are browned
- Remove to a paper towel lined plate
- Add the Brussels sprouts, water and 1/2 tsp. salt to the skillet and increase the heat to medium high
- Cover and simmer until the sprouts are bright green, about 9-10 minutes
- Uncover and cook until the liquid has evaporated and the sprouts are tender, about 5 minutes longer
- Remove pan from heat and add the bacon and shallot mixture, butter and vinegar

- Season with salt and pepper to taste

114. So Good They Cant Be Brussel Sprouts Recipe

Serving: 4 | Prep: | Cook: 20mins | Ready in:

Ingredients

- # 1 lb. Brussels sprouts
- # 8 strips of bacon
- # 2 tbsp butter
- # salt and pepper to season
- 1/2 of a lemon

Direction

- Cut the cores from the sprouts and discard.
- Peel off the leaves, reserving them, and discard or thinly slice the tight, innermost heads.
- Heat a sauté pan and fry the bacon until crisp; remove to paper towel to drain. Pour all but a tablespoon of fat from the pan (I left it all in).
- Add the butter, to melt. Toss the leaves in, and sauté until tender, 5 t 10 minutes. Season, crumble over the bacon, and Squeeze the Lemon over top and serve.

115. Southern Style Brussel Sprouts Recipe

Serving: 8 | Prep: | Cook: 30mins | Ready in:

Ingredients

- 5 slices thick cut bacon,cut in 1/2" pieces
- 2 cloves garlic,sliced
- 3lbs. brussel sprouts(fresh),peeled,stems removed and cut in half
- 11/2c water
- 2 Tbs unsalted butter

- 1tsp sugar
- 1/2tsp kosher salt
- 1/8tsp black pepper
- 1c chopped pecans

Direction

- In a Dutch oven, cook bacon over med-high heat until brown. Add garlic and cook 1 min. Drain bacon and garlic; set aside, discarding grease.
- To Dutch oven, add Brussels sprouts, water, butter, sugar, salt and pepper. Simmer over med-high heat, stirring occasionally, for approx. 15 mins. or till almost all water has evaporated from pan.
- Add reserved bacon and garlic and pecans. Cook 2 minutes. Serve

---

116. Spicy Fried Brussels Sprouts Recipe

Serving: 0 | Prep: | Cook: 20mins | Ready in:

Ingredients

- 2lbs small Brussels sprouts, trimmed and cut in half
- 1/4 cup butter, melted, or, can sub 1/4 cup salad quality olive oil
- juice from 2 lemons
- 1T honey
- 1-2t Sirracha(also known as "Rooster sauce", or, sub your favorite hot sauce)
- 1/2-1t red pepper flakes
- 3 cloves garlic, minced
- kosher or sea salt and fresh ground black pepper
- peanut or olive oil for frying

Direction

- Heat about 1 inch of oil in large, heavy pan or skillet. (I used cast iron)

- Meanwhile, whisk together butter, lemon juice, honey, Sriracha, red pepper flakes garlic, and a little salt and pepper in large bowl, until combined, then set aside.
- Fry sprouts in batches in 350 oil just for about 2 minutes or so each side. They will turn a beautiful golden brown.
- Set on paper towels or brown paper bags to drain while finishing the rest. The oil shouldn't cool down too much, since you are frying so quickly, but it's important to not let it get too hot, either. So, watch your temp, and keep it right around 350.
- When all are fried and drained, toss with the dressing, sprinkle with a little more salt and pepper and serve immediately.
- Don't worry, though, if these aren't steaming hot, they were good at room temp...the dressing is full enough that it made this almost like a fried sprout salad :)
- **During frying, some of the outer leaves will fall off into the oil... get them out quick, but don't discard them... just add 'em to the dressing, too...or, just munch on those while you're finishing the dish...they are crispy and delicious. :) Don't leave them in the oil, though, because they will burn quickly.

---

117. Sports Illustrated Brussels Sprouts Recipe

Serving: 2 | Prep: | Cook: 15mins | Ready in:

Ingredients

- 3 garlic cloves, minced
- 2 slices bacon (I used apple wood smoked, thick cut)
- 1/2 pound Brussels sprouts, trimmed, tough leaves removed, halved
- 1/2 tsp sugar
- 1/4 cup chicken broth
- sea salt & black pepper, freshly ground - to taste

Direction

- Heat medium skillet over medium heat. Add bacon and cook until crisp. Transfer to paper towel lined plate to cool. Put sprouts into skillet, cut side down. Cook until they begin to brown, about 3 minutes. Add garlic, season with s&p and sauté for another 1-2 minutes. Increase heat to medium-high, then add sugar and broth, scraping browned bits from bottom of pan and mix well. Cover and cook for another 2 minutes. Meanwhile, cut bacon into small pieces. Toss bacon with sprouts before serving.

118. Surprisingly Delicious Brussel Sprouts Recipe

Serving: 4 | Prep: | Cook: 20mins | Ready in:

Ingredients

- 1 pound of Brussels sprouts
- 2 (or 3 or 4 or 5....) slices of thick bacon
- kosher salt and pepper to taste
- perhaps some olive oil, depending on how much your bacon puts out ;)

Direction

- First, slice the Brussels sprouts in half. Slice them vertically down through the stems so the leaves will stay together. If they're exceptionally large, quarter them.
- Then chop up the bacon into pieces, like large bacon bits. In a skillet, cook the bacon over medium high heat. Once the bacon is done, take a slotted spoon and remove the bacon tidbits, but leave the grease.
- While still on med-high heat, add sprouts and toss to coat. Add a heavy pinch of kosher salt and pepper. You want to cook the sprouts until they are tender, but still have a little bit of a bite to them. During cooking, if you notice that the pan is getting too dry, splash a bit of

olive oil in the pan to lube the sprouts back up. Add a lid (for if the oil is spitting at you, but it also helps it cook faster, keeping the heat in and kind of steaming the veggies as they brown). Cook for about 7 to 10 minutes until the leaves have turned soft on the outside but still hold their shape. Remove from heat, reintroduce the bacon, and serve!

119. Totally Awesome Brussel Sprouts Recipe

Serving: 4 | Prep: | Cook: 10mins | Ready in:

Ingredients

- fresh brussel sprouts
- 2 tbsp salted butter
- pepper
- garlic salt
- fresh lemon juice
- balsamic vinegar

Direction

- Pre heat oven to 350 F
- Wash Brussels sprouts, trim 1/8" off bottoms and halve
- Blanch sprouts in boiling water for 2 min.
- Arrange sprouts cut side up in a baking dish
- Sprinkle with salt and pepper, dab with butter
- Bake for 10 min
- Before serving, sprinkle with lemon juice and vinegar

120. Whuebel And ChefMeows Marinated Brussel Sprouts Recipe

Serving: 8 | Prep: | Cook: 20mins | Ready in:

Ingredients

- 1/3 cup salad oil
- 2 tablespons brown sugar
- 1 teaspoon salt
- 1/8 teaspoon freshly ground black pepper
- 1/2 large onion thinly sliced
- 1/2 cup white wine
- 1/2 cup red wine vinegar
- 2 cloves garlic crushed
- 1/2 lemon sliced and squeezed OR 3 tablespoons chopped dill pickle
- 2 pounds Brussels sprouts trimmed and cut in half
- 3 tablespoons chopped dill pickle

Direction

- Combine wine, vinegar, sugar and garlic in heavy sauce pan and bring to boil then add sprouts.
- Reduce heat then over and simmer 10 minutes.
- Transfer sprouts and liquid to serving bowl.
- Add lemon and lemon squeezings or dill pickle - use either dill pickles or lemon but not both.
- Put in refrigerator overnight to allow flavors to blend and be absorbed.
- Serve at room temperature.
- Note: This recipe was developed as a result of the combined efforts of chefmeow and whuebl.

121. Brussel Sprouts On A Skewer Recipe

Serving: 4 | Prep: | Cook: 10mins |Ready in:

Ingredients

- 1 lb brussel sprouts
- 1 red onion
- juice and zest from 1 lemon
- 2 cloves garlic, minced
- 3 Tb butter, melted
- 3 Tb olive oil

- chives, parsley, or green onions
- sea salt and cracked pepper to taste

Direction

- Get grill ready
- Steam Brussels sprouts 5 minutes
- Cut off ends
- Prepare red onion for skewers
- Alternate red onion and Brussels sprouts on skewers
- Combine remaining ingredients in a mixing bowl
- Baste on veggies as you grill until desired doneness is achieved

122. Brussels Sprouts With Shallot And Capers Recipe

Serving: 4 | Prep: | Cook: 20mins |Ready in:

Ingredients

- Brussels sprouts
- olive oil
- shallot
- chicken broth
- capers
- cold butter

Direction

- Wash and trim Brussels sprouts
- Steam until fork tender
- In separate pan cook sliced shallot in olive oil until translucent
- Add cooked sprouts
- Add chicken broth until about 1/3 way up the sprouts
- Cook on low until most of the chicken broth is gone
- Add capers and butter until butter is melted

123.　　煎烤的球芽甘蓝 Chinese Style Brussel Sprouts Recipe

Serving: 0 | Prep: | Cook: 20mins | Ready in:

Ingredients

- 1kg small Brussels sprouts
- 8 tbsp hoisin sauce
- sesame oil
- A
- 3 tbsp ginger, minced
- 3 gloves of garlic, minced
- B
- 3 tbsp rice wine
- 1 tbsp soy sauce
- 1 tsp sugar

Direction

- Wash Brussels sprouts, trim ends, then cut bulbs into halves.
- Heat large wok, add 3 tbsp. oil. Add A, and stir-fry over medium heat until fragrant.
- Add Brussels sprouts and stir-fry over very high heat until color turns.
- Add B, and cook for about 5 minutes, stirring regularly, until Brussels sprouts start to become tender.
- Stir in hoisin sauce. Continue to cook for about 2-3 minutes more.
- Drizzle with a little sesame oil, and serve.

Chapter 2: Awesome Vegetable Side Dish Recipes

***

124.　　1015 ONION RINGS Recipe

Serving: 6 | Prep: | Cook: 5mins | Ready in:

Ingredients

- 3 large Texas 1015 onions
- 2 c. buttermilk
- 1 c. all-purpose flour
- 1 1/2 tsp. baking powder
- 1 tsp. salt
- 1/4 tsp. red pepper
- 2/3 c. water
- 1 beaten egg
- 1 T. vegetable oil
- 1 tsp. lemon juice
- vegetable oil for frying
- salt, if desired

Direction

- Peel and slice onions into separate rings.
- Pour buttermilk into a large shallow pan.
- Add onion rings and soak 30 minutes.
- Combine flour, baking powder, salt, red pepper, water, egg, 1 T. oil, and lemon juice; stir until smooth.
- Heat oil to 375 degrees.
- Remove onion rings from buttermilk and dip into batter.
- Fry in hot oil until golden brown.
- Drain on absorbent paper.
- Sprinkle with salt, if desired
- The cook time is for each batch or load...
- DO NOT OVER FILL FRYER OR THEY WILL BE GREASY AND SOGGY.

125.　　African Spinach Recipe

Serving: 4 | Prep: | Cook: 5mins | Ready in:

Ingredients

- 2 bunches spinach

- 250 ml water
- 2 ml salt
- 50 g peanuts

Direction

- Clean the spinach in cold water. Remove the stalks and discard. Chop the leaves. Bring the water to the boil in a saucepan, add the chopped leaves.
- Cook until wilted, 1 min
- Pour off most of the water
- Meanwhile roast the peanuts in a frying pan then add the salt.
- Simmer gently for a few min
- Add the peanuts to the cooked spinach mix in and serve.

126.   Amaretto Carrots Recipe

Serving: 8 | Prep: | Cook: 20mins | Ready in:

Ingredients

- 1 lb carrots , sliced (reserve green tops)
- 1/4 teaspoon salt
- 2 teaspoons amaretto liqueur
- 2 teaspoons almond extract
- 2 tablespoons butter
- 1 tablespoon cornstarch
- 1/3 cup honey

Direction

- Place carrots in a medium saucepan; cover with water (about 1 1/2 cups). Add salt; cook over medium heat until fork-tender, about 10 minutes.
- Wash green tops and chill in ice water.
- Remove carrots to a warm dish and set aside. Ladle a tablespoon or two of cooking liquid into a small dish and set aside to cool.
- Add amaretto, almond extract and butter to saucepan; stir constantly until butter is melted.

- Whisk cornstarch into the small dish of reserved (cool) liquid; whisk cornstarch mixture into saucepan and continue cooking until sauce is thickened.
- Stir in honey.
- Return carrots to pan and heat through.
- Garnish with green carrot tops.

127.   Artichoke Pilaf Recipe

Serving: 6 | Prep: | Cook: 20mins | Ready in:

Ingredients

- 1-1/2 cups basmati rice
- 4 large cloves garlic
- 1/4 teaspoon olive oil
- 1/8 teaspoon dried thyme
- 1/8 teaspoon dried marjoram
- 1/8 teaspoon basil
- 3 cups water
- 8 canned artichoke hearts

Direction

- Rinse rice several times until rinse water runs clear.
- Sauté garlic and herbs in olive oil until fragrant about two minutes.
- Add rice and sauté another three minutes.
- Add artichoke hearts and sauté another minute.
- Add water and bring to a boil.
- Cover then reduce heat and cook about fifteen minutes.
- Turn off burner and let sit five more minutes.
- Fluff with fork.

128.   Artichoke Tart Recipe

Serving: 8 | Prep: | Cook: 30mins | Ready in:

Ingredients

- 8-12 artichoke hearts
- 1/8 stick of butter
- 1 cup sweet onion chopped
- 1/4 cup red bell pepper, small diced
- 1 tablespoon minced garlic
- 1/8 teaspoon oregano
- 1/8 teaspoon thyme
- 4 eggs
- 1 teaspoon creole mustard
- 1 teaspoon creole seasoning
- 1/2 cup panko bread crumbs
- 1/4 teaspoon hot sauce
- 1/2 teaspoon grated parmesan cheese
- 1 cup grated cheddar
- 1 teaspoon freshly ground black pepper
- 1/4 cup minced green onion
- frozen pie crust thawed.

Direction

- Preheat oven to 325 degrees. Place pie crust in for ten minutes while crust is baking.
- Melt butter in a small sauté pan over medium heat. Add onion and red bell pepper and cook 3 to 4 minutes. Add garlic, oregano, thyme and cook 2 to 3 minutes more. Remove both from heat and cool.
- Roughly chop the artichokes. Whip the eggs in a large mixing bowl, and mix in the rest of the ingredients.
- Spread the mixture into the pie. Bake 30 minutes.
- Let cool to room temp

129.   Asian Cole Slaw Recipe

Serving: 8 | Prep: | Cook: | Ready in:

Ingredients

- 1 small head napa cabbage, sliced thinly
- 1 bunch green onions, chopped thinly

- 1 pkg chicken flavored ramen noodles, broken up
- salt and pepper to taste
- handful toasted almonds
- For Dressing:
- 1/2 cup veggie oil
- 1/4 - 1/2 cup white wine vinegar (depending on your taste)
- seasoning packet from noodles
- handful toasted sesame seeds
- 1 tsp dark sesame oil

Direction

- Combine all ingredients together to make the dressing.
- Pour dressing over cabbage, onions and noodles and mix well.
- Add salt and pepper to taste
- Let set overnight for seasonings to blend and noodles to soften
- Add almonds before serving

130.   Asian Sesame Grilled Asparagus Recipe

Serving: 4 | Prep: | Cook: 20mins | Ready in:

Ingredients

- 1 pound asparagus spears
- 2 tablespoons sesame oil
- 1 tablespoon soy sauce
- 1 clove garlic minced
- 1 teaspoon salt
- 1 teaspoon freshly ground black pepper
- 2 tablespoons sesame seeds

Direction

- Soak skewers or toothpicks in water 1 hour before using then drain.
- Snap off bases of asparagus then skewer 5 asparagus spears together with.

- In small bowl combine oil, soy sauce and garlic and stir to mix.
- Brush on asparagus on both sides and season with salt and pepper.
- Place asparagus on grill and cook until nicely browned turning to brown both sides.
- Sprinkle with sesame seeds as they grill.

131.   Asian Slaw Recipe

Serving: 6 | Prep: | Cook: | Ready in:

Ingredients

- 1 (3-inch) piece ginger, grated fine
- 1/2 cup rice wine vinegar
- 1 tablespoon soy sauce
- 1 lime, juiced
- 2 tablespoons sesame oil
- 1/2 cup peanut butter
- 1 head napa cabbage, sliced thin
- 1 red bell pepper, julienne fine
- 1 yellow bell pepper, julienne fine
- 2 serrano chiles, minced fine
- 1 large carrot, grated fine with a peeler
- 3 green onions, cut on the bias, all of white part and half of the green
- 2 tablespoons chiffonade cilantro
- 2 tablespoons chiffonade mint
- 1/2 teaspoon ground black pepper
- ****
- Optional Additions That I Like:
- Chopped peanuts

Direction

- In a small bowl, or food processor combine ginger, vinegar, soy sauce, lime juice, oil, and peanut butter.
- In a large bowl, combine all other ingredients and then toss with dressing.
- You can save some of the dressing to dress noodles that can be added to this dish along with stir fried pork to make an entire meal.

132.   Asparagus And Parmesan Foldovers Recipe

Serving: 10 | Prep: | Cook: 10mins | Ready in:

Ingredients

- 2 loaves sandwich bread
- butter, softened
- parmesan cheese
- 3 cans Jolly Green Giant asparagus spears, drained and placed on paper towel to absorb the moisture

Direction

- Trim the crusts from the bread (save for crumbs, or homemade croutons)
- Roll bread flat between two pieces of waxed paper
- Spread each slice with softened butter and sprinkle with Parmesan cheese
- Place 1 spear on corner of bread and roll up
- Secure with toothpick*
- Brush each roll with melted butter and sprinkle with cheese
- Place on a cookie sheet
- Bake at 400 degrees for about 10-12 minutes
- *This can be done the day before, refrigerate, then baked the next day

133.   Asparagus And Toasted Pine Nuts With Lemon Vinaigrette Recipe

Serving: 6 | Prep: | Cook: 20mins | Ready in:

Ingredients

- 1 pound fresh asparagus spears
- 3 tablespoons pine nuts
- 1/4 cup olive oil
- 1 tablespoon fresh lemon juice

- 1 clove garlic crushed
- 1/2 teaspoon salt
- 1/2 teaspoon dried whole basil
- 1/2 teaspoon dried whole oregano
- 1 teaspoon freshly ground black pepper

Direction

- Snap off tough ends of asparagus then remove scales from stalks with vegetable peeler
- Place spears in a steaming rack over boiling water then cover and steam 5 minutes.
- Transfer to a serving platter.
- Sauté pine nuts in a small skillet over medium heat for 3 minutes then set aside.
- Combine olive oil and remaining ingredients in saucepan then stir with wire whisk to blend.
- Cook over medium heat 3 minutes or until thoroughly heated stirring constantly.
- Pour over asparagus then sprinkle with pine nuts.
- Let stand to room temperature before serving.

134. Asparagus Artichoke And Shitake Risotto Recipe

Serving: 4 | Prep: | Cook: 45mins | Ready in:

Ingredients

- 5 cups chicken broth
- 1 cup water
- 1 lb thin to medium aspargus, trim and cut 1/4 inch slice, tips - 1-1/4 inch
- 3/4 lb fresh shitake mushrooms, discard stem, slice cap - 1/4 inch thick
- 2 large fresh artichoke hearts
- 2 shallots, finely chopped
- 3/4 cup dry white wine
- 1 Tbsp EVOO
- 1/2 stick unsalted butter
- 1 cup grated Parmesan-Reggiano
- 1-1/2 cups Arborio (Italian) rice
- 2 garlic cloves

- 1 Bay leaf
- 1 Tbsp white vinegar

Direction

- Artichokes: Remove all the outer leaves, choke, and stem of a whole artichoke. Cut heart into 1/4 slices and immediately place in a bowl with juice of 1 lemon, completely coating the artichoke slices to prevent browning. In a small pot, pour 1/4 cup white wine, 2 smashed garlic cloves, bay leaf, 1-1/2 cups water, & 1 Tbsp./splash white vinegar, and bring to a boil. Add the artichoke hearts with the lemon juice, reduce heat and let simmer for ~ 10 minutes or until tender. Drain and set aside.
- In a 4 quart pot, bring broth and water to a boil, add the asparagus and cook uncovered ~3 to 4 minutes until crisp-tender. Transfer to bowl of iced water with a slotted spoon to stop cooking. Drain and pat dry.
- Keep broth at a very slow simmer, covered.
- In a heavy 4 quart saucepan, heat oil with 1 Tbsp. of butter over med-high heat until foam subsides. Add mushrooms and sauté until browned, ~ 4 minutes. Season with salt and pepper, then transfer to a bowl.
- Cook shallots in 2 tablespoons of butter in a saucepan over medium to med-low heat until tender, ~3 minutes. Add rice, stirring and cook for ~1 minute. Add 1/2 cup white wine, cook while stirring until absorbed, ~1 minute.
- Now add 1 cup of the simmering broth to the rice and cook at a strong simmer while stirring until absorbed, ~ 2 minutes. Continue simmering and adding broth 1/2 cup at a time, stirring frequently. Let the broth be absorbed before making each addition and cook until rice is barely tender and looks creamy, ~ 20 minutes. Reserve leftover broth for thinning later.
- Remove from heat, stir 1/2 cup of cheese, remaining butter, then salt and pepper to taste.
- Gently stir in asparagus, artichokes, and mushrooms. Cover pan and let set for ~ 1

minute. If needed thin rice with some of the leftover broth.

- Serve immediately and garnish as desired with remaining cheese.

135.   Asparagus Au Gratin Recipe

Serving: 4 | Prep: | Cook: 40mins | Ready in:

Ingredients

- 4 tablespoons butter
- 1/4 cup all purpose flour
- 1-3/4 cup chicken stock
- 1/4 cup half and half
- 3/4 cup grated cheddar cheese
- 1/4 cup grated parmesan cheese
- 1 teaspoon salt
- 1 teaspoon freshly ground black pepper
- 3 bunches hot freshly cooked asparagus spears

Direction

- Preheat oven to 450.
- Butter a casserole dish.
- In a saucepan melt the butter then add the flour and stir with a wire whisk until blended.
- Meanwhile bring chicken stock and half and half to a boil and add all at once to butter flour mixture stirring vigorously with the whisk until sauce is thickened and smooth then add the cheddar, Parmesan, salt and pepper and stir until the cheeses melt.
- Alternate layers of sauce and asparagus in a buttered casserole ending with a layer of sauce.
- Sprinkle with additional Parmesan cheese and brown quickly under a preheated broiler or bake in preheated oven for 5 minutes.

136.   Asparagus Casserole Recipe

Serving: 4 | Prep: | Cook: 30mins | Ready in:

Ingredients

- 2 cans asparagus spears
- 1 can cream of chicken soup
- 2 cups sharp cheese, grate
- 4 hard boiled eggs
- 12 saltine crackers, crushed

Direction

- Heat soup with juice from one can of asparagus and set aside. Layer asparagus, sliced eggs, crushed crackers, then grated cheese in dish; pour soup over this layer. On the top layer, pour soup after crackers so cheese is last (on top).
- Cook until bubbly at 350 degrees.

137.   Asparagus On The Grill Recipe

Serving: 4 | Prep: | Cook: 10mins | Ready in:

Ingredients

- 1 1/2-2 lbs. asparagus
- olive oil
- salt and pepper to taste
- garlic powder (optional)

Direction

- Soak wooden skewers in water for 20 minutes
- About 3/4-1 inch from end of asparagus, push skewer through and push to other end of skewer.
- Repeat with 5 more asparagus
- Take another skewer and from the other end of the asparagus do the same thing with all
- Now it should look like a raft

- 6 asparagus and two skewers
- Brush with olive oil
- Season with salt and pepper and garlic powder if desired
- Grill over medium heat flipping once until done

138. Asparagus Parmesan Recipe

Serving: 2 | Prep: | Cook: 15mins | Ready in:

Ingredients

- 16 spears asparagus, trimmed, peeled and blanched in boiling salted water
- 1 tbsp. parmesan cheese, grated
- 1 egg, large, beaten + 1 tbsp. cold water
- 1/2 cup flour
- 1 cup bread crumbs, fresh made, crust removed I used boxed unseasoned
- 1/2 tsp. garlic, freshly minced and peeled
- 1/2 tsp. salt
- 1 pinch ground white pepper

Direction

- Trim, peel and blanch the asparagus in boiling salted water for one minute.
- Remove and cool in cold water; drain well.
- Dip the spears in the flour that has been seasoned with the salt and pepper, then into the beaten egg and water mixture, then into the bread crumbs (to which the grated cheese and garlic has been added); coat well with the crumbs.
- In a frying pan heat the oil over medium-high heat, add half of the spears and sauté on all sides until golden in color, drain on paper towels and keep warm while you cook the remaining spears.
- Serve with a marinara sauce and additional grated cheese over freshly cooked thin spaghetti.

- First time I made... I did not bother with spaghetti!
- Enjoy!

139. Asparagus Squares Recipe

Serving: 6 | Prep: | Cook: 40mins | Ready in:

Ingredients

- 4 c. fresh asparagus, coarsely chopped
- 1 medium onion, chopped
- 1 c. whole wheat or all purpose flour
- ½ c. shredded cheddar cheese
- ¼ c. fresh parsley, chopped
- 4 eggs
- 1/3 c. sour cream
- 2 TB water

Direction

- In large bowl, toss asparagus, onion, flour, cheese and parsley until well combined; set aside.
- In small bowl, beat eggs, sour cream and water until well blended. Pour into asparagus mixture. Mix until well blended.
- Pour into greased 9 x 13 inch (3 L) baking dish. Bake in preheated 350 F (180 C) oven for 35 to 45 minutes or until firm. Cut into squares.

140. Asparagus Strudel Recipe

Serving: 16 | Prep: | Cook: 40mins | Ready in:

Ingredients

- 2 -cups water
- 3/4- pound fresh asparagus, trimmed and cut into 1-inch pieces
- 2- medium leeks (white portion only), thinly sliced

- 1-1/4 cups butter, divided
- 2 cups (8 ounces) shredded gruyere or swiss cheese
- 3 -eggs, lightly beaten
- 2- tablespoons lemon juice
- 2- tablespoons minced fresh parsley
- 1- tablespoon minced fresh mint
- 1 -tablespoon minced fresh dill
- 1/3 -cup sliced almonds, toasted
- Dash cayenne pepper
- 32 sheets phyllo dough, (14 inches x 9 inches)

Direction

- In a large skillet, bring water to a boil.
- Add asparagus; cover and boil for 3 minutes.
- Drain and immediately place asparagus in ice water.
- Drain and pat dry. In the same skillet, sauté leeks in 1/4 cup butter for 5 minutes or until tender.
- In a large bowl, combine the asparagus, leeks, cheese, eggs, lemon juice, parsley, mint, dill, almonds and cayenne.
- Melt remaining butter.
- Place one sheet of phyllo dough on a work surface (keep remaining dough covered with plastic wrap and a damp towel to avoid drying out).
- Brush with butter. Repeat layers seven times.
- Spoon a fourth of the vegetable mixture along the short end of dough to within 1 in. of edges.
- Fold long sides 1 in. over filling.
- Roll up jelly-roll style, starting with a short side. Place seam side down on a greased baking sheet.
- Repeat, making three more strudels.
- Brush tops with remaining butter. Bake at 350° for 40-45 minutes or until golden brown.
- Cool for 10 minutes before slicing. Yield: 4 strudels 8 slices each.

141.   Asparagus And Irish Cheese Gratin Recipe

Serving: 6 | Prep: | Cook: 20mins | Ready in:

Ingredients

- 20 asparagus spears
- 1 medium white onion quartered
- 4 whole garlic cloves peeled
- 3 ounces white wine
- 6 ounces heavy cream
- 1 teaspoon Dijon mustard
- 2 ounces breadcrumbs
- 2 ounces Irish cheese
- 1 tablespoon Irish butter softened
- 1/2 teaspoon salt
- 1 teaspoon freshly ground black pepper

Direction

- Snap tough ends off asparagus then wash and save.
- Cook asparagus tips in boiling water for a few minutes then cool.
- Put ends into a pot with onion, garlic, wine and 12 ounces of the asparagus water.
- Bring to boil and keep at a lively simmer for 15 minutes or until the water is reduced by half.
- Strain off vegetables and return stock to pan.
- Pour in cream and add mustard then cook sauce at a rolling boil until reduced to thick sauce.
- Season with salt and pepper then make a crumble by combining crumbs cheese and butter.
- Arrange asparagus on individual plates then pour sauce on top and sprinkle with crumble.
- Place each plate under broiler until crumble browns and cheese begins to melt.
- Serve immediately.

142. Asparagus With Blue Cheese Recipe

Serving: 4 | Prep: | Cook: 10mins | Ready in:

Ingredients

- 1 pound asparagus cleaned and tough ends trimmed
- 2 teaspoons red wine vinegar
- 2 tablespoons olive oil
- 2 tablespoons chives minced
- 4 tablespoons blue cheese crumbled
- 1 teaspoon freshly ground white pepper

Direction

- Snap ends off asparagus spears.
- Fill medium skillet with 1 inch water and bring to a boil.
- Add asparagus in single layer and cook 10 minutes.
- Drain well and arrange on a serving plate.
- Stir together vinegar and oil in small bowl.
- Add blue cheese and chives and mix well then pour over hot asparagus.
- Season with white pepper.
- Set aside until tepid then serve.

143. Asparagus With Lemon Butter Recipe

Serving: 6 | Prep: | Cook: 10mins | Ready in:

Ingredients

- 2 bunches thin asparagus
- 1/2 stick butter
- 1/2 lemon, juice and grated peel
- salt
- 1/4 c. soft bread crumbs

Direction

- Cut 1 T. of the butter into small bits and reserve.
- Preheat the broiler.
- Steam the asparagus just until done. Melt the remaining butter and mix with the lemon juice and peel. Salt to taste, and pour over the asparagus in a baking dish. Cover with bread crumbs and butter bits and broil until crumbs are nice and brown.

144. Avocado And Corn Salsa Recipe

Serving: 4 | Prep: | Cook: | Ready in:

Ingredients

- frozen corn
- 1 avocado, cubed
- lime juice
- 1/'2 red onion, peeled and chopped
- coriander leaves (we used parsley as we're not fans of coriander)
- cumin powder
- splash of olive oil
- salt
- spicy hot sauce.

Direction

- In a bowl mix together the ingredients together

145. BAKED MEDITERRANEAN VEGETABLES Recipe

Serving: 4 | Prep: | Cook: 45mins | Ready in:

Ingredients

- 1 small eggplant, cubed

- 1 large red bell pepper, cubed
- 1 zucchini, sliced
- 1 small red onion, cut into wedges
- 2 garlic cloves, sliced
- 2 bay leaves
- 1 tsp. basil
- 1 tsp. rosemary
- salt and pepper to taste
- 2 TB olive oil
- 1 (6oz) jar marinated artichoke hearts, drained (reserving liquid)

Direction

- In a shallow baking dish; combine vegetables with garlic, bay leaves, basil, rosemary, salt and pepper. Drizzle with olive oil and reserved artichoke marinade. Bake in preheated 400 F (200 C) oven for about 40 minutes stirring every 10 minutes until vegetables are fork-tender. Cut artichoke hearts into 1/2 inch (1 cm) pieces and stir into vegetables. Bake 5 minutes more and discard bay leaves.

146. Bacon Wrapped Grilled Corn On The Cob Recipe

Serving: 8 | Prep: | Cook: 10mins | Ready in:

Ingredients

- 8 ears corn
- 1 lb bacon
- water, for soaking
- butcher string

Direction

- Carefully expose the corn kernels by pulling back the husk, but do NOT remove the husk.
- Remove the corn silk (you can use a soft brush to ensure that all the silk is removed).
- Put water in a large container, add the corn, and soak the corn in the husks for 30 minutes –

this will help prevent the husks from charring on the grill.
- Preheat your grill to medium temperature.
- Remove the soaked corn from the water and pat dry.
- Wrap strips of bacon around the corn kernels on each ear, then fold the husks back over the bacon and kernels.
- Tie the husks down with butcher string; repeat with all ears of corn.
- Grill over medium coals/heat, turning occasionally, for about 15 to 20 minutes and the bacon is cooked and the corn is tender.
- Cut the butcher string away from the husks and serve.
- Note: you can make these earlier in the day if you store them in a container in the fridge, wrapped in moistened towels.
- I've also found that I like to pre-cook the bacon a little so that it's partially cooked, drizzled the small amount of fat mixed with a bit of oil or butter over the cobs, wrapped the bacon around, then gone on with the steps. Otherwise the bacon doesn't cook completely on the cob and is generally tossed away uneaten.

147. Bacon Wrapped Asparagus Recipe

Serving: 3 | Prep: | Cook: 10mins | Ready in:

Ingredients

- 10 fresh asparagus spears, trimmed
- 1/8 teaspoon pepper
- 5 bacon strips, halved lengthwise

Direction

- Place the asparagus on a sheet of waxed paper; coat with nonstick cooking spray. Sprinkle with pepper, turning to coat. Wrap a bacon piece around each spear; secure ends with toothpicks.

- Grill, uncovered, over medium heat for 4-5 minutes on each side or until bacon is crisp. Discard toothpicks.

148.   Baked Artichokes And Tomatoes Recipe

Serving: 8 | Prep: | Cook: 30mins | Ready in:

Ingredients

- 1 stick butter, melted
- 1lb(about) artichoke hearts
- 2pts cherry tomatoes or the same amount regular tomatoes, wedged
- 1 cup seasoned bread crumbs, croutons or stuffing mix, crushed
- 6oz fresh mushrooms, sliced
- 1/2 cup freshly grated parmesan cheese
- salt and pepper

Direction

- In 9X13 baking dish, place artichokes, mushrooms and tomatoes.
- Pour about 1/2 the butter over them and sprinkle with salt and pepper.
- Combine rest of butter, bread crumbs, cheese, and a bit more salt and pepper (if needed, depending on bread crumbs, used) in bowl.
- Sprinkle bread crumb topping over vegetables.
- Bake at 350 for about 30 minutes, until heated through and topping is crunchy.

149.   Baked Avocado Vinaigrette Recipe

Serving: 8 | Prep: | Cook: 15mins | Ready in:

Ingredients

- 4 medium avocados, halved

- 1 tsp salt
- 1/2 tsp pepper
- 6 Tbsp olive oil
- 1 Tbsp finely chopped chives
- 3 Tbsp tarragon vinegar
- 3 Tbsp finely chopped dill pickle
- 1 Tbsp finely chopped parsley

Direction

- Place the avocado halves (seeded) cut side up in a shallow baking pan with some hot water.
- Bake for 15 minutes at 325.
- Mix remaining ingredients into a vinaigrette while baking the avocados.
- Fill each cavity with the vinaigrette and serve.

150.   Baked Breaded Eggplant Slices Recipe

Serving: 6 | Prep: | Cook: 30mins | Ready in:

Ingredients

- 2 eggplants, washed, unpeeled, ½ inch sliced
- 1 cup bread crumbs
- 1/2 cup Parmesan or other sharp grated cheese
- 2 Tbsp parsley flakes
- 1/4 cup toasted sesame seeds
- ½ cup mayonnaise
- salt and pepper

Direction

- Preheat oven to 400°F
- Arrange eggplant slices on a shallow baking pan and brush them with mayonnaise.
- Sprinkle with salt and pepper, being careful since cheese has salt too.
- In a small bowl mix bread crumbs, grated cheese, parsley and toasted sesame seeds.
- Dip eggplant slices in the bread mixture and coat thoroughly, pressing to stick mixture on both sides.

- Place eggplant slices on a shallow clean and ungreased baking pan and bake for 15-20 minutes or until nicely brown. Turn slices and let brown for 10-15 minutes more.
- They are terrific as a first veggie course as well as side dish for meat or fish.

151.   Baked Carrot Fries Recipe

Serving: 4 | Prep: | Cook: 25mins | Ready in:

Ingredients

- 1 lb peeled, skinny baby carrots (or regular carrots, peeled and cut into sticks)
- 1 tbsp olive oil
- salt and pepper, to taste

Direction

- Preheat oven to 400 F.
- If baby carrots are on the thick side, slice them lengthwise in halves or quarters. Toss carrots with olive oil and season w/ salt and pepper.
- Place carrots in a single layer on a baking sheet lined w/ parchment paper.
- Bake for 20-25 minutes or until they start to crisp.
- Serve as is or with your favourite dip. Garlic aioli is great w/ these!

152.   Baked Carrots Recipe

Serving: 6 | Prep: | Cook: 90mins | Ready in:

Ingredients

- 1 pkg. baby carrots
- 1/3 C. butter
- 1/2 C. sugar
- 1/2 tsp. salt
- 1/2 tsp. cinnamon

- 1/3 C. boiling water

Direction

- Preheat oven to 350°
- Place carrots in casserole dish.
- Cream butter, sugar, salt and cinnamon together.
- Add water to sugar mixture blend well then pour over carrots and bake covered for 1 1/2 hours.

153.   Baked Spinach Casserole Recipe

Serving: 4 | Prep: | Cook: 60mins | Ready in:

Ingredients

- 1 1/4 pounds spinach
- 1/4 cup all-purpose flour
- 3 eggs, beaten
- 3/4 cup shredded cheddar cheese or goat cheese
- 1/2 cup dried bread crumbs
- 2 tablespoons chopped fresh parsley (optional)
- 1/4 cup butter, melted
- 1 cup milk or you can use LACTAID
- 1/2 teaspoon salt
- 1/8 teaspoon ground black pepper

Direction

- Preheat oven to 350 degrees F (175 degrees C). Grease a 2 quart baking dish.
- Clean spinach thoroughly. Remove all excess water. Chop spinach. Arrange spinach and flour in layers, nestle beaten eggs about midway between the layers.
- Combine cheese and bread crumbs. Mix in optional parsley, if desired. Sprinkle over top of spinach. Mix butter or margarine, milk, salt and pepper. Pour over all ingredients. Bake at 350 degrees F for 50 minutes to one hour.
- Great with a steak!

154. Baked Stuffed Avocado Recipe

Serving: 4 | Prep: | Cook: 15mins | Ready in:

Ingredients

- 1 large white onion
- 1 tablespoon butter
- 2 large ripe avocado pears halved and stones removed
- 4 ounces chopped almonds
- 4 ounces gruyere cheese diced
- 4 tablespoons grated parmesan cheese
- 2 tablespoons chopped parsley
- 2 tablespoons sherry
- 1 teaspoon salt
- 1 teaspoon freshly ground black pepper

Direction

- Preheat oven to 400.
- Fry onion in butter for 10 minutes.
- Meanwhile scoop flesh out of the avocado skins with a teaspoon taking care not to damage the skins then dice the flesh.
- Add onion to the avocado together with the Brazil nuts, cheeses, parsley and sherry.
- Season with salt and pepper.
- Pile mixture back into the avocado shells and place in a shallow ovenproof dish.
- Bake for 12 minutes.
- Serve immediately.

155. Baked Stuffed Vidalia Onions Recipe

Serving: 6 | Prep: | Cook: 20mins | Ready in:

Ingredients

- 1/2 cup uncooked white rice
- 6 large vidalia onions
- 3/4 pound ground spicy pork sausage
- 1/4 cup chopped green bell pepper
- 1 egg, beaten
- 1 (8 ounce) package cream cheese, softened
- 1/2 teaspoon dried oregano
- 2 tablespoons chopped fresh parsley
- 2 tablespoons butter, melted
- 1/2 teaspoon paprika

Direction

- Preheat oven to 400 degrees F (200 degrees C). Lightly grease a baking dish.
- In a saucepan bring 1 cup water to a boil. Add rice and stir. Reduce heat, cover and simmer for 20 minutes. Meanwhile, bring a large pot of salted water to a boil. Peel onions and slice off the tops; boil for 12 to 15 minutes, or until tender but not mushy. Drain, cool and remove the centers, leaving the shell intact. Chop onion centers and reserve 1/2 cup.
- Place sausage in a large, deep skillet. Cook over medium high heat until evenly brown. Drain and set aside, reserving drippings. Sauté green pepper and 1/2 cup chopped onion in sausage drippings.
- In a large bowl combine green pepper, onion, sausage, egg, 1 cup cooked rice, cream cheese, oregano and parsley. Spoon mixture into onion shells and place in prepared dish. Combine melted butter and paprika; brush tops of onions.
- 5. Cover and bake in preheated oven for 15 minutes. Uncover, and bake an additional 5 minutes.

156. Baked Tomatoes Stuffed With Cheesy Potatoes Recipe

Serving: 6 | Prep: | Cook: 15mins | Ready in:

Ingredients

- 6 large, firm, unpeeled tomatoes
- 3 cups mashed potatoes (using fresh potatoes or instant potato flakes prepared according to package directions)
- 1/4 cup fresh, chopped chives
- 1/2 teaspoon dried thyme
- 1 - 2 teaspoons pepper
- 1 1/4 cup shredded cheddar cheese, divided
- 1/4 cup dry bread crumbs
- 3 teaspoons paprika
- salt to taste

Direction

- Preheat oven to 350°F.
- Using a paring knife, remove the stem end of each tomato. Using a grapefruit spoon, small melon baller or a teaspoon, carefully hollow out each tomato, removing seeds and juice. Sprinkle the inside of each tomato with a little salt and place the tomatoes upside down on a cooling rack to drain for about 15 minutes.
- In a medium mixing bowl, combine the potatoes, chives, thyme, pepper and 1 cup of the cheddar cheese. Fill tomato cups with the potato mixture using a teaspoon.
- In a small bowl, combine bread crumbs, remaining 1/4 cup cheddar cheese and paprika; sprinkle on top of each tomato.
- Place filled tomatoes in non-stick or well-oiled muffin cups. Bake 10 - 15 minutes until topping is crisp and tomatoes are heated through.

---

157.   Balsamic Vinegar Glazed Vegetables Recipe

Serving: 4 | Prep: | Cook: 15mins | Ready in:

Ingredients

- 2 tbls. olive oil
- 1 red bell pepper, cut into 1/4 inch strips
- 1 yellow bell pepper, cut into 1/4 inch strips
- 1 onion, sliced thinly

- 2 zucchini, cut into 1/2 inch thick disks
- 2 yellow summer squash, cut into 1/2 inch disks
- 2 tbls. balsamic vinegar
- salt and pepper to taste

Direction

- Heat oil in large skillet to medium high
- Add peppers and onion and sauté until tender
- Add zucchini and squash and sauté until tender, about 8 minutes
- Add vinegar and boil until liquid is reduced to glaze and coats all vegetables
- Salt and pepper

---

158.   Barley Mushroom Bake Recipe

Serving: 4 | Prep: | Cook: 75mins | Ready in:

Ingredients

- 3 T. oil
- 1/2 cup chopped onion
- 1/2 cup uncooked pearl barley
- 3 cups chicken broth
- 4 cups sliced fresh mushrooms
- 3 T. dry sherry wine (optional, I didn't use the sherry)
- 3 T. toasted sliced almonds

Direction

- Heat oven to 350.
- Lightly oil a 1 quart baking dish.
- Heat 1 T. oil in large skillet. Add onion and cook over medium high heat 3 to 4 minutes. Stir often until tender.
- Add barley, cook, stirring often, until barley is golden; transfer to prepared baking dish.
- Add chicken broth.
- Bake uncovered 30 minutes.
- Meanwhile, heat remaining 2 T. oil in same skillet.

- Add mushrooms and cook over medium high heat. Stir occasionally 5 to 7 minutes until liquid from mushrooms has evaporated and they are lightly golden.
- Remove from heat and sprinkle with sherry and stir into barley mixture. Continue baking uncovered 45 minutes or until broth is absorbed and barley is tender.
- Sprinkle with almonds.

159. Beekeepers Cabbage Recipe

Serving: 2 | Prep: | Cook: 155mins | Ready in:

Ingredients

- 1   red cabbage (1-1/2 to 2 lbs)
- 1   onion
- 1   parsnip
- 1 lg apple
- 1 tb honey
- 1/2 oz butter
- 2 tb fruit vinegar (or more)
- -- preferably raspberry
- caraway seeds
- 1/4 pt yoghurt or sour cream; optional

Direction

- Cut cabbage into quarters. Remove and discard the tough central stalk. Shred the cabbage and put it into a large mixing bowl. Peel and finely chop the onion and add it to the cabbage. Cut the parsnip and apple into small pieces, peeling them first if you wish, and add them to the bowl.
- Drizzle on the honey. Add a good seasoning of salt and pepper and scant 1/2 teaspoon caraway seeds. Sprinkle on the vinegar, use 3 tablespoons if the apple you are using is the dessert variety, just 2 tablespoons if it is a cooking apple. Mix everything together well using your hands -- a little messy, but spoons are not as effective -- then pile the mixture into

a buttered casserole. Lay a sheet of thickly buttered greaseproof paper directly on top of the vegetables and cover the casserole with a well-fitting lid to prevent drying out.
- Cook at 300 F (150 C) gas mark 2 for about 2-1/2 hours until the vegetables are beautifully tender, if possible stir the mixture once or twice as it cooks. Remove the greaseproof paper and check seasoning immediately before serving. Serve the vegetable mixture just as it is, or top at the last minute with 1/4 pint cold creamy yoghurt or soured cream into which you have stirred a few bruised and lightly crushed caraway seeds. Or hand round the bowl of flavoured cream separately, so that those who want it can help themselves.

160. Beer Braised Cabbage Recipe

Serving: 4 | Prep: | Cook: 15mins | Ready in:

Ingredients

- 2Tbs unsalted butter
- 1 onion,chopped fine
- 1/2c beer,preferably light -bodied lager
- 1Tbs whole grain mustard
- 1/2tsp minced fresh thyme
- 1 small head green cabbage(about 1 ;b.),halved,cored and sliced thin
- 2tsp cider vinegar
- salt and pepper

Direction

- Melt butter in large skillet over medium -high heat. Cook onion until softened, about 5 mins. Stir in beer, mustard and thyme and simmer until slightly thickened, about 2 mins.
- Add cabbage and vinegar and cook covered, stirring occasionally, until wilted and tender, about 8 mins. Season with salt and pepper.

161. Beet With Orange Puree Recipe

Serving: 8 | Prep: | Cook: 45mins | Ready in:

Ingredients

- 2 large beets
- 1 small potato
- 1 orange, juiced and zested

Direction

- Wrap the beets and potato in foil and roast in a 400 degree oven 20 minutes for the potato, 45 minutes for the beets, until cooked through.
- When the beets and potato are cool enough to handle, peel and dice them.
- Transfer to a food processor or blender and add 1/2 cup of the orange juice and process.
- It may take a little while, but it should become a smooth mixture, add more orange juice if necessary to get the desired consistency.
- Add a bit of salt or coriander if desired.
- Place in a serving dish and grate the fresh zest over top.

162. Beets Roasted In Wine Recipe

Serving: 6 | Prep: | Cook: 30mins | Ready in:

Ingredients

- 1 bunch beets peeled and cubed
- 1 cup red wine
- 1/4 cup honey
- 2 tablespoons butter

Direction

- Place beets in saucepan then add remaining ingredients and enough water to barely cover.

- Simmer until tender then pour into baking dish and bake at 350 for 30 minutes.

163. Beets With Maple Syrup Recipe

Serving: 4 | Prep: | Cook: 60mins | Ready in:

Ingredients

- 8 beets washed
- 1/2 cup maple syrup
- 4 tablespoons butter
- 1/4 teaspoon sugar
- 1/4 teaspoon cinnamon
- 1/4 teaspoon cloves

Direction

- Bake beets in 350 oven for 45 minutes.
- Remove from oven and peel and slice.
- Put beets, butter, maple syrup and seasonings in a baking dish.
- Bake at 350 for 15 minutes.

164. Beets With Mushrooms Recipe

Serving: 8 | Prep: | Cook: 10mins | Ready in:

Ingredients

- 1 medium onion, finely chopped
- 1/2 cup cooking oil
- 4 cups cooked beets, cut into thin strips
- 1 cup sliced cooked mushrooms
- 3 cloves crushed garlic
- 1 tbsp sugar
- 2 tbsp vinegar
- 1/4 tsp salt
- 1/4 tsp pepper

Direction

- Sauté onion in cooking oil until golden, but not brown. Add remaining ingredients and stir gently. Chill overnight in the refrigerator.
- We use fresh beets, so the cooking time would be increased.

---

165.   Black Bean Salad With Couscous Recipe

Serving: 8 | Prep: | Cook: 10mins | Ready in:

Ingredients

- 1 cup uncooked couscous
- 1 1/4 cups chicken broth
- 3 tablespoons extra virgin olive oil
- 2 tablespoons fresh lime juice
- 1 teaspoon red wine vinegar
- 1/2 teaspoon ground cumin
- 8 green onions, chopped
- 1 red bell pepper, seeded and chopped
- 1 cup seedless green grapes chopped in half
- 1/4 cup chopped fresh cilantro
- 1 cup frozen corn kernels, thawed
- 2 (15 ounce) cans black beans, drained
- salt and pepper to taste

Direction

- Bring chicken broth to a boil in a 2 quart or larger sauce pan and stir in the couscous. Cover the pot and remove from heat. Let stand for 5 minutes.
- In a large bowl, whisk together the olive oil, lime juice, vinegar and cumin. Add green onions, red pepper, cilantro, corn, grapes and beans and toss to coat.
- Fluff the couscous well, breaking up any chunks. Add to the bowl with the vegetables and mix well. Season with salt and pepper to taste and serve at once or refrigerate until ready to serve.

---

166.   Black Beans And Rice Recipe

Serving: 4 | Prep: | Cook: 10mins | Ready in:

Ingredients

- 2 teaspoons olive oil
- 2 white onions minced
- 2 green bell peppers,diced
- 3 garlic cloves minced
- 2 cans black beans drained and rinsed
- 2 teaspoons dried oregano
- 2 teaspoons balsamic vinegar
- 2 red bell peppers diced
- 4 cups hot cooked rice
- 4 tomatoes chopped
- 2 cups shredded sharp cheddar cheese
- hot sauce

Direction

- In large saucepan heat the oil.
- Add onions, green peppers and garlic.
- Sauté for 3 minutes.
- Add black beans and oregano.
- Bring to a boil then cook over medium heat for 5 minutes.
- Add balsamic vinegar and remove from heat.
- Stir in red peppers.
- To serve place rice in individual serving bowls and spoon beans on top.
- Sprinkle with tomatoes, cheese and hot sauce.

---

167.   Black Eyed Pea Salad Recipe

Serving: 8 | Prep: | Cook: | Ready in:

Ingredients

- 2 cans black-eyed peas, rinsed and drained
- 1 ripe avocado, peeled and chopped

- 1 medium tomato, chopped
- 1 medium onion, chopped
- 1/2 cup Catalina salad dressing

Direction

- Combine all ingredients in a large bowl.
- Toss well.
- Cover and chill for about 8 hours.

---

168. Bok Choy Apple Slaw Recipe

Serving: 8 | Prep: | Cook: | Ready in:

Ingredients

- 1/3 cup sour cream
- 1/3 cup mayonnaise
- 2 tablespoons white wine vinegar
- 2 teaspoons honey
- 1/2 teaspoon celery salt
- 1/4 teaspoon salt
- 6 cups very thinly sliced bok choy
- 1 large Granny Smith apple julienned or shredded
- 1 large carrot julienned or shredded
- 1/2 cup slivered red onion

Direction

- Whisk sour cream, mayonnaise, vinegar, honey, celery salt and salt in a large bowl until smooth.
- Add bok choy, apple, carrot and onion.
- Toss to coat.

---

169. Bourbon Baked Beans Recipe

Serving: 16 | Prep: | Cook: 60mins | Ready in:

Ingredients

- 5 cans baked beans
- 1 tablespoon molasses
- 1/4 teaspoon dry mustard
- 1/2 cup chili sauce
- 1/2 cup bourbon
- 1/3 cup strong coffee
- 15 ounce can crushed pineapple well drained
- 1/2 cup brown sugar
- 8 slices bacon

Direction

- Mix together beans, molasses, mustard, chili sauce, bourbon and coffee.
- Let stand for 3 hours.
- Preheat oven to 300 and bake beans for 30 minutes.
- Add pineapple and brown sugar and bake for another 30 minutes.
- Meanwhile fry bacon until crisp then drain well and crumble.
- Serve beans garnished with the bacon.

---

170. Braised Cauliflower With Anchovies Garlic And White Wine Recipe

Serving: 4 | Prep: | Cook: 20mins | Ready in:

Ingredients

- 21/2 tbs evoo
- 1 medium head cauliflower cut into florets
- 2 medium anchovy fillets, minced to a paste
- 3 cloves garlic, pressed
- 1/2 tsp red pepper flake
- 1/3 c dry white wine
- 1/3 c low-sodium chicken broth
- 2 tbs minced fresh parsley
- salt

Direction

- Heat 2 tbsp. evoo in large skillet over medium-high heat until shimmering.
- Add cauliflower and cook, stirring occasionally until the florets begin to brown, about 6-7 minutes.
- Clear a space in the center of the pan and add the anchovies, garlic, red pepper flake and remaining 1/2 tbsp. evoo.
- Mash and stir the garlic mixture in the center of the pan until it becomes fragrant, about one minute.
- Stir to combine with the florets and cook one minute longer.
- Add white wine and broth and cover, cooking until florets are tender but not mushy, about 4-5 minutes.
- Add parsley and season with salt and serve immediately!

- Make sure to fry them half-cooked only. The outer side are almost brown.
- Remove the eggplants and place them on paper towels.
- Pour off the cooking oil in the pan until only about 2 Tsp remains.
- Sauté the onions.
- Add the garlic .Sauté until golden brown but make sure not to overcook!
- Add the oyster sauce, sugar, light soy sauce, and chili bean sauce.
- Mix well.
- Add the eggplants. Mix then lower the heat and simmer for about 3 mins.
- Turn off the heat. Drizzle sesame seed oil and give the dish a final stir.
- When serving, garnish with bottled minced garlic on top.

171. Braised Eggplants Recipe

Serving: 3 | Prep: | Cook: 20mins | Ready in:

Ingredients

- 3 eggplants (the long ones)
- 2 Tbsp of minced garlic
- 2 sweet onions (the small ones)
- 2 Tbsp of oyster sauce
- 2 Tsp of sugar
- 4 Tbsp light soy sauce
- 1/2 Tsp bottled chili bean sauce
- 1 Tsp sesame seed oil
- 125ml or 1/2 cup of cooking oil
- 63ml or 1/4 cup of water
- Bottled minced garlic.

Direction

- Cut the onions into halves and slice thinly.
- Cut off the tips of the eggplants and slice into halves lengthwise.
- Cut each half into 3-4 pieces.
- Pour the cooking oil in a nonstick pan and fry the eggplants.

172. Braised Greens And Garlic Recipe

Serving: 4 | Prep: | Cook: 20mins | Ready in:

Ingredients

- 1 lb kale, mustard greens or chard, (about 8 cups)
- 1 Tbs extra virgin olive oil
- 5 cloves garlic, minced
- 1/2 tsp salt
- lemon wedges

Direction

- Wash greens thoroughly by soaking in lots of cold water.
- Drain.
- Chop greens into about 3-inch pieces.
- Heat oil in a large skillet.
- Sauté garlic for 2 minutes.
- Add greens to skillet.
- (They do not have to be dried off, as the water will evaporate during cooking.)

- Cover and cook over medium heat for 10 minutes, stirring once in a while to coat all the greens with garlic and oil.
- Sprinkle with salt.
- Serve with lemon wedges.

173. Braised Kale Recipe

Serving: 8 | Prep: | Cook: 15mins | Ready in:

Ingredients

- 1 tablespoon olive oil
- 2 cups sliced white onions
- 1 teaspoon salt
- 1 teaspoon freshly ground black pepper
- 2 tablespoons minced garlic
- 8 cups firmly packed stemmed torn kale
- 2 cups chicken stock

Direction

- Heat oil in a large skillet over high heat.
- Add onions, salt and pepper then stir fry 2 minutes.
- Add garlic, kale and stock then cook stirring occasionally for 3 minutes.

174. Braised Red Cabbage With Apple And Onion Recipe

Serving: 4 | Prep: | Cook: 30mins | Ready in:

Ingredients

- Ingredients and directions together.

Direction

- In a large Dutch oven or heavy pot, melt 1 Tbs butter over medium. Add 1 medium onion, halved and thinly sliced, and 1 Gala or Fuji apple, halved, cored and sliced and cook, stirring, until onion softens, 4 to 6 mins.
- Stir in 1 head red cabbage (2lbs), cored, quartered, and thinly sliced, and season with coarse salt and ground black pepper. Add 3 Tbs cider vinegar, 4 tsp. sugar and 1/2 c water. Bring to a boil; reduce to a simmer, cover, and cook until cabbage is tender, 20 to 25 mins. Season with salt, pepper and sugar.

175. Broccoli Rice Casserole Recipe

Serving: 8 | Prep: | Cook: 30mins | Ready in:

Ingredients

- 1.5 lb bag frozen broccolit florets
- 2 Cans cream of celery soup, approx. 10.5 oz can
- 2 Cups Shredded cheddar cheese
- 1 Cup milk
- 3/4 Cup butter, melted
- 1 Cup cooked rice

Direction

- Boil broccoli until just slightly cooked. Drain between paper towels.
- Mix in balance of ingredients and place in greased baking dish.
- Bake at 300 degrees for 30 minutes or until bubbly.

176. Broccoli Cream Cheese Casserole Recipe

Serving: 12 | Prep: | Cook: 40mins | Ready in:

Ingredients

- 4 packages frozen broccoli

- 8 ounces cream cheese softened
- 1 stick margarine softened
- 6 slices American cheese
- 1 can cream of celery soup
- bread crumbs for topping

Direction

- Cook broccoli according to package directions then drain.
- Combine cream cheese, margarine, cheese and soup then melt together and mix with broccoli.
- Pour into greased casserole dish and top with bread crumbs.
- Bake at 350 for 40 minutes.

177. Broccoli Deluxe Recipe

Serving: 10 | Prep: | Cook: | Ready in:

Ingredients

- 2 10 oz. packages frozen cut broccoli
- 4 Tbsps. butter or margarine
- 2 Tbsps. all-purpose flour
- 1/4 tsp. salt
- Dash pepper
- 1 c. milk
- 1 3 oz. pkg. cream cheese, cut up
- 1 c. soft bread crumbs
- 1/4 c. (1 pz.) grated parmesan cheese

Direction

- Cook broccoli according to package directions; drain.
- In saucepan, melt 2 tablespoons of butter or margarine; blend in flour, salt, and pepper.
- Add milk all at once; cook and stir till thick and bubbly.
- Reduce heat; blend in cream cheese till smooth.
- Stir in the broccoli; turn into 1 1/2 quart casserole.
- Bake in 350 oven for 20 minutes.

- Melt remaining butter; toss with bread crumbs and parmesan cheese.
- Sprinkle crumbs over casserole; bake 15 to 20 minutes more.
- Makes 10 servings.

178. Broccoli For Garlic And Almond Lovers Recipe

Serving: 4 | Prep: | Cook: 8mins | Ready in:

Ingredients

- 2 crowns of fresh broccoli - make sure it's stiff, dark healthy green and crisp and not soggy and sad looking
- 2 or more cloves of garlic minced
- 1 teaspoon salt
- 1/2 teaspoon sugar
- 1/2 cup of almonds - slithered, blanched, whatever kind you have on hand is fine.
- 3-5 tablespoons olive oil
- Equipment needed: Steamer, I have a 'double boiler' type steamer which sits right inside my 3 quart pot which I find is perfect.

Direction

- Rinse broccoli and cut up high on its stalks. Separate little florettes and place inside steamer. Sprinkle with half of salt and all of sugar. Fill bottom part with water and place lid on pot.
- Let water come to a boil, then turn down heat on low and allow broccoli to steam over the simmering water.
- Sautee or brown/toast up almonds either in your oven or in a skillet with a little olive oil or butter. These brown quickly so don't walk away.
- After 6 minutes, check on broccoli and check for doneness - cook a little longer if you like your broccoli a little softer but still with some bite (al dente).
- Once done, turn off heat.

- In bowl, place minced garlic and add cooked broccoli.
- Save water if you want for when you make vegetable soup otherwise discard.
- Drizzle olive oil over broccoli and add additional salt if you like. Toss till well coated then sprinkle toasted almonds on top - and serve to happy and healthy eaters.

179.   Broccoli Salad Recipe

Serving: 8 | Prep: | Cook: 20mins | Ready in:

Ingredients

- 1 package of bacon, cooked to a crisp
- 1 head of fresh broccoli, just the florets
- 1/4 cup of red onion, chopped (optional)
- 1/2 cup raisins
- 1/4 cup of sunflower seeds
- 1 cup of mayonnaise
- 1/2 cup of white sugar
- 3 tablespoons of apple cider vinegar

Direction

- Place bacon in a large skillet, cook until crispy. Drain on paper towel, crumble and set aside.
- Chop broccoli florets into bite size pieces. In a medium mixing bowl, combine broccoli with the red onions, raisins, crumbled bacon and sunflower seeds.
- In a small bowl, whisk together mayonnaise, apple cider vinegar and sugar. Pour over broccoli mixture and toss until well combined.
- Refrigerate for a couple of hours before serving.

180.   Buffalo Chili Onions Recipe

Serving: 8 | Prep: | Cook: 10mins | Ready in:

Ingredients

- 4 large onions - cut into 1/2 inch thick slices
- 1/2 cup hot sauce
- 1/2 cup butter - melted
- 1/4 cup chili sauce
- 2 tsp chili powder

Direction

- Mix together hot sauce, butter, chili sauce & chili powder in a small bowl
- Brush on both sides of onion slices
- Place onions on grill over medium heat
- Grill onions 10 mins or until tender, turning & basting often with chili mixture.
- Onions can be prepared ahead & grilled just before serving

181.   Butterbeans Bacon And Tomatoes Recipe

Serving: 6 | Prep: | Cook: 60mins | Ready in:

Ingredients

- 3 bacon slices, chopped
- 1 medium onion, finely chopped
- 1 small green bell pepper, chopped
- 3 garlic cloves, minced
- 1 bay leaf
- 3 medium size tomatoes, chopped (of coarse this is better when tomatoes are in season)
- 4 cups chicken broth
- 4 cups fresh or frozen butterbeans, thawed
- 2 tablespoons minced parsley
- 1 teaspoon salt
- 1 teaspoon pepper
- 1 teaspoon worcestershire sauce
- 1/2 teaspoon hot sauce (your choice)

Direction

- Cook bacon in a Dutch oven until crisp.

- Stir in onion and next 3 ingredients; sauté until vegetables are tender.
- Stir in tomato, and cook for 3 minutes.
- Stir in broth and butterbeans; bring to a coil.
- Cover, reduce heat, and simmer, stirring occasionally, 30 minutes.
- Simmer uncovered, 20 minutes, stirring often.
- Stir in parsley and remaining ingredients.
- Cook stirring often, 5 minutes.
- Discard bay leaf.

182.   CABBAGE ON THE GRILL Recipe

Serving: 4 | Prep: | Cook: 40mins | Ready in:

Ingredients

- 1 medium head cabbage
- 4 teaspoons butter or margarine, softened
- 1 teaspoon salt
- ½ teaspoon garlic powder
- ¼ teaspoon pepper
- 2 teaspoons grated parmesan cheese
- 4 bacon strips

Direction

- Cut cabbage into four wedges; place each on a piece of double-layered heavy-duty foil. Spread cut sides with butter. Sprinkle with salt, garlic powder, pepper and Parmesan cheese. Wrap a bacon strip around each wedge.
- Fold foil around cabbage and seal tightly. Grill, covered, over medium heat for 40 minutes or until the cabbage is tender, turning twice.

183.   CAMPFIRE POTATOES Recipe

Serving: 46 | Prep: | Cook: 37mins | Ready in:

Ingredients

- 5 medium potatoes, peeled and thinly sliced
- 1 medium onion, sliced
- 6 tablespoons butter or margarine
- 1/3 cup shredded cheddar cheese
- 1 tablespoon worcestershire sauce
- salt and pepper to taste
- 1/3 cup chicken broth

Direction

- Place the potatoes and onion on a large piece of heavy-duty foil; dot with butter.
- Combine the cheese, Worcestershire sauce salt and pepper; sprinkle over potatoes.
- Fold foil up around potatoes and add broth. Seal the edges of foil well. Grill, covered, over medium coals for 35 to 40 minutes or until potatoes are tender.

184.   COLLARD GREENS Recipe

Serving: 8 | Prep: | Cook: 90mins | Ready in:

Ingredients

- 4 bunches collard greens
- 2 lg. ham hocks
- 1 med. onion
- salt and pepper to taste
- .

Direction

- Remove leaves from stems of collard greens and discard stems. Wash thoroughly insuring all grit and grime has been removed from the greens.

- Wash ham hocks and boil with chopped onion until almost done. (Do this ahead of time making sure meat has cooked long enough)
- Add greens, salt, and pepper to ham hocks.
- Bring greens to a boil, reduce heat and cook until greens are tender

185. CREAMED GREEN BEANS Recipe

Serving: 8 | Prep: | Cook: 60mins | Ready in:

Ingredients

- 1 pound or more of fresh green beans. Kentucky Wonder if your lucky.
- 1/2 onion minced
- 1 clove garlic
- basil to taste
- salt
- pepper
- 6 slices of bacon minced
- water to cover
- 1/2 stick oleo
- 2 table spoon flour
- 1/4 cup water
- Carnation Evaporated Milk

Direction

- In a cast iron skillet cook bacon until it renders some fat.
- Add onion and stir.
- Add garlic and stir.
- Add green beans that have been "snapped" into pieces
- Add basil, salt, pepper
- Cover with water and cook on low until done.
- Mix flour with water and add to the bean stock to thicken, add Carnation milk to desired thickness.
- Adjust seasonings.
- Now this and some cornbread... Heaven.

186. Cabbage Smothered And Southern Recipe

Serving: 8 | Prep: | Cook: 60mins | Ready in:

Ingredients

- 2 SMALL heads of cabbage OR 1 GOOD SIZE MEDIUM CABBAGE (I DON'T USE THE LARGE heads of cabbage)
- 2 LARGE yellow onions
- seasoning (I USE NATURES seasoning)
- black pepper
- salt (ADD TOWARDS THE END OF THE COOKING PROCESS, TASTE BEFORE AND AFTER ADDING salt)
- sugar OR SPLENDA (TO YOUR DESIRED TASTE. PEOPLE DIFFER, SOME LIKE IT SWEET SOME NOT. sugar TAKES THE bitter OUT OF THE cabbage IN MY OPINION)
- MEAT (YOUR CHOICE OF bacon, SMOKED pork (WHICH I USE), ham OR ham hocks).

Direction

- CLEAN YOUR CABBAGE, AND I CUT MINE INTO SMALL QUARTERS.
- IN A LARGE POT, PLACE YOUR CABBAGE, MEAT AND SEASONINGS.
- ADD 1/2 CUP OF WATER (CABBAGE TENDS TO MAKE ITS OWN JUICE)
- BRING TO A BOIL FOR A FEW MINUTES
- TURN DOWN TO A MEDIUM HEAT. PLACE A SEE THROUGH LID ON TOP OF YOUR POT SO YOU CAN KEEP YOUR SOUTHERN EYE ON THE CABBAGE.
- STIR CABBAGE A FEW TIMES TO HELP THE SMOTHERING PROCESS
- TASTE YOUR CABBAGE HALFWAY THROUGH, YOU MAY HAVE TO ADD A LITTLE BIT OF THIS OR A LITTLE BIT OF THAT. LOL!

187.   Cabbage Torta Recipe

Serving: 8 | Prep: | Cook: 50mins | Ready in:

Ingredients

- .....pie dough.....
- 3 cups flour
- 6 large eggs
- 1 tablespoon baking powder
- 1/3 cup plus 1 tbs. Crisco
- pinch salt and pepper
- .....Filling:....
- 3 cups Shredded cabbage
- 1 large onion chopped
- 1/2 pound mushrooms
- basil, marjoram -- tarragon
- salt and pepper
- 4 ounces cream cheese
- 4 Hard boiled eggs -- sliced
- Fresh chopped dill or basil

Direction

- Prepare pie dough. You can use this or a favorite rich pie dough.
- Some torta dough contain a bit of wine in the dough and butter instead of Crisco.
- Combine dry ingredients.
- Cut in Crisco to form coarse crumbs. Beat eggs and stir in.
- Dough should be soft but pliable.
- Cover and chill while preparing filling.
- Sauté shredded cabbage and onion and sliced mushrooms in a skillet with a bit of olive oil and cook and stir until cabbage is wilted and very tender, about 20 minutes.
- Season to taste with basil, marjoram, tarragon and salt and pepper or as desired.
- Divide dough and roll out 1/2 on lightly floured surface to fit a 10 inch deep pie dish (could be spring form pan also).
- Spread bottom crust with the softened cream cheese.
- Layer on the sliced eggs. Add cooked and cooled cabbage filling.

- Cover with chopped dill or basil. Add top crust and crimp and seal edges.
- Slit top crust in several places to let steam escape.
- Brush with an egg glaze.
- Bake at 350 degrees for about 30 minutes.

188.   California Spinach Casserole Recipe

Serving: 6 | Prep: | Cook: 30mins | Ready in:

Ingredients

- 2 (6 ounce) jars marinated artichoke hearts, drained
- 1 (16 ounce bag) cut spinach, thawed and squeezed dry
- 1/4 cup sweet onion, finely diced
- 8 ounces cream cheese, softened
- 1/3 cup milk
- 3 tablespoons butter, softened
- 1/2 cup parmesan cheese, shredded

Direction

- Arrange artichoke hearts in bottom of greased 8 inch baking dish.
- Layer spinach over artichoke hearts.
- Sprinkle with onion.
- Beat together cream cheese, milk and butter. Spread over onion layer.
- Sprinkle with Parmesan cheese.
- (At this point, can be covered and chilled up to a day ahead.)
- Bake, uncovered, at 350 degrees for 30 to 40 minutes.

189.   Candied Carrots Recipe

Serving: 8 | Prep: | Cook: 20mins | Ready in:

Ingredients

- 2lbs carrots, cut into sticks (I've also used baby carrots)
- 1/4 Cup butter
- 1/4 Cup packed brown sugar
- 1/4 tsp. salt
- 1/8 tsp. white pepper (I do use black)

Direction

- Place cut carrots in a large saucepan with about an inch of water.
- Bring to a boil, reduce heat; cover & simmer for10-15 minutes or until crisp tender. (Be sure to watch that the water has not boiled off)
- Drain & set aside.
- In the same pan, combine butter, sugar, salt & pepper.
- Cook & stir until butter is melted.
- Return carrots to the pan; cook & stir over medium heat for 5 minutes or until glazed.

190.　　　Candied Pickled Baby Beets Recipe

Serving: 2 | Prep: | Cook: 40mins |Ready in:

Ingredients

- 8-10 red baby beets
- 3 Tbsp. extra virgin olive oil
- 1 to 1 1/2 cups Elderflower
- 1/4 cup red wine vinegar

Direction

- Pre-heat oven to 400 F. Coat the beets with the oil, then loosely wrap each beet individually with aluminum foil and roast until tender, about 40-50 minutes. Remove from foil and let cool. When cool, remove skins and either finely dice or slice into rounds.
- In a non-reactive container, place the cooled beets inside. Add the elderflower and red wine vinegar. The beets should be completely

submerged in the liquid. Marinate the beets overnight in the fridge.

191.　　　Carrots Souffle Recipe

Serving: 4 | Prep: | Cook: 30mins |Ready in:

Ingredients

- 1 lb. carrots, chopped
- 1/4 cup butter, melted
- 1/2 cup sugar
- 1 Tbsp. plus 1 1/2 tsp. flour
- 1/2 tsp. baking powder
- 1/2 tsp. vanilla
- 2 eggs, beaten

Direction

- Preheat oven to 350F.
- In a saucepan, over medium heat, cook carrots until tender, drain and mash.
- Add all the other ingredients.
- Pour into a 2-quart casserole dish.
- Bake for 30 minutes.
- Sprinkle with powdered sugar when cooled.
- NOTE...
- I sometimes add raisins for a change.

192.　　　Cauliflower With Bacon And Cheese Sauce Recipe

Serving: 4 | Prep: | Cook: 10mins |Ready in:

Ingredients

- 1 large head cauliflower
- 2 quarts boiling water
- 1 Tbsp. salt
- 8 slices bacon, cut into 1/2-inch pieces
- Cheese Sauce:
- 3 Tbsp. butter or margarine

- 3 Tbsp. all-purpose flour.
- 1 1/2 cups milk mixture boils
- 1/2 cup whipping cream
- 1 tsp. salt
- 1/2 tsp. black pepper
- 1/8 tsp. nutmeg
- 1/2 cup shredded Jarlsberg or mild swiss cheese.

Direction

- Wash cauliflower. Trim and cut into flowerets. Drop into boiling salted water and cook 10 min. or until just barely tender. Drain and place into serving dish. Keep warm.
- Meanwhile fry bacon until crisp over medium heat. Drain and keep warm.
- Prepare Cheese Sauce: Melt 3 Tbsp. butter or margarine in heavy saucepan. Stir in 3 Tbsp. all-purpose flour. Cook over medium heat, stirring for 2 min. Slowly whisk in 1 1/2 cups warmed milk and heat, stirring, until mixture boils. Whisk until smooth. Add 1/2 cup whipping cream, 1 tsp. salt, 1/2 tsp. black pepper, 1/8, tsp. nutmeg and 1/2 cup shredded Jarlsberg or mild Swiss cheese.
- Pour over cauliflower and top with bacon. Serve immediately.
- To prepare ahead: place cooked cauliflower into buttered ovenproof or microwave proof dish. Top with sauce and bacon. Cover and refrigerate. Reheat at 350°F for 20 min. or until heated through, or place into microwave oven for 5 min. on High power.

193. Charcoal Roasted Beets And Red Onions Recipe

Serving: 6 | Prep: | Cook: 90mins | Ready in:

Ingredients

- 6 small fresh beets trimmed of all but 2 inches of greens and unpeeled
- 2 medium red onions unpeeled

- 2 tablespoons extra virgin olive oil
- 1/3 cup chicken broth
- 3 tablespoons balsamic vinegar
- 1-1/2 teaspoons fresh thyme leaves divided
- 1 teaspoon salt
- 2 teaspoons freshly ground black pepper

Direction

- Prepare a moderately hot charcoal fire in a grill unit that has a cover.
- Place beets and red onions in a cast iron skillet and drizzle with olive oil then place skillet on grill rack over fire and cover the grill unit and roast the vegetables for 1-1/2 hours.
- Remove vegetables from skillet with tongs.
- Add broth, vinegar and 1 teaspoon thyme to the skillet then place over high heat and boil liquid scraping bottom of skillet for about 4 minutes.
- Season with salt and pepper.
- Peel beets and onions when cool enough to handle.
- Slice beets into julienne strips and onions into thin rings then spoon liquid over onions and beets.
- Add remaining 1/2 teaspoon thyme and stir well to combine.
- Heat briefly and serve.

194. Cherry Tomato And Zucchini Saute With Basil And Pine Nuts Recipe

Serving: 4 | Prep: | Cook: 5mins | Ready in:

Ingredients

- 1 tbsp olive oil
- 3 small zucchini, halved lengthwise and thinly sliced
- 2 cups cherry tomatoes, halved
- 2 green onions, sliced
- 2 tsp balsamic vinegar

- salt and freshly ground pepper
- 2 tbsp chopped fresh basil
- 2 tbsp lightly toasted pine nuts

Direction

- Heat oil in a large non-stick skillet over high heat.
- Add zucchini and cook, stirring, for 1 minute.
- Add cherry tomatoes, green onions and balsamic vinegar.
- Cook, stirring, for 1 to 2 minutes or until zucchini is crisp-tender and tomatoes are heated through.
- Season with salt and pepper.
- Sprinkle with basil and pine nuts and serve immediately.

195.   Chinese Restaurant Style Sauteed Green Beans Recipe

Serving: 3 | Prep: | Cook: 10mins | Ready in:

Ingredients

- 1Tbs. less-sodium soy sauce
- 1Tbs honey
- 1Tbs unsalted butter
- 2Tbs extra-virgin olive oil
- 12 oz. green beans,trimmed
- kosher salt
- 1Tbs. minced garlic

Direction

- Combine soy sauce, honey and 1Tbs water in a small dish and set near the stove. Set a shallow serving dish near the stove too.
- In a 10" straight sided sauté pan, heat the butter with the olive oil over med-high heat. When the butter is melted, add the green beans and 1/2tsp salt and toss with tongs to coat well Cook, turning the beans occasionally, until most are well browned, shrunken, and

tender,7-8 mins.(The butter in the pan will have turned dark brown.

- Reduce heat to low, add the garlic, and cook, stirring constantly with a heatproof rubber spatula, until the garlic is softened and fragrant, 15-20 seconds. Carefully add the soy mixture (you'll need to scrape the honey into the pan. Cook, stirring, until the liquid reduces to a glazy consistency that coats the beans, 30-45 secs.
- Immediately transfer the beans to a serving dish, scraping the pan with a spatula to get all the garlicky sauce. Let sit for a few minutes and serve warm.

196.   Chipotle Glazed Vegetable Kebabs Recipe

Serving: 6 | Prep: | Cook: 8mins | Ready in:

Ingredients

- 2 medium-large zucchini, trimmed, chunked
- 18 small white mushrooms, stems trimmed flat with the caps
- 18 large cherry tomatoes, stemmed
- green sweet peppers, chunked
- onions, chunked
- 3/4 cup Chipotle vinaigrette (recipe follows)
- salt and freshly ground black pepper
- ====================================
==========
- Chipotle vinaigrette
- This dressing is not too fiery hot, and can be used on salads ranging from plain (though not delicate) greens to main-dish salads featuring meat, poultry, or seafood.
- It only takes minutes to prepare.
- 3 tablespoons sherry wine vinegar
- 1 tablespoon balsamic vinegar
- 2 garlic cloves, chopped
- 2 canned chipotles en adobo, chopped
- 2 tablespoons adobo sauce from the chipotle can

- 1/2 teaspoon salt
- 2/3 cup olive oil
- freshly ground black pepper
- *****chipotle chile:
- This hot chile is actually a dried, smoked JALAPEÑO. It has a wrinkled, dark brown skin and a smoky, sweet, almost chocolaty flavor.
- Chipotles can be found dried, pickled and canned in adobo sauce.
- Chipotles are generally added to stews and sauces; the pickled variety are often eaten as appetizers.

Direction

- Cut each zucchini crosswise into 9 equally thick slices.
- Trim the slices to form cubes.
- Divide the vegetables, alternating them, among 6 flat metal skewers.
- Be certain to arrange the flat sides of the zucchini cubes and the stem ends of the mushrooms so they will get the maximum exposure to the fire.
- Light a direct heat charcoal fire and let it burn down to medium-hot (5 seconds to "ouch") or preheat a gas grill to medium-high.
- Position the rack about 6 inches above the heat source.
- When the grill is ready, lightly brush the kebabs with some of the vinaigrette.
- Lay the kebabs on the rack, cover and grill, turning every 2 minutes and basting often with the vinaigrette, until it is used up and the vegetables are lightly colored by the grill, 6 to 8 minutes total.
- Season with salt and pepper and slide the vegetables off the skewers onto plates.
- Serve hot.
- The Chipotle Vinaigrette:
- 1. In a food processor or blender, combine the sherry vinegar, balsamic vinegar, garlic, chipotles, adobo and its sauce, and salt. Process until smooth. With the motor running, gradually add the oil through the hole in the lid: the dressing will thicken. Season with

pepper and pulse to blend. Adjust the seasoning and pulse again just before using.
- 2. Use immediately or cover tightly and refrigerate for up to 3 days. The dressing may separate; return to room temperature, then rewhisk to blend.

197.   Cider Glazed Roots With Cinnamon Walnuts Recipe

Serving: 6 | Prep: | Cook: 80mins |Ready in:

Ingredients

- 3lbs assorted root vegetables(beets,celeriac,carrots,parsnips,rutabags,turnip)cut into 1" pieces
- 1c apple cider
- 1/4c dark brown sugar.
- 1/2tsp salt,plus more to taste
- 1/4tsp pepper1/2c chopped walnuts
- 1Tbs butter
- 1/8tsp ground cinnamon

Direction

- Preheat oven to 400
- If using parsnips, quarter lengthwise and remove woodsy core before cutting into 1: pieces. Whisk cider, brown sugar, 1/2tsp of salt and pepper in a 9x13" baking dish till sugar is dissolved. Add root vegetables and toss to coat. Cover the baking dish with foil.
- Bake 20 mins. Uncover, stir the vegetables. Continue cooking, uncovered, stirring every 20 mins. or so till the vegetables are glazed and tender, about 1 hour more.
- Meanwhile, place walnuts in a small skillet and cook over med-low heat, stirring constantly, till fragrant and lightly browned, 2 to 6 mins.
- Remove from heat and add butter, cinnamon and a pinch of salt. Stir till butter melts and nuts are coated. Spread on plate to cool slightly.

- Transfer vegetables to serving dish and sprinkle with cinnamon walnuts.

198. Collard Greens Recipe

Serving: 8 | Prep: | Cook: 120mins | Ready in:

Ingredients

- House Seasoning:
- 1 c salt
- 1/4 c black pepper
- 1/4 c garlic powder
- Collards:
- 1/2 lb smoked turkey wings
- 1 T House seasoning
- 1 T seasoned salt
- 1 T hot red pepper sauce
- 1 large bunch collard greens
- 1 T butter

Direction

- House Seasoning:
- Mix ingredients together and store in an airtight container for up to 6 months.
- Collards:
- In a large pot, bring 3 quarts of water to a boil and add smoked meat, House Seasoning, seasoned salt and hot sauce.
- Reduce heat to medium and cook for 1 hour.
- Wash the collard greens thoroughly.
- Remove the stems that run down the center by holding the leaf in your left hand and stripping the leaf down with your right hand.
- The tender young leaves in the heart of the collards don't need to be stripped.
- Stack 6 to 8 leaves on top of one another, roll up, and slice into 1/2 to 1-inch thick slices.
- Place greens in pot with meat and add butter.
- Cook for 45 to 60 minutes, stirring occasionally.
- When done taste and adjust seasoning.

199. Colourful Veggies With Serious Kick Recipe

Serving: 6 | Prep: | Cook: 50mins | Ready in:

Ingredients

- 4 cups vegetable broth
- 2 cups canned diced tomatoes
- ½ cup chopped onions
- ½ cup diced carrots
- ½ cup sliced celery
- 2 cups shredded green cabbage
- 1 tablespoon lemon juice
- ½ teaspoon oregano
- 1 bay leaf
- Pinch black pepper
- 1 ½ cups cooked lentils
- ¼ - ½ tsp Tabasco

Direction

- Bring all ingredients except lentils and Tabasco to a boil.
- Cover, lower heat to simmer 20 minutes.
- Add lentils and Tabasco, stir and re-cover.
- Cook 30 minutes, remove bay leaf, and serve

200. Corn Pudding 11 Recipe

Serving: 0 | Prep: | Cook: 45mins | Ready in:

Ingredients

- 1 can cream style corn
- 2 Tbsps. flour
- 1 tsp. salt
- 2 Tbsps. margarine
- 2 Tbsps. sugar
- 2 eggs
- 1 c. milk or Half & Half

Direction

- Mix and bake in 350 degree oven for 45 minutes or until sets.

201.   Cranberry Coleslaw Anthonys Home Port Seattle Recipe

Serving: 8 | Prep: | Cook: | Ready in:

Ingredients

- 1 cup dried cranberries
- 2 cups red cabbage, thinly sliced (about 1/4 of a cabbage)
- 2 cups green cabbage
- 1/4 cup red onion very thinly sliced
- 1/3 cup apple cider vinegar
- 1/3 cup canola oil
- 1/4 cup granulated sugar
- 1 tablespoon coarse salt (sea salt or kosher salt)
- 1 teaspoon celery seed
- 1/4 cup shredded carrot (optional)

Direction

- In a food processor combine vinegar, oil, sugar, salt and celery seed. Reserve this mixture.
- Put the slicing blade onto the food processor and thinly slice red and green cabbage and red onion. Combine this with the dressing, stirring well.
- Add cranberries, mix and refrigerate several hours, stirring occasionally.
- Drain liquid from the coleslaw before serving.
- This is extremely simple to prepare and involves little preparation or clean-up. Can be made up to two days in advance and keeps well for a week. Enjoy!

202.   Creamed Corn With Bacon And Blue Cheese Recipe

Serving: 6 | Prep: | Cook: 10mins | Ready in:

Ingredients

- 5 medium ears fresh corn with husks and silk removed
- 4 oz (about 4 slices) of bacon cut into 1/2 inch pieces
- 1 medium shallot, minced
- 1 medium garlic clove, minced
- 1 1/2 c heavy cream
- 1/2 tsp minced fresh thyme leaves
- Pinch cayenne pepper
- 2 oz blue cheese crumbled (about 1/2 cup)
- salt and ground black pepper

Direction

- Cut the kernels from 3 ears of corn and transfer them into a medium bowl.
- Firmly scrape the cobs with the BACK of a butter knife to collect the pulp and milk in the same bowl.
- Grate the remaining 2 ears of corn on the coarse side of a box grater set in the bowl with cut kernels.
- Firmly scrape these cobs with the back of a butter knife to collect the pulp and milk in the same bowl.
- Cook the bacon in a large non-stick skillet over med-high heat until crisp and browned, about 5 minutes.
- Transfer onto a paper towel lined plate to drain.
- Remove and discard all but 2 tbs of the bacon drippings from the pan.
- Add the shallot and cook until softened but not browned, 1-2 minutes.
- Add the garlic and cook until aromatic, about 30 seconds.
- Stir in the corn kernels and pulp, the cream, thyme and cayenne.
- Bring the mixture to a simmer and cook, adjusting the heat as necessary and stirring

occasionally, until the corn is tender and the mixture has thickened, 10-15 minutes.
- Remove the pan from the heat and stir in the cheese.
- Adjust the seasonings with salt and pepper and serve immediately.

---

203. Creamed Peas Recipe

Serving: 5 | Prep: | Cook: 10mins | Ready in:

Ingredients

- 1-16 oz package frozen peas
- 4 Tablespoons butter (or more if you like)
- 2 Tablespoons flour
- 1 cup half & half
- heaping teaspoon sugar
- 1/2 teaspoon salt

Direction

- Cook peas in boiling water for ten minutes; pour into colander and drain. (I reserve some of the liquid to add if my cream sauce is too thick from not measuring my flour)
- Using same sauce pan melt butter over medium heat and stir in flour. Gradually add half & half, stirring constantly until thick and creamy.
- Stir in sugar, salt and peas. Taste.
- Add more salt or sugar if you like

---

204. Crockpot Stewed Tomatoes Recipe

Serving: 6 | Prep: | Cook: 22mins | Ready in:

Ingredients

- 6 - 8 ripe tomatoes
- 2 Tab. butter or margarine
- 1 med. onion, thinly sliced

- 3/4 cup chopped celery
- 1/2 cup chopped green pepper
- 3 Tab. sugar (more or less)
- 1 small bay leaf
- 1 teas. salt
- 1/8 teas. pepper

Direction

- Core tomatoes
- Place in boiling water for about 15 - 20 seconds, then in ice water to cool quickly peel.
- Cut tomatoes in wedges.
- In crock pot, combine all ingredients.
- Cover and cook on low 8 - 9 hours.
- Remove bay leaf.
- Sprinkle top with parsley, if desired.
- Serve as a side dish, or freeze in portions for soups or other recipes

---

205. Dads Style BBQ Corn Recipe

Serving: 6 | Prep: | Cook: 12mins | Ready in:

Ingredients

- 6 ears fresh, husk-on corn
- ½ cup unsalted, very soft butter
- 1 tbsp BBQ seasoning
- 1 tsp salt

Direction

- Soak ears of corn 8 minutes in cold water.
- Preheat BBQ to medium.
- Dry off corn husks and place on hot grill.
- Cover and cook 10-12 minutes. Turn every 4 minutes.
- Combine butter, BBQ seasoning and salt in a bowl.
- Serve butter with corn.

206. Dans Fried Green Tomatoes Recipe

Serving: 4 | Prep: | Cook: 10mins | Ready in:

Ingredients

- 1/2 Cup all-purpose flour
- 3 eggs, beaten
- 1/2 Cup yellow cornmeal
- 1 Lbs green tomatoes, sliced 1/2 thick
- 1/2 canola oil
- kosher salt

Direction

- Place the flour, eggs and cornmeal in three separate shallow bowls.
- Dip the tomatoes first in the flour, then the eggs (letting any excess run off) and finally the cornmeal, pressing gently to help it adhere.
- Heat the oil in a large skillet over medium high heat. Working in batches, cook the tomatoes until golden, 1 to 2 minutes per side.
- Transfer to a paper towel-lined plate. Season with salt before serving.
- Enjoy!

207. Delicious Creamed Cabbage With Bacon Recipe

Serving: 6 | Prep: | Cook: 10mins | Ready in:

Ingredients

- 2 slices bacon, crisp-cooked and crumbled
- 1/2 cup finely diced, cooked country ham
- 1/2 cup chopped onion
- 7 cups shredded green cabbage
- 1/2 cup heavy cream
- pepper to taste

Direction

- In a large pot, layer in order: bacon, ham, onion, cabbage, pepper
- Pour cream over all
- Bring to a simmer, reduce heat to medium
- Cook 10 minutes, stirring gently, occasionally OR until cabbage is soft and liquid is reduced to a niche thick sauce
- Delicious!

208. Delicious Onion Rings Recipe

Serving: 20 | Prep: | Cook: 2mins | Ready in:

Ingredients

- 2 eggs beaten
- 1 pt milk
- 10 oz cake flour
- 2 tsp baking powder
- 1/2 tsp salt
- 1/2 tsp garlic powder (NOT garlic salt!)
- 1 oz parsley flakes
- 1/2 tsp paprika (optional: for added color)
- 3 lb onions -- large
- as needed --- flour

Direction

- Combine the eggs and milk in a bowl.
- Mix the flour, baking powder, salt, garlic powder, parsley flakes, and paprika together and add to the milk.
- Mix well.
- The batter should have the consistency of a thin pancake batter.
- Peel the onions and cut crosswise into 1/4 inch slices.
- Separate into rings (save unusable pieces for another purpose).
- Place the onions in cold water if they are not used immediately to maintain crispness.
- Drain and dry the onions thoroughly.

- Dredge with flour and shake off excess. (This step isn't always necessary, but it helps the batter adhere.)
- Dip a few pieces at a time in the batter and fry in deep fat (350°F) until golden brown. This only take a minute or two.
- Drain and serve immediately.
- Note:
- There are some variations listed below you might also enjoy!
- Beer Batter
- Substitute light beer for the milk.
- Omit baking powder because the carbonation of the beer acts as a leavener.
- Buttermilk Batter
- Substitute buttermilk for the milk and use 1 tsp. baking soda instead of the 2 tsp. baking powder.
- Other Fried Vegetables:
- Try this with sweet potatoes, kohlrabi, and cauliflower for a taste variety!
- ENJOY!

209.   Double Broccoli Quinoa Recipe

Serving: 4 | Prep: | Cook: 40mins | Ready in:

Ingredients

- 3 cups cooked quinoa (see instructions below)
- 5 cups raw broccoli, cut into small florets and stems
- 3 medium garlic cloves
- 2/3 cup sliced or slivered almonds, toasted
- 1/3 cup freshly grated Parmesan
- 2 big pinches salt
- 2 tablespoons fresh lemon juice
- 1/4 cup olive oil
- 1/4 cup heavy cream
- Optional toppings: slivered basil, fire oil (optional)**, see below , sliced avocado
- crumbled feta or goat cheese

Direction

- Heat the quinoa and set aside see more below!
- Now barely cook the broccoli by pouring 3/4 cup water into a large pot and bringing it to a simmer.
- Add a big pinch of salt and stir in the broccoli.
- Cover and cook for a minute, just long enough to take the raw edge off.
- Transfer the broccoli to a strainer and run under cold water until it stops cooking.
- Set aside.
- To make the broccoli pesto puree two cups of the cooked broccoli, the garlic, 1/2 cup of the almonds, Parmesan, salt, and lemon juice in a food processor.
- Drizzle in the olive oil and cream and pulse until smooth.
- Just before serving, toss the quinoa and remaining broccoli florets with about 1/2 of the broccoli pesto.
- Taste and adjust if needed, you might want to add more of the pest a bit at a time, or you might want a bit more salt or an added squeeze of lemon juice.
- Turn out onto a serving platter and top with the remaining almonds, a drizzle of the chile oil, and some sliced avocado or any of the other optional toppings.
- *To cook quinoa: rinse one cup of quinoa in a fine-meshed strainer.
- In a medium saucepan heat the quinoa, two cups of water (or broth if you like), and a few big pinches of salt until boiling.
- Reduce heat and simmer until water is absorbed and quinoa fluffs up, about 15 minutes.
- Quinoa is done when you can see the curlicue in each grain, and it is tender with a bit of pop to each bite.
- Drain any extra water and set aside.
- **To make the red chile oil:
- You'll need 1/2 cup extra-virgin olive oil and 1 1/2 teaspoons crushed red pepper flakes.
- If you can, make the chile oil a day or so ahead of time by heating the olive oil in a small saucepan for a couple minutes - until it is

about as hot as you would need it to sauté some onions, but not so hot that it smokes or smells acrid or burned.

- Turn off the heat and stir in the crushed red pepper flakes.
- Set aside and let cool, then store in refrigerator.
- Bring to room temp again before using.

210. Easy Easy Country Corn Casserole Recipe

Serving: 8 | Prep: | Cook: 50mins | Ready in:

Ingredients

- EASY easy COUNTRY corn CASSEROLE
- ~~~~~~ ~~~~~~
- 1 box Jiffy cornbread mix
- 1 can whole kernel corn, drained
- 1 can cream corn
- 8 oz. sour cream
- 1/2 stick butter
- 1 cup shredded Cheddar

Direction

- Preheat oven to 350 degrees F.
- In a large bowl, stir together the 2 cans of corn, corn muffin mix, sour cream, and melted butter.
- Pour into a greased 9 by 13-inch casserole dish. Bake for 45 minutes, or until golden brown.
- Remove from oven and top with Cheddar. Return to oven for 5 to 10 minutes, or until cheese is melted.
- Let stand for at least 5 minutes and then serve warm.
- ~~~~~~ ~~~~~~

211. Easy Easy Greek Style Green Beans Recipe

Serving: 6 | Prep: | Cook: 20mins | Ready in:

Ingredients

- 1/2 cup chopped onion
- 1 clove garlic, minced
- 1 tablespoon olive oil
- 1 28-ounce can diced tomatoes
- (or, halved grape tomatoes, chopped fresh tomatoes with juice)
- 1/4 cup sliced pitted ripe olives
- 1 teaspoon dried oregano, crushed
- 2 9-ounce packages or one 16-ounce package frozen French-cut green beans, thawed and drained
- (or equivalent of fresh, cooked til tender)
- 1/2 cup crumbled feta cheese (2 ounces)

Direction

- In a large skillet cook onion and garlic in hot oil about 5 minutes or until tender.
- Add undrained tomatoes, olives, and oregano.
- Bring to boiling; reduce heat.
- Boil gently, uncovered, for 10 minutes.
- Add beans.
- Return to boiling.
- Boil gently, uncovered, about 8 minutes or until desired consistency and beans are tender.
- Transfer to a serving bowl; sprinkle with cheese.
- ***NOTE***
- Fresh green beans and tomatoes are always way better than anything canned, and I use them often. If canned is what you have (or a combination of canned / fresh) it's a great recipe to make them taste even better!

212.   Easy Pesto Cauliflower Recipe

Serving: 4 | Prep: | Cook: 12mins | Ready in:

Ingredients

- 1 head cauliflower
- 1 bunch basil
- handful of nuts (pine nuts are traditional, but we've used almonds, walnuts, and pistachios)
- 1 clove garlic
- olive oil
- salt
- pepper
- Optional: kalamata olives, chopped

Direction

- Cut cauliflower into chunks, microwave it in a covered dish for about 8 minutes.
- While cauliflower is cooking, put basil, nuts, garlic, salt and pepper in food processor. Drizzle in olive oil until you have a nice thick paste, but nothing too runny.
- A little at a time, drop in cauliflower and blend until smooth.
- Fold in Kalamata olives and serve.
- Yum!

213.   Easy N Delicious Country Onion Casserole Recipe

Serving: 8 | Prep: | Cook: 30mins | Ready in:

Ingredients

- Easy n delicious Country Onion Casserole
- ~~~~~~~~~~~~~~~~~~~~~~~~~~~~~~~~~~~~ ~~~~~~~~~~~~~
- 2 large bermuda onions, sliced and separated into rings
- 2 tablespoons of butter
- 1/2 pound of swiss cheese, grated

- 1/4 teaspoon of black pepper
- 1/2 cup of milk
- 1 can of cream of chicken soup
- 1 teaspoon of soy sauce
- 8 slices of French bread, buttered

Direction

- Simmer onions in butter until tender. Place in a casserole dish.
- Top this with the grated Swiss cheese and black pepper.
- Heat the soup and milk until well blended then add the soy sauce and stir well.
- Pour this mixture over the onions and cheese in the casserole dish. Stir lightly.
- Overlap the bread slices on the top of the casserole. Bake at 350 degrees for a total of 30 minutes.
- After the casserole has baked for about 15 minutes, push the bread down into the cheese and onions and continue baking for the remaining 15 minutes.
- You can use any type of onions that you like and also lots more than are called for.

214.   Eggplant Al Fresco Recipe

Serving: 6 | Prep: | Cook: 45mins | Ready in:

Ingredients

- * 1 large American eggplant (or 3 Italian eggplants)
- * 2 green bell peppers
- * 1 red bell pepper
- * 2-3 large cloves of garlic
- * ½ cup fruity olive oil
- * sea salt
- * parsley

Direction

- Preheat oven to 350 degrees F.

- Cut the eggplant into ½-inch cubes. Cut the bell peppers into ½-inch squares. Mix them in a large ceramic bowl.
- Add 2 to 3 cloves of finely minced garlic and the finely chopped Italian parsley. Stir in 1 teaspoon of sea salt. Then add the olive oil and mix together with a large spoon.
- Bake uncovered in the oven for 45 to 60 minutes, stirring every 15 minutes. The eggplant should be tender, but not mushy.
- Once the eggplant is tender, remove the bowl from the oven and allow to cool, stirring twice during the cooling. Once the dish is cool, taste test to determine if more salt is required.
- With a slotted spoon, place the eggplant in a ceramic serving dish or pie plate. Garnish with parsley. Serve at room temperature.
- Of course, you have to enjoy *wink*

- Mash, season with salt and pepper and a little lemon juice
- Fry bacon in large skillet, slowly.
- When nearly done, push to the edge of the pan; add onion and celery.
- Continue to cook very slowly until the vegetables are clear but not brown.
- Add two tablespoons of cracker crumbs to the eggplant mixture along with the bacon, onion and celery mixture. Mix well.
- Add the adobo seasoning (sub grill seasoning if you want).
- Stir in eggs and cheese.
- Pour into a buttered 1 1/2 quart to 2 quart casserole.
- Sprinkle rest of cracker crumbs on top.
- Dot with butter.
- Bake at 325 degrees for one hour.
- Delicious reheated too!

215. Eggplant Deluxe Casserole Recipe

Serving: 6 | Prep: | Cook: 80mins | Ready in:

Ingredients

- 2 large eggplants, peeled
- 4 strips of bacon cut fine
- 1 large onion minced
- 2 stalks of celery minced (tough strings removed)
- 2 teaspoons of adobe seasoning
- 2 eggs beaten
- 4 tablespoons of finely crushed cracker crumbs
- 1 cup of finely shredded cheddar cheese
- 1/2 teaspoon of salt
- 1/4 teaspoon of pepper
- squeeze of lemon juice
- 1 tablespoon of butter cut in little pieces

Direction

- Peel eggplant, cut in one inch chunks,
- Steam in colander over boiling water until very easily pierced with a fork.

216. Eggplant Fans Recipe

Serving: 4 | Prep: | Cook: 90mins | Ready in:

Ingredients

- 3 medium eggplants ends trimmed
- 2 large firm tomatoes halved lengthwise cored and thinly sliced
- 1/2 cup olive oil
- 1 large white onion finely chopped
- 4 garlic cloves thinly sliced
- 4 tender artichokes
- 1/2 cup small pitted black olives rinsed
- 2 bay leaves crumbled
- 1 teaspoon mixed dried thyme, oregano and savory
- 1/2 teaspoon salt
- 1 teaspoon freshly ground black pepper

Direction

- Preheat oven to 450.
- Split eggplants lengthwise.

- Place the halves split side down on a chopping board and cut each half lengthwise/
- Leave slices attached at the stem end to form fans.
- Slip tomato slices into the slits of the eggplant halves.
- Oil a large gratin dish with 2 tablespoons of the olive oil.
- Scatter half the onion and garlic over the bottom.
- Arrange eggplant halves gently forced together side by side in the dish.
- Pour remaining olive oil into a bowl.
- Pare artichokes to the hearts and quarter them.
- Removing chokes and place the hearts immediately into the oil turning to coat completely.
- Force the quartered artichoke hearts and olives into crevices around the eggplant fans.
- Fit in the bay leaf fragments then scatter remaining onion and garlic over the surface.
- Sprinkle with herbs, salt and pepper.
- Press everything into place to form as regular a surface as possible.
- Dribble the oil left over from the artichokes over the entire surface adding more if necessary.
- Place a sheet of aluminum foil loosely over the surface and bake for 1-1/2 hours.
- After 15 minutes reduce heat to 350.
- When done the stem ends of the eggplants should be soft to the touch.
- Serve at room temperature.

217.   Eggplant Fingers Recipe

Serving: 6 | Prep: | Cook: 25mins | Ready in:

Ingredients

- 2 eggplants
- olive oil
- 1 1/2 cups Italian bread crumbs
- 1 cup parmesan cheese

Direction

- Cut skin off eggplant and slice into one half to three-quarter inch rounds. Cut rounds into fingers about 1/2 to 3/4 inch sticks. Coat with olive oil. Mix parmesan and bread crumbs. Roll fingers in bread, cheese mixture and place on baking sheet. Bake at 375 until golden brown.

218.   Elaines Pepper Stir Fry Recipe

Serving: 4 | Prep: | Cook: 20mins | Ready in:

Ingredients

- 2 whole yellow sweet peppers
- 2 whole green sweet peppers
- 2 whole orange sweet peppers
- 4 large shallots
- 6 to 8 green onions
- mushrooms, no set amount

Direction

- Slice the peppers into long strips.
- Slice the shallots and onions thinly.
- Slice mushrooms to your preference.
- Place on a hot grill, on a baking sheet or tinfoil.
- Cook, turning frequently, until peppers are moderately soft, and the shallots are nicely caramelized.
- Add salt, pepper, whatever- to your taste.

219.   Elaines Roasted Onions Recipe

Serving: 6 | Prep: | Cook: 25mins | Ready in:

Ingredients

- 6 large Spanish onions

- 2 tbsp each:
- basil
- thyme
- oregano
- lemon pepper (unsalted)
- minced garlic
- tinfoil

Direction

- Cut off both ends of the onions, and remove the outer peel
- Combine in a bowl: basil, thyme, oregano, lemon pepper and garlic
- Combine thoroughly
- Cut crosswise slits into the onions, and add a generous amount of the mixture of herbs and spices
- Envelope with heavy-duty tinfoil, and set onto the barbecue grill, lid closed. Cook at medium-high heat for 25 minutes, or until done to your preference.

220.   FRIED GREEN TOMATOES Recipe

Serving: 4 | Prep: | Cook: 112mins | Ready in:

Ingredients

- 3 slices of bacon
- 4 medium green tomatoes
- 1 C. cornmeal
- salt and pepper to taste
- 1/2 C. milk

Direction

- Fry the bacon in heavy skillet.
- Transfer it to absorbent paper.
- Cut each tomato into 1/2" thick slices.
- Put sliced tomatoes on absorbent paper.
- Mix together the cornmeal, salt and pepper.
- Dip tomato slices into a small bowl of milk remove and coat with your cornmeal mixture.

- Fry tomatoes in the bacon fat over medium heat until the cornmeal browns, about 1 1/2 minutes on each side.

221.   Fiery Hot Green Beans Recipe

Serving: 4 | Prep: | Cook: 10mins | Ready in:

Ingredients

- 2 cups water
- 3/4 cup white vinegar
- 2 tablespoons granulated sugar
- 1 tablespoon crushed mustard seeds
- 4 garlic cloves thinly sliced
- 4 bay leaves
- 2 teaspoons salt
- 1 teaspoon cayenne pepper
- 1 pound fresh green beans trimmed

Direction

- Combine all ingredients except beans in a large saucepan and bring to a boil over high heat.
- Cover then reduce heat and simmer 5 minutes.
- Add beans then cover and simmer 10 minutes until beans are cooked but still crisp.
- Transfer beans and liquid to a shallow serving dish and refrigerate covered overnight.
- Serve cold or at room temperature.

222.   Fontina Aparagus Bake Recipe

Serving: 4 | Prep: | Cook: 15mins | Ready in:

Ingredients

- Ingredients:
- butter, for greasing

- 2 and 1/4 lb asparagus, spears trimmed
- 2 cooked ham slices, cut into strips
- 4 oz Fontina cheese, sliced
- 2 eggs
- 2 tablespoons parmesan cheese, freshly grated
- salt and pepper
- Squares of toasted Italian bread - season with Italian herbs

Direction

- Directions:
- Preheat the oven to 350deg F
- Grease an ovenproof dish with butter. Line the sides with the flavored toasted bread squares.
- Cook the asparagus in salted, boiling water for 10 minutes.
- Drain and place in the prepared dish and top with the ham and Fontina.
- Beat the eggs with the Parmesan cheese, season with salt and pepper and pour over the asparagus.
- Bake for 15-20 minutes until the Parmesan has melted and the eggs have set.
- Let's Eat!

223. Fresh Sweet Corn Cakes Recipe

Serving: 4 | Prep: | Cook: 15mins | Ready in:

Ingredients

- 4 thin slices bacon, diced
- 2 ears fresh sweet corn
- 1 or 2 jalapeno peppers (to your liking), cut in half and seeds removed, then diced finely
- 1 small sweet onion, diced (a good cup or so)
- ½ cup yellow cornmeal
- 1 or 2 tablespoons sugar (depending on how sweet you like your corn cakes)
- 1 teaspoon baking powder
- ½ teaspoon sea salt
- ¼ teaspoon baking soda

- a pinch or more of cayenne pepper (or to your taste)
- 5 tablespoons buttermilk
- 1 medium egg
- 4 ounces grated pepper jack cheese, or Mexican Blend grated cheese
- Topping:
- 2 green onions, sliced (whites and part of the greens)
- 2 ounces crumbled queso fresco cheese
- salsa, optional
- guacamole, optional
- sour cream, optional
- peanut oil (or whatever oil you prefer to fry in)

Direction

- Fry diced bacon in a cast iron skillet (or any heavy skillet that doesn't have a non-stick coating…pans with non-stick coatings will tend to not give you the browning you want for this recipe).
- Remove bacon from skillet and drain on paper toweling, leaving 2 tablespoons bacon grease in the pan.
- Stand corn cobs on end in a deep bowl and use a very sharp knife to run down the sides of the corn, top to bottom, cutting the kernels from the cob; measure out 1 heaping cup of kernels (save any extra for another use).
- In the hot bacon grease in the skillet, sauté the corn, diced jalapeno, and diced onion until onions turn golden, about 10 to 12 minutes; remove pan from heat and set aside.
- In a mixing bowl, combine corn meal, sugar, baking powder, sea salt, baking soda and cayenne pepper.
- In a small bowl, whisk together buttermilk and egg; gently stir into cornmeal mixture just until moistened.
- Add bacon, sautéed veggies and grated cheese to batter, stirring only enough to incorporate all of the ingredients together.
- Return cast iron skillet to medium/medium-high heat, and add oil to generously cover the bottom of the pan.

- When oil is sizzling hot, drop the corn cakes into 4 "patties" in the skillet; fry for approximately 2 minutes, until well browned on bottom; flip corn cakes and fry an additional 2 minutes on the other side.
- NOTE: It is very important to have a very hot oil when you fry the cakes – if the cakes linger too long in the pan to brown, they will become dry. The key is quick, HOT frying!
- Serve immediately, topped with green onions, crumbled cheese, and any other optional toppings

224. Fried Corn Tennessee Style Recipe

Serving: 4 | Prep: | Cook: 20mins | Ready in:

Ingredients

- 6 ears fresh corn (Though not as flavorful as fresh corn, frozen corn kernels also can be used.)
- 4 slices bacon
- 1/2 cup milk
- 1 tsp. salt
- 1/4 tsp. freshly ground black pepper
- Pinch sugar

Direction

- With sharp knife, cut corn kernels from cob. Also scrape pulp out with back of knife. Set aside.
- Cut bacon in half and fry in heavy iron skillet until crisp. Drain on paper towelling.
- Discard all but 4 Tbsp. bacon fat. Add corn. Cook, without stirring, until bottom is browned (lift corn from the side with a spatula to check).
- When well browned, add milk and seasonings, stirring until well combined. Cover and cook over low heat 10 min. longer. Arrange bacon over the top and serve.

225. GARLICKY BRAISED KALE WITH SUN DRIED TOMATOES Recipe

Serving: 4 | Prep: | Cook: 20mins | Ready in:

Ingredients

- 2 tablespoons extra virgin olive oil
- 5 cloves garlic cut in half then smashed and peeled
- 2 tablespoons finely chopped oil packed sun-dried tomatoes well drained
- 1/2 large bunch kale washed and cut into 1" ribbons
- 1/2 teaspoon salt
- 1 teaspoon freshly ground black pepper
- 1/2 cup chicken stock
- 1/2 teaspoon balsamic vinegar
- 1/2 ounce crumbled goat cheese

Direction

- Heat the olive oil in a soup pot over medium heat.
- Add garlic and sauté stirring for 3 minutes.
- Add tomatoes and stir to combine.
- Add kale tossing to coat well with the oil.
- Season with salt and pepper then continue stirring until kale is wilted.
- Add stock then bring to a boil and reduce to a simmer.
- Cover and cook until kale has softened about 8 minutes.
- Uncover then turn heat to high and boil away the remaining liquid stirring frequently.
- Take pan off heat then season with vinegar and stir to combine.
- Transfer to a small serving dish and top with crumbled goat cheese.

226. GERMAN SWEET AND SOUR RED CABBAGE Recipe

Serving: 10 | Prep: | Cook: 75mins | Ready in:

Ingredients

- 1 red cabbage, sliced
- 1 onion, diced
- 1 Large apple
- 1 c. vinegar
- 1/2 c. sugar (I used splenda)
- 1 c. water
- 4 tbsp. bacon drippings

Direction

- In a large kettle, gently brown one diced onion in bacon drippings. Then add red cabbage, cut in 1/3 inch slices and stir fry.
- Add the cooking apple, peeled and cut up.
- Add the vinegar, sugar, and water, simmer until cabbage is tender with the lid on the pan, approximately 1 hours.

227. GUACAPICO AKA PICO DE GALLO WITH AVOCADO Recipe

Serving: 4 | Prep: | Cook: | Ready in:

Ingredients

- 2 cups onion, coarsely chopped, about 3/8-1/2"
- 2 cups ripe roma tomato, deseeded and coarsely chopped, about 3/8-1/2"
- 3 cup avocados, coarsely diced, about 3/8-1/2"
- 1-2 fresh jalapeno pepper(s), deseeded and chopped (adjust for your heat tolerance)
- 1/4 cup cilantro, chopped, placed loose in measuring cup
- juice of 2 limes
- Generously salt and pepper to taste

Direction

- Mix ingredients in non-reactive bowl and refrigerate for a minimum of 1 hour to allow flavors to blend.
- Serve cold or room temp.

228. Garden Casserole Recipe

Serving: 12 | Prep: | Cook: 85mins | Ready in:

Ingredients

- 1 cup chopped onion
- 1 green pepper, chopped
- 1 sweet red pepper, chopped
- 1/4 cup butter or margarine, melted
- 1 1/2 cups uncooked long-grain rice
- 2 (10- 3/4 ounce) can chicken broth, undiluted
- 3/4 cup water
- 2 ripe tomatoes, chopped
- 1 tablespoon tomato paste
- 1/4 to 1/2 teaspoon pepper
- 1/2 teaspoon dried whole saffron, crushed
- or 1/4 teaspoon ground saffron
- Dash of worcestershire sauce
- 3/4 pound broccoli, cut into 1-1inch
- pieces
- 2 small zucchini, cut into 1/2-inch pieces
- 10 ounces fresh shucked green peas
- 12 fresh asparagus spears cut into 1-inch pieces

Direction

- Sauté onion, green pepper, and red pepper in butter in a heavy oven proof Dutch oven until tender.
- Stir in rice and next 7 ingredients, and bring to a boil.
- Remove from heat; cover and bake at 350 degrees for 30 minutes.
- Stir remaining vegetables into rice mixture.

- Cover and bake an additional 45 minutes or until liquid is absorbed and vegetables are crisp-tender.

229. Garden Zucchini Gratin Recipe

Serving: 8 | Prep: | Cook: 8mins | Ready in:

Ingredients

- 1 1/2 Tbs butter
- 8 Cups Thinly sliced zucchini OR (combo of 4 cups of zucchini and 4 cups of yellow squash)
- 1 cup sliced white onion
- 2 cloves garlic, minced
- 1/2 cup fat-free half-and-half (of course you can use regular!)
- 4 Tbs reduced-fat cream cheese (of course you can use regular!)
- 3/4 cup panko bread crumbs (Japanese-style bread crumbs), divided (a must)
- 3/4 cup grated parmesan cheese, divided.
- 1/2 teaspoon salt
- 1/4 teaspoon ground black pepper
- nonstick cooking spray

Direction

- Preheat oven to 450 degrees. In a large skillet, melt the butter over medium heat; add zucchini, onion and garlic. Cook, stirring occasionally until vegetables are tender, about 6 to 8 minutes.
- Add the half-and-half and cream cheese to the vegetable mixture; stir to combine, allowing the cream cheese to melt.
- Set aside 4 tablespoons of the panko and 5 tablespoons of the Parmesan cheese. Add the remaining 6 tablespoons of the panko and 5 tablespoons of Parmesan cheese, salt and pepper to the vegetable mixture; stir to combine.
- Coat a 2-quart shallow baking dish with nonstick spray. Spoon mixture into the baking dish. Sprinkle the top with remaining panko and Parmesan cheese.
- Bake until top is golden brown, about 10 to 12 minutes.
- Enjoy!
- 104 calories and 5g of fat per serving!

230. Garlic Asparagus And Pasta With Lemon Cream Recipe

Serving: 6 | Prep: | Cook: 10mins | Ready in:

Ingredients

- 8 ounces dried rotini
- 1 tablespoon butter
- 2 cups fresh asparagus cut into 2-inch pieces
- 8 baby sunburst squash and/or pattypan squash halved
- 2 cloves garlic minced
- 1/2 cup whipping cream
- 2 teaspoons finely shredded lemon peel

Direction

- Cook pasta according to package directions
- Drain pasta and keep warm.
- Melt butter in a large skillet.
- Add asparagus, squash and garlic.
- Cook stirring frequently until vegetables are crisp-tender then remove with a slotted spoon and add to pasta.
- Combine whipping cream and lemon peel in skillet then bring to boiling and boil 3 minutes.
- To serve pour cream mixture over pasta mixture and toss gently to coat.

231. Garlic Butter Green Beans Ci Recipe

Serving: 6 | Prep: | Cook: 15mins | Ready in:

Ingredients

- 2lb fresh green beans, cleaned
- 6-8 cloves garlic, minced
- 1 stick butter
- salt and pepper

Direction

- Place beans in large saucepan and add water to just cover.
- Boil, then reduce heat and cook until just tender but still crisp (7-10 min), drain
- In large skillet, melt butter and add garlic.
- Add beans, toss to coat and cook just till heated through.
- Add fresh ground pepper and sea or kosher salt just prior to serving.
- *please note, these are even better if beans are steamed rather than boiled, then tossed in garlic butter*

---

232. Garlic Sesame Kale Recipe

Serving: 6 | Prep: | Cook: 15mins | Ready in:

Ingredients

- 2 bunches kale, trimmed and chopped
- 1 tsp. olive oil
- 2 cloves garlic, minced
- 1/4 tsp. cayenne pepper
- 2 tsp toasted sesame oil
- 2 tsp sesame seeds, toasted

Direction

- In Dutch oven, bring 1 c. water to boil.
- Add kale; cover and cook for 4 min, stirring occasionally.
- Uncover and cook until water evaporates, about 3 min.
- Heat olive oil in heavy skillet over medium heat.

- Sauté garlic and cayenne pepper of 1 min.
- Add kale.
- Cook and stir for 3 min.
- Transfer kale to bowl.
- Toss with sesame oil.
- Season with salt and pepper to taste.
- Garnish with sesame seeds.

---

233. German Onion Cake Recipe

Serving: 10 | Prep: | Cook: 45mins | Ready in:

Ingredients

- 2 cups onions, coarsely chopped
- 2 tablespoons butter (1/4 stick)
- 1 teaspoon salt
- 1/4 teaspoon dried marjoram
- 1/4 teaspoon black pepper
- 2 cups all-purpose flour
- 1/4 cup cornstarch
- 4 teaspoons baking powder
- 5 tablespoons vegetable shortening
- 3/4 cup milk (may need up to 1 cup)
- 1 egg, well beaten
- 3/4 cup sour cream
- 2 teaspoons poppy seeds
- 1/4 teaspoon paprika

Direction

- In a medium skillet, sauté the onions in butter over low heat until they just begin to brown, about 15 minutes.
- Season with ¼ teaspoon of the salt, the marjoram, and the pepper. Set aside to cool. Preheat oven to 450 degrees.
- In a food processor bowl place flour, cornstarch, baking powder, and the remaining salt, mix. Add the shortening and process just until it is the texture of soft crumbs. Add the milk and mix quickly to form a soft dough.

- Oil a 10-inch round cake pan and lightly use your fingers to spread the dough out evenly. Spread the cooked onion over the top.
- Beat the egg and sour cream together. Spoon the mixture over the onion, and spread it out to the very edge of the pan.
- Sprinkle lightly with poppy seeds and paprika.
- Bake for 20 minutes. Let cool slightly, then cut into wedges.

234.   German Red Cabbage Recipe

Serving: 6 | Prep: | Cook: 35mins | Ready in:

Ingredients

- 1 medium red cabbage
- 1 large apple
- 1 onion, sliced
- 1½ tablespoons brown sugar
- 3 tablespoons red wine vinegar
- ½ teaspoon caraway seeds
- 2 tablespoons butter
- salt and pepper to taste

Direction

- Chop the cabbage into 4 quarters, cut out the central core and shred.
- Peel and core apple. Chop into small pieces.
- Place all ingredients into a large pan with about 1 ¼ cups water. Bring to the boil, cover and simmer on low heat, for about 30 minutes, stirring once or twice.
- The cabbage should be tender but not soft with little liquid left.
- Serve hot. If making ahead, cool and chill. Reheat thoroughly to serve.

235.   Ginger Carrots Recipe

Serving: 4 | Prep: | Cook: 15mins | Ready in:

Ingredients

- 1/2 cup chinablue tangy ginger SAUCE
- 1 cup chicken broth or water
- 1 pound baby carrots, peeled and trimmed
- 1/4 cup toasted, sliced almonds

Direction

- Marinate carrots in china blue tangy ginger SAUCE for 5 minutes.
- In large sauté pan bring chicken broth simmer.
- Add carrots and marinade, bring back to simmer, cover and cook for 15-20 minutes, until tender.
- Uncover and continue cooking for 2-3 minutes until liquid is almost entirely evaporated and carrots are glazed.
- Remove from heat.
- Sprinkle with almonds.
- Serve hot or at room temperature.

236.   Glazed Carrots Recipe

Serving: 8 | Prep: | Cook: 25mins | Ready in:

Ingredients

- 1 packages 16 oz.fresh baby carrots or cut regular size carrots into smaller pieces.
- 1/4 C. butter or margarine
- 1/4 C. packed brown sugar
- 1 envelope ranch salad dressing mix

Direction

- Place carrots in a saucepan; add 1 inch of water.
- Bring to a boil. Reduce heat; cover and cook for 8 to 10 minutes or until crisp-tender.
- Drain and set aside.

- In the same pan, combine butter, brown sugar and salad dressing mix until blended.
- Add carrots.
- Cook and stir over medium heat for 5 minutes or until glazed.

237. Greek Tomatoes Recipe

Serving: 5 | Prep: | Cook: 25mins | Ready in:

Ingredients

- 3 small plum tomatoes, cut in half.
- 1 tablespoon dry breadcrumbs
- 2 tablespoons crumbled feta cheese with basil and tomato
- 1/4 teaspoon dried oregano
- 1/8 teaspoon pepper

Direction

- Preheat toaster oven to 350 degrees
- Place tomato halves on toaster oven pan coated with cooking spray; cut side up
- Sprinkle breadcrumbs over each tomato half, and top with cheese.
- Sprinkle with oregano and pepper.
- Bake at 350 degrees for 20 minutes.
- Serve warm.
- To bake in a conventional oven, place tomato halves on a baking sheet and bake for 25 minutes at 350 degrees.
- These will look like little stuffed tomatoes.

238. Greek Zucchini Patties Recipe

Serving: 8 | Prep: | Cook: 6mins | Ready in:

Ingredients

- 1 pound zucchini, grated

- 1 teaspoon kosher salt or 3/4 teaspoon table salt
- 3/4 cup crumbled feta cheese
- 1 large egg, lightly beaten
- 3 green onions, thinly sliced
- 3 tablespoons all-purpose flour
- 1/4 cup chopped pine nuts
- 1 tablespoon chopped fresh dill, or 1 teaspoon dried
- 1 1/2 teaspoons chopped fresh oregano leaves, or 1/2 teaspoon dried
- 1 garlic clove, finely chopped
- 1/4 teaspoon freshly milled black pepper
- olive oil

Direction

- Combine the grated zucchini and kosher salt. Set aside for 5 minutes (no more, or it will be mush). Rinse in cold water and squeeze dry in a kitchen towel or press in a strainer or colander until dry.
- Combine the cheese, egg, green onions, flour, pine nuts, dill, oregano, garlic, and pepper in a large bowl; fold in the zucchini. Form into 24 small cakes (about 2 tablespoons of mixture for each) and sauté in olive oil, turning once, until browned, about 3 minutes on each side. Serve immediately.

239. Green Bean Casserole Recipe

Serving: 6 | Prep: | Cook: 30mins | Ready in:

Ingredients

- 1 can (10 3/4 oz.) Campbell's® condensed cream of mushroom soup OR Campbell's® Condensed 98% Fat Free Cream of Mushroom Soup
- 1/2 cup milk
- 1 tsp. soy sauce
- Dash ground black pepper
- 4 cups cooked cut green beans

- 1 1/3 cups French's® French fried onions

Direction

- MIX soup, milk, soy, black pepper, beans and 2/3 cup onions in 1 1/2-qt. casserole.
- BAKE at 350°F. for 25 min. or until hot.
- STIR. Sprinkle with remaining onions. Bake 5 min.
- TIP: Use 1 bag (16 to 20 oz.) frozen green beans, 2 pkg. (9 oz. each) frozen green beans, 2 cans (about 16 oz. each) green beans or about 1 1/2 lb. fresh green beans for this recipe.
- For a change of pace, substitute 4 cups cooked broccoli flowerets for the green beans.
- For a creative twist, stir in 1/2 cup shredded Cheddar cheese with soup. Omit soy sauce. Sprinkle with 1/4 cup additional Cheddar cheese when adding the remaining onions.
- For a festive touch, stir in 1/4 cup chopped red pepper with soup.
- For a heartier mushroom flavor, substitute Campbell's® Condensed Golden Mushroom Soup for Cream of Mushroom Soup. Omit soy sauce. Stir in 1/4 cup chopped red pepper with green beans.

240.   Green Bean Salad Recipe

Serving: 8 | Prep: | Cook: 10mins | Ready in:

Ingredients

- 2 lbs green bean, stem ends removed
- 1/3 cup diced red onion
- 1/3 cup chopped flat leaf parsley
- 1/3 cup diced roasted red pepper
- 1 tsp minced garlic
- 1 1/2 Tbsp red wine vinegar
- 1 1/2 Tbsp Dijon mustard
- 3 Tbsp extra virgin olive oil
- a handful walnut, toasted and chopped

Direction

- Cook green bean in a pot of boiling water until crisp tender, about 5 to 6 minutes.
- Remove to a bowl filled with ice water to stop the cooking.
- Drain and dry with paper towels then place in a serving bowl
- Mix the sauce (vinegar, mustard, olive oil)
- Toss with remaining ingredients. Season, to taste, with salt and pepper.
- Let sit at room temperature, at least 30 minutes.

241.   Green Bean And Mushroom Casserole Recipe

Serving: 10 | Prep: | Cook: | Ready in:

Ingredients

- 2 (15.5 oz) cans of French cut green beans, liquid removed
- 1 pound small Portobello mushrooms, cut into slices
- 1 (10.75 ounce) can roasted garlic, cream of mushroom condensed
- 4 slices of bacon
- 1 cup cheddar cheese, shredded
- 1/2 medium onion, diced
- 1/4 cup olive oil
- 1/3 tsp white pepper
- 3 garlic cloves, finely diced
- 1/2 cup almonds, slivered
- 3/4 tsp seasoned salt, with no msg

Direction

- Preheat the oven to 375 degrees F.
- Fry bacon in a large skillet, over medium-high heat, until crisp. Remove, place onto paper towels and drain. Reduce heat to medium then pour oil into skillet. When oil becomes hot, stir in mushrooms and onion and cook, stirring regularly until the onions become translucent. Add the garlic, and fry for an additional few minutes, until fragrant. Mix in the soup and

almonds, then bring to boil. Season with white pepper and salt, then crumble bacon and add to the mixture. Carefully, stir in the green beans, and place the mixture into a casserole dish.

- Bake, uncovered, for 30 minutes. Remove, and sprinkle Cheddar cheese on the top. Place into the oven for an additional 5 minutes, (until cheese has melted). Allow to stand 5 minutes prior to serving.

242.   Green Beans With Red Peppers And Garlic Recipe

Serving: 6 | Prep: | Cook: 5mins | Ready in:

Ingredients

- 1 lb green beans, stems trimmed
- 2 teaspoons olive oil
- 1 red bell pepper (capsicum), seeded and cut into julienne
- 1/2 teaspoon chile paste or red pepper flakes
- 3 cloves garlic, finely chopped
- 1/2 teaspoon salt
- 1/4 teaspoon pepper
- handful sliced almonds (optional)

Direction

- Cut the beans into 2-inch (5cm) pieces. Bring a large saucepan three-quarters full of water to a boil. Add the beans and blanch until they turn bright green and are tender crisp, about 90 seconds. Drain the beans and plunge into an ice-water bath or rinse them heavily with very cold water to stop the cooking. Set aside.
- In a large frying pan, heat the olive oil over medium heat. Add the bell pepper and toss and stir for 1 minute.
- Add the beans and sauté for 1 minute longer.
- Add the chili flakes or paste and garlic and cook for one minute longer. The beans will be tender and bright green.

- Drizzle with a touch of olive oil, season with salt and pepper, and garnish with the sliced almonds. Serve immediately.

243.   Green Tomato Casserole Recipe

Serving: 8 | Prep: | Cook: 45mins | Ready in:

Ingredients

- 2 1/2 lbs green tomatoes, peeled and sliced
- 1 tsp salt
- 1 tsp basil
- 1/2 cup Italian bread crumbs
- 1 tsp sugar
- 1 tsp thyme
- 1/3 tsp black pepper
- 2 tbs butter, divided use

Direction

- Layer peeled and sliced tomatoes and seasonings (alternate) in buttered casserole and dot with butter. Bake at 350 uncovered for 45 minutes

244.   Grilled Cabbage Recipe

Serving: 4 | Prep: | Cook: 180mins | Ready in:

Ingredients

- 1 large cabbage
- cream cheese
- butter
- Minced garlic
- salt & pepper
- Grated Romano and parmesan cheese

Direction

- Core cabbage (not all the way through)

- Layer Ingredients and pack into core
- Salt & pepper, Butter & garlic, Grated Romano and Parmesan cheese, and Cream cheese.
- Repeat layers and top with Cream cheese
- Pack it as tight as you can.
- Wrap in foil and place on grill core side up.
- The directions say directly over coals but I would argue for indirect and longer cooking
- Cook until tender.

245.   Grilled Corn With Ancho Avocado Butter Recipe

Serving: 6 | Prep: | Cook: 10mins | Ready in:

Ingredients

- 1/2 to 1 small ancho chili pepper
- 2 tablespoons lime juice
- 3 tablespoons butter or margarine, softened
- 1/2 of a small avocado, seeded, peeled, and chopped
- 1/8 teaspoon salt
- 6 ears white and /or yellow sweet corn

Direction

- In a small saucepan combine ancho pepper, lime juice, and 2 tablespoons water; cook on low heat, covered, for 10 minutes or until pepper turns soft.
- Drain and cool.
- Remove stem and seeds of pepper.
- Finely chop pepper and combine with softened butter or margarine.
- Slightly mash the avocado with the salt.
- Stir into butter.
- Cover and chill or spoon into small mold or cup lined with plastic wrap; chill.
- Remove husks and silk from ears of corn.
- If desired, leave a few leaves of the husks intact for presentation.
- In a large saucepan cook corn, covered, in a small amount of boiling water for 5 to 7 minutes.

- Drain.
- Grill on an uncovered grill directly over medium coals for 10 minutes, turning several times.
- Remove butter from mold.
- Remove plastic wrap.
- Serve corn with ancho-avocado butter.

246.   Grilled Romaine Lettuce Recipe

Serving: 4 | Prep: | Cook: 5mins | Ready in:

Ingredients

- 2 Heads romaine lettuce - cut in half lengthwise and washed.
- 1/2 cup olive oil
- 1/4 cup balsamic vinegar
- 1/2 tsp. dried minced onion
- 1/2 tsp. garlic powder
- 1/4 tsp. oregano
- 1/2 tsp. salt
- 1/4 tsp. pepper

Direction

- Place split heads of Romaine lettuce in a freezer bag .Mix all other ingredients together in a separate bowl and pour in bag.
- Lay bag flat in fridge for 15 minutes.
- Then turn bag over and lay flat again for another 15 minutes.
- Pre heat grill.
- On medium heat, grill Romaine for about 2 minutes on each side.
- Serve warm.

247.   Grilled Veggies With Basil Mayonnaise Recipe

Serving: 6 | Prep: | Cook: 8mins | Ready in:

Ingredients

- vegetables Ingredients:
- 2 medium red and/or yellow peppers, cut into 8 wedges
- 2 medium zucchini and/or yellow squash, cut diagonally into 1-inch pieces
- 8 small carrots with 1-inch greens intact
- 6 green onions and/or red scallions, cut into 3-inch pieces
- 2 tablespoons butter, melted
- 1/2 teaspoon coarsely ground pepper
- 1/4 teaspoon salt
- 1 teaspoon finely chopped fresh garlic
- ==========================
- basil mayonnaise Ingredients:
- 1/2 cup mayonnaise
- 1 teaspoon finely chopped fresh garlic
- 2 tablespoons fresh lemon juice
- 1/3 cup coarsely chopped fresh basil leaves

Direction

- Heat gas grill on medium or charcoal grill until coals are ash white. Make aluminum foil grilling pan with rectangle of double thickness heavy-duty aluminum foil or use purchased foil pan. Place peppers, squash, carrots and onions in grilling pan. Drizzle with melted butter; sprinkle with pepper, salt and 1 teaspoon garlic. Place on grill. Cover; grill, stirring occasionally, until vegetables are roasted (8 to 12 minutes).
- Meanwhile, stir together all basil mayonnaise ingredients in small bowl. Serve with roasted vegetables.

248. Guacamole Full On No Holds Barred Recipe

Serving: 4 | Prep: | Cook: 10mins | Ready in:

Ingredients

- 3 medium sized ripe avocados

- 1 medium size white onion
- 1 medium size red onion
- 1- 6 cloves of fresh garlic
- 3 small bird-eye chilli peppers
- A large bunch of chopped cilantro or coriander leaves
- 3 tablespoons of lime juice
- 1 tablespoon of lemon juice
- 1/2 teaspoon of salt
- 1/2 teaspoon of cracked black pepper

Direction

- As each item is prepared, place all contents in a suitable plastic container or in your food processor/blender.
- Cut avocados in half and then remove stones.
- Fully scoop out flesh of each half and then chop roughly into 1cm/1/2 inch cubes.
- Coarsely chop both onions into small cubes.
- Crush 1 to 6 cloves of garlic, according to taste.
- Slice and de-seed 1-3 birds' eye chillies, according to preference.
- Finely chop a bunch of cilantro/coriander leaves.
- Put all of the ingredients so far into a plastic container or into your blender.
- Add the lime and lemon juice.
- Finally add the salt and black pepper.
- Then either mash/stir manually or using the lowest setting or burst mode on your blender until you have a semi-smooth mixture.
- For best results, serve after 2 hours in the fridge or immediately if time is of the essence.
- (I prefer the light use of a blender as it produces a finer texture but you can simply mash the ingredients in the plastic container if you wish.)

249. Guacamole With Roasted Corn And Chipotle In Adobo Sauce Recipe

Serving: 4 | Prep: | Cook: 30mins | Ready in:

Ingredients

- 4-6 ripe avocados (about 1 1/2 pounds), halved, pitted, peeled (I used Haas)
- 2 tablespoons fresh lime juice
- 2-3 ears of fresh corn
- 2-3 plum/roma tomatoes, seeded, diced
- 4 green onions, chopped
- 1/4 - 1/2 cup canned chipotle chile with adobo, finely chopped (can use more or less because they pack a fiery punch)
- 1/2 cup sour cream
- 1/2 cup cilantro, chopped

Direction

- Put your corn in the oven at a preheated 400 F for 30 minutes. Leaves the shucks and silks in place and place on the oven rack.
- Remove corn and let cool until you can handle it without injury - about 15 minutes. Shuck and de-silk.
- ~~~~
- Mash avocados with lime juice in medium bowl.
- Using sharp knife, remove corn kernels from cob and add to avocado mixture.
- Stir in tomato and green onions.
- Combine chipotle and sour cream in small bowl; whisk to blend. Stir cream mixture into avocado mixture. Season with salt.
- **Can be made 4 hours ahead. Place plastic wrap directly onto surface of guacamole and refrigerate. Bring to room temperature before serving.

250.   Guinness Battered Onion Rings Recipe

Serving: 4 | Prep: | Cook: 20mins | Ready in:

Ingredients

- 4 cups vegetable oil, for frying
- 2 cups flour

- 1/4 teaspoon cayenne pepper
- 1 teaspoon baking powder
- 2 teaspoons cornstarch
- 1/2 teaspoon salt, plus more for seasoning
- 1/2 teaspoon ground white pepper
- 1 (12-ounce) bottle Guinness, at room temperature
- 1 large yellow onion, peeled and cut into 1/2-inch thick rings

Direction

- In a deep stockpot or deep-fryer, preheat oil to 360 degrees F.
- Place 1/2 cup of the flour and the cayenne pepper in a resealable plastic bag or paper bag and set aside.
- In a medium mixing bowl, combine the remaining flour, the baking powder, cornstarch, salt, and white pepper. Whisk in Guinness until smooth.
- Place the onion rings in the bag containing the flour mixture and toss to coat well. Working in batches, transfer the floured onion rings to the beer batter, making sure that each ring is thoroughly coated with the batter. Remove the rings from the batter and allow excess batter to drip off from the onion rings and immediately place in the preheated oil. Fry, in batches, until golden brown, turning rings as needed, about 2 to 3 minutes per batch. Remove the onion rings, place on a paper towel-lined plate, and season with salt. Repeat with remaining onion rings. Serve hot.

251.   Harvard Beets Recipe

Serving: 8 | Prep: | Cook: 60mins | Ready in:

Ingredients

- 12 small beets cooked and cut in slices, cubes or fancy
- 1/4 cup water
- 1/2 cup sugar

- 1/4 cup vinegar
- 1/2 tbsp cornstarch
- 2 tbsp butter

Direction

- Pre-cook beets until tender.
- Mix sugar and cornstarch in a medium pot.
- Add vinegar and water and boil 5 minutes.
- Add beets to hot sauce and let stand for at least 30 minutes.
- Just before serving bring to a boiling point and add butter

252. Hashbrown Casserole Recipe

Serving: 11 | Prep: | Cook: 60mins | Ready in:

Ingredients

- 2 lbs. of frozen hash browns
- 1 pt. of sour cream
- 1/2 c. of chopped onions
- 2 c. of grated cheddar cheese
- 1/2 c. of melted margarine
- 1 can of cream of chicken soup
- 1 tsp. of salt
- 1/4 tsp. of pepper

Direction

- First you want to add all the ingredients in a bowl.
- Mix well.
- Add to a buttered casserole dish.
- Bake at 350 degrees approx. 45 min.
- Enjoy!

253. Healthy Oven Fried Vegetables Recipe

Serving: 4 | Prep: | Cook: 12mins | Ready in:

Ingredients

- 1/4 c. fine dry bread crumbs
- 1 T. parmesan cheese
- 1/8 t. paprika
- 2/3 c. 1/4" sliced mushrooms
- 2 T. Italian salad dressing
- 2/3 c. 1/4" thick sliced onion rings
- 2/3 c. 1/4" thick sliced cauliflower

Direction

- Preheat oven to 450 degrees.
- Spray a baking sheet with cooking oil spray.
- Set aside.
- Stir together breadcrumbs, parmesan cheese and paprika in a 9" pie plate until well mixed.
- Place vegetables in a medium bowl.
- Drizzle salad dressing over vegetables and toss till coated.
- Roll vegetables in crumb mixture till coated.
- Place the coated vegetables in a single layer on the baking sheet. Bake for 10-12 minutes or until golden.
- NUTRITION FACTS:
- Serving Size: 1
- Servings per Recipe: 4
- Calories 101
- Calories from Fat 58
- Total Fat 6g
- Saturated Fat 1g
- Mono Fat 0g
- Cholesterol 1mg 0%
- Sodium 340mg 14%
- Total Carbs 9g 3%
- Dietary Fibre 1g 5%
- Sugars 1g

254. Heart Healthy N Hearty Layered Broccoli Salad Recipe

Serving: 4 | Prep: | Cook: | Ready in:

Ingredients

- 6 cups chopped broccoli flowerets
- 1 small red onion, very thinly sliced
- 1 1/2 cups (6 ounces) grated 50% light cheddar cheese
- 2/3 cup dried, sweetened cranberries or raisins
- 1/2 cups sliced canned beets (drained-rinsed)
- 1/2 cup plain fat free yogurt
- 3 tablespoons honey
- 2 tablespoons Light (no fat)mayonnaise
- 2 tablespoons apple cider vinegar
- 1/4 cup unsalted, dry roasted, hulled sunflower seeds or chopped walnuts
- 1ounce (2 tablespoons) 50% less fat bacon pieces

Direction

- In a large, glass serving bowl, layer broccoli, onion and cranberries. In a small bowl, whisk together yogurt, honey, mayonnaise and vinegar. Drizzle the yogurt dressing over the layered salad. Layer cheese on top. Cover and refrigerate until ready to serve. Sprinkle with sunflower seeds and bacon pieces just before serving.
- Nutritional Facts:
- Calories: 230
- Fat: 12 g
- Saturated Fat: 4.5 g
- Cholesterol: 25 mg
- Sodium: 350 mg
- Calcium: 25% Daily Value
- Protein: 14 g
- Carbohydrates: 29 g

255. Heart Healthy Pumpkin And Black Bean Soup Recipe

Serving: 4 | Prep: | Cook: 30mins | Ready in:

Ingredients

- Heart Healthy pumpkin and black bean Soup
- 1- 1/2 tablespoon extra-virgin olive oil
- 1 medium onion, finely chopped
- 4 cups canned or fresh low-sodium
- Swanson's 98% fat free chicken stock
- 1 can (14 1/2 ounces) diced tomatoes in juice
- 1 can (15 ounces) black beans, drained
- 2 cans (15 ounces) pumpkin puree
- 1/2 cup light cream
- 1 teaspoon curry powder
- 1/2 teaspoons ground cumin
- 1/4 teaspoon cayenne pepper
- coarse salt
- fresh chives for garnish

Direction

- Heat soup pot over medium heat. Add oil.
- When oil is hot, add onion.
- Sauté onions 5 minutes.
- Add broth, tomatoes, black beans and pumpkin puree.
- Stir to combine ingredients and bring soup to a boil.
- Reduce heat to medium low and stir in cream, curry, cumin, cayenne and salt, to taste.
- Simmer 5 minutes, adjust seasonings and serve garnished with chives.

256. Herb Stuffed Tomatoes Recipe

Serving: 8 | Prep: | Cook: 30mins | Ready in:

Ingredients

- 8 tomatoes
- salt and pepper

- 1Tbs unsalted butter
- 4Tbs olive oil
- 1/2 onion,fine chopped
- 4 garlic cloves,fine chopped
- 3c fresh bread crumbs
- 2Tbs. chopped chives
- 2Tbs chopped fresh parsley
- 2Tbs chopped fresh basil
- 1tsp dried oregano
- 1c grated parmesan
- 1 large egg,beaten

Direction

- Preheat oven to 375. Cut tomatoes in half and spoon out flesh. Put flesh in a sieve set over bowl and press down to release juices; reserve. Season inside of tomatoes with salt and pepper; invert over a baking sheet lined with a kitchen towel.
- Melt butter with 2Tbs oil in a skillet over low heat. Add onion and sauté for 5 mins. Add garlic and sauté 3 mins. Remove from heat. Stir in bread crumbs, herbs and parmesan. Stir in 1/4c of tomato juices, then egg.
- Stuff tomatoes with breadcrumb mixture. Grease a 9x13 baking dish. Place tomatoes in a dish in a single layer. Drizzle with 2 Tbs. oil. Bake for 30 mins, until topping is browned and crisp.

257.   Holiday Vegetable And Hass Avocado Saute Recipe

Serving: 4 | Prep: | Cook: 10mins | Ready in:

Ingredients

- 1-1/2 Tbs avocado oil or olive oil
- 2 tsp finely chopped garlic
- 1/2 large shallot,finely chopped
- 1/2 Tbs fresh thyme leaves
- 3 zucchini,cut in half lengthwise and sliced 1/4' thick
- 1/2 red bell pepper,cut in 1" squares

- 1 Tbs grated lemon peel
- 1-1/2 Tbs fresh lemon juice
- 1 ripe,fresh hass avocado,seede,peeled,cut in chunks

Direction

- In large skillet, heat oil over med-high heat. Add garlic, shallot and thyme, sauté for 3 mins.
- Mix in zucchini, bell pepper and lemon peel, stir and cook for 2 mins. Lower heat and cover, cooking 3 mins.
- In a small bowl, combine lemon juice with avocado. Add to skillet and gently mix. Cook for 2 mins to allow flavors to blend.
- Makes a great accompaniment to roasted meat and poultry.

258.   Honey Baked Squash Recipe

Serving: 2 | Prep: | Cook: 40mins | Ready in:

Ingredients

- 2 small acorn squash halved width wise and deseeded
- 3 tablespoons butter
- 3 ounces honey
- 4 ounces dried figs chopped
- 1 ounce chopped almonds
- 1/2 teaspoon ground cinnamon
- 1/4 teaspoon freshly ground nutmeg

Direction

- Preheat oven to 350. Place squash cut sides down in shallow ovenproof dish and add enough boiling water to come to a depth of 1/2 inch. Cover with foil and bake 25 minutes. Place butter in a small saucepan and melt over low heat then add the honey, figs, almonds, cinnamon and nutmeg and mix well. Carefully pour off water from baking tin containing squash and turn squash cut sides up. Fill the hollows with fig mixture then return to the oven uncovered and bake 15 minutes longer. Serve immediately.

259. Honey Roasted Beets Recipe

Serving: 8 | Prep: | Cook: 20mins | Ready in:

Ingredients

- 3-1/2 pounds assorted medium size fresh beets greens trimmed
- cooking spray
- 1/3 cup honey
- 1/4 cup sherry vinegar
- 2 tablespoons unsalted butter softened
- 2 tablespoons water
- 1 teaspoon finely grated orange rind
- 1 teaspoon minced fresh thyme leaves
- 1/4 teaspoon salt
- 1/8 teaspoon ground black pepper

Direction

- Pierce beets with fork tines then arrange beets and 3 cups water in a microwave safe dish.
- Seal airtight with double layer of plastic wrap then microwave on high for 10 minutes.
- Drain beets and let cool to the touch.
- Peel off and discard skins.
- Cut beets into quarters and crosswise slices then place in large bowl.
- Heat oven to 425 then coat a large non-stick baking pan with cooking spray.
- In small bowl combine honey, vinegar, butter, water, orange rind, thyme, salt and black pepper then pour over beets and toss.
- Transfer beets to a baking pan and roast in oven turning occasionally for 20 minutes.
- To serve transfer beets to a bowl and serve warm.

260. Honey Dijon Glazed Baby Carrots Recipe

Serving: 6 | Prep: | Cook: 1mins | Ready in:

Ingredients

- 3 Tbs. honey
- 3 Tbs. Dijon mustard
- 1 package frozen baby carrots, I slice mine so they cook quicker.

Direction

- Prepare carrots using the method you normally use (boil, steam, etc. until fork tender).
- Drain excess water.
- Set carrots aside in a separate bowl.
- Return pan to stove and add honey and mustard.
- Heat until bubbly, then return carrots to honey mixture, coat evenly with the sauce and cook for one minute.
- Serve immediately.

261. Hop In John Recipe

Serving: 8 | Prep: | Cook: 240mins | Ready in:

Ingredients

- 1 lb. of dried black eyed peas
- 2 smoked ham hocks or one meaty ham bone (great use of leftovers)
- 2 medium yellow onions chopped
- 3 cloves of minced garlic
- 1 bay leaf
- 1 cup of long grain rice
- 1 can of diced tomatoes with chile peppers, keep the juice
- 1 1/2 chopped bell pepper, red is prettiest for the holiday but I use green to economize

- 3 ribs of celery chopped
- 1 serrano pepper, minced, seeds and veins removed
- 2 teaspoons of favorite Cajon seasoning (The BAM man is my favorite)
- 1/2 tsp of dried thyme leaves
- 3/4 tsp of cumin
- 3/4 tsp of salt
- 4 green onions, diced, tops and all

Direction

- In a large Dutch oven combine the peas, your ham bone and 6 cups of water.
- Add one half of one of the onions along with 1 big tsp. of the chopped garlic.
- Add the bay leaf.
- Bring to a boil, reduce the heat and simmer gently for 2 to 2 1/2 hours.
- Remove the ham bone and cut off the meat and dice.
- Drain the black-eyed peas.
- Discard the bay leaf.
- Bring 2 1/2 cups of water to boil
- Add rice and cover and simmer until the rice is nearly done about 15 minutes.
- Mince the remaining onions/garlic and add to the rice along with peas, tomatoes, peppers, celery, seasoning, thyme, cumin and salt.
- Cook another 10 minutes until the rice is tender.
- Stir in chopped ham and diced green onions.
- Serve with additional Crystal Hot sauce on the side.
- Cracklin' cornbread, collards are a must.

262. Imam Bayildi Recipe

Serving: 6 | Prep: | Cook: 10mins |Ready in:

Ingredients

- 4 medium aubergines (eggplants)
- 3 tablespoons olive oil
- 1 onion, finely chopped

- 2 garlic, cloves crushed
- 1 green pepper (capsicum)
- 1 red pepper (capsicum)
- parsley, good handful chopped
- 3 large tomatoes, blanched, skinned and coursely chopped
- 1/2 teaspoon ground cinnamon
- black pepper
- salt
- 1/2-1 teaspoon sugar
- 1/2 lemon, juice of

Direction

- Heat oven to 375°F.
- Slice each aubergine in half lengthwise.
- Scoop out the flesh from the aubergines and chop.
- Blanch the aubergine shells in boiling water for 2 minutes then drain upside down.
- Heat 3 tbsp. of oil in a pan and sauté the onion until soft and golden.
- Add crushed garlic and fry for 2 minutes.
- Add parsley, chopped aubergine, tomatoes, green and red pepper, cinnamon, salt and black pepper and cook for about 5 minutes.
- Add lemon juice and sugar to taste.
- Arrange the aubergine boats in a baking dish and fill each one with the filling.
- Cover the dish with aluminium foil.
- Bake in the oven for about 25 minutes.

263. Italian Kabobs Recipe

Serving: 4 | Prep: | Cook: 20mins |Ready in:

Ingredients

- 12 large mushrooms
- 2 small zucchini , bias sliced into 1 inch pieces
- 3 tablespoons Italian salad dressing
- 2 tablespoons lemon juice
- 1 teaspoon worcestershire sauce
- 12 cherry tomatoes
- 1/4 teaspoon salt

Direction

- Preheat both sides of gas grill on high for 10 minutes
- Pour boiling water over mushrooms.
- Let stand 1 minute and then drain the mushrooms.
- Thread mushrooms and zucchini onto 4 skewers.
- Mix salad dressing, lemon juice, Worcestershire sauce, and 1/4 teaspoon salt.
- Turn both sides of grill to medium.
- Place skewers on grids.
- Close hood and cook 12 minutes.
- Turn and baste often.
- Add tomatoes to skewers.
- Grill 5 to 8 minutes more.
- Baste often.

264.   Italian Stuffed Zucchini Recipe

Serving: 4 | Prep: | Cook: 30mins | Ready in:

Ingredients

- 4 medium zucchini halved lengthwise
- 2 tablespoons regular olive oil (not extra virgin)
- 3/4 cup finely minced onions
- 3 large cloves garlic
- 3 eggs beaten
- 1/2 cup chopped tomato
- 3/4 cup grated parmesan cheese
- 2 tablespoons chopped parsley (optional)
- 2-3 tablespoon fresh chopped basil (crucial!)
- 1/2 teaspoon salt
- 1 teaspoon freshly ground black pepper
- 1/4 teaspoon plain bread crumbs

Direction

- Scoop out inside of zucchini.
- Chop scooped zucchini into bits and cook in oil with onions and garlic until onions are soft.

- Combine sautéed ingredients with tomatoes cheese, herbs, eggs, salt and pepper.
- Fill each zucchini with mixture and dust with breadcrumbs and some extra cheese.
- Bake at 375 for 30 minutes in a lightly oiled glass baking dish.

265.   Janets Zucchini Surprise Recipe

Serving: 16 | Prep: | Cook: 75mins | Ready in:

Ingredients

- 1-1/2 lbs zucchini, cut into 1/2" slices
- 1 cup onion chopped
- 1/2 jar of drained roasted peppers (more if you like) chopped
- 6 scallions chopped
- 5 eggs slightly beaten
- 1/2 cup milk
- 1/2 - 3/4 cup sour cream
- 2 cups of mozzerella cheese shredded
- 1 cup of cheddar cheese shredded
- 1 tsp salt
- 2 tsp baking powder
- 3 tbsp flour
- 1/2 bag of stuffing cubes
- 1/2 cup bread crumbs
- garlic powder
- pepper
- butter

Direction

- Combine eggs, milk, sour cream, cheeses, seasonings, baking powder and flour.
- Stir in zucchini, onions, scallions & peppers into egg mixture
- Butter a 9 x 13 pan
- Spread stuffing cubes over pan
- Pour zucchini/egg mixture over cubes
- Sprinkle bread crumbs over top
- Dot with butter over bread crumbs

- Bake in 350 oven
- Cook at least 60 minutes.
- Mixture in pan should be firm not giggly and eggs should be cooked thru
- Rest 5 minutes before serving

---

266. Judys Mediterranean Quinoa Salad Recipe

Serving: 18 | Prep: | Cook: 20mins | Ready in:

Ingredients

- 1 14 oz. package quinoa
- 1 ½ quart water
- 4 large cloves garlic, crushed
- ½ cup green onions, chopped
- ¾ cup carrots, diced small
- ½ cup celery, chopped small (include the tops, adds additional flavor)
- 3 tbls fresh mint, chopped
- 2 tbls cilantro, chopped
- 1 cup flat-leaf parsley, chopped
- 2 cups arugula
- Zest from 2 large lemons
- ½ cup freshly squeezed lemon juice (2 large lemons)
- ½ cup extra virgin olive oil
- ½ cup toasted pine nuts
- 1 cup dried cranberries
- ½ cup black olives, pitted
- ½ cup crumbled feta cheese (I used the basil and tomato flavored feta)
- salt and freshly ground pepper to taste
- NOTE: This recipe serves 18 if you are serving a 1/3 cup of this salad as a side dish.

Direction

- Rinse quinoa thoroughly by running fresh water over the quinoa in a pot and draining. "Rinsing is recommended to wash away any naturally occurring bitter tasting saponins remaining after processing.*" Place quinoa and water in a saucepan and bring to a boil, then reduce heat and simmer until all of the water is absorbed (10-15 mins.). When done, the grains will be translucent and the outer germ layer will separate. You will end up with approximately 3 cups of cooked quinoa.
- Add the lemon zest while the quinoa is still warm, this will enhance the flavour of the natural oils from the lemon zest. Let quinoa cool to room temperature, then transfer to a serving bowl.
- After quinoa has cooled to room temp, mix in the garlic and scallions thoroughly, then add the remaining chopped herbs, vegetables, dried cranberries, and toasted pine nuts. Finally, mix in the feta cheese and kalamata olives and season with salt and freshly ground pepper.
- Refrigerate for at least 1 hour before serving to allow the flavours to meld and develop.
- "*Saponins are soap-like substances that occur on the outside of the quinoa grains. It is believed they are put there by nature to deter insects and birds." "Quinoa was a staple a staple of the ancient Incas and means" the mother grain". It's high in iron and has a distinctive flavour and fluffy texture. You can use it in casseroles, pilaf, salads, and in baking recipes. Have fun creating your own recipes with this wonderful grain. Judy

---

267. Lanas Accidental Healthy Vegan Ginger Stir Fry

Serving: 4 | Prep: | Cook: 10mins | Ready in:

Ingredients

- 1 tablespoon cornstarch
- 1 clove garlic, crushed
- 1 teaspoons chopped fresh ginger root
- 3-4 Tbs. EVOO divided =EVOO is extra virgin olive oil
- 1 1/2 cups cut white or other sweet potato

- (I had white and they were incredible)
- 1/2 cup chopped carrots
- 1 cup yellow or other squash rounds
- 3/4 cup red bell pepper
- 1 to 2 tablespoons low sodium soy sauce
- 4 tablespoons water
- 1 cup chopped onions
- salt and fresh pepper to taste (if desired)

Direction

- In a bowl, blend cornstarch, garlic, and 2 tablespoons EVOO until cornstarch is dissolved.
- Add 1 teaspoon ginger; mix.
- To heated skillet or wok (with EVOO), add carrots, sweet potatoes, peppers, squash, (onions last).
- Add water as needed.
- Cook vegetables in EVOO (to your desired crispness level), stirring constantly to prevent burning.
- Stir in soy sauce and water.
- Add sauce (mixed) and cook for a couple more minutes.
- Cook in medium heat, stirring very often, until vegetables are tender but still crisp.

268.   Lanas Southern Style Beer Batter Onion Rings Recipe

Serving: 4 | Prep: | Cook: 30mins | Ready in:

Ingredients

- 1 1/3 cup all-purpose flour
- 1 teaspoon salt
- 1/2 teaspoon ground pepper
- 2 large sweet onions, sliced (I use from VIDALIA, Ga. !! :)
- 1 tablespoon vegetable oil
- 2 egg yolks
- 3/4 cup beer

Direction

- Mix together the flour, salt, pepper, oil, and egg yolks.
- Gradually whisk in the beer.
- Refrigerate the batter 3 to 4 hours before using.
- Slice onions into rings; separate rings and dip in the batter.
- Deep-fry in batches in 370° oil until golden brown.

269.   Lemon Glazed Carrots Recipe

Serving: 6 | Prep: | Cook: 15mins | Ready in:

Ingredients

- 2 pounds baby carrots, the fresh already cleaned ones.
- 3 tablespoons butter
- 3 tablespoons brown sugar
- 2 - 3 tablespoons fresh-squeezed lemon juice, according to taste
- 1/4 teaspoon salt
- 2 tablespoons finely chopped parsley

Direction

- Place a steamer basket in a 3- or 4-quart pot; add 1-inch water to pot.
- Place carrots in basket and bring to a boil over Medium-High heat.
- Cover pot; reduce heat to Medium-Low and cook 10 to 15 minutes or until tender.
- Drain.
- Return empty cooking pot to Medium heat.
- Add butter; melt and blend with sugar, 2 tablespoons lemon juice and salt.
- Stir and cook until sugar dissolves. If desired, stir in additional lemon juice, to taste.
- Add carrots and parsley; toss to coat. Serve hot.
- I always end up adding more butter... I love my butter!

270.　　Lovely Black Bean And Corn Salad Recipe

Serving: 6 | Prep: | Cook: | Ready in:

Ingredients

- Lovely black bean and corn Salad
- WISK TOGETHER:
- 4 tablespoons of white balsamic vinegar
- 1 tablespoon canola oil
- 1/2 teaspoon each: salt, pepper, cumin and chili powder
- then add:
- 1 can of black beans, drained and rinsed
- 1 1/2 cups frozen corn, rinsed to take the chill off
- 1 red bell pepper, diced
- 1/2 red onion, diced
- Handful of cilantro, chopped

Direction

- MIX ALL WELL AND CHILL & SERVE!

271.　　Mandarin Coleslaw Recipe

Serving: 8 | Prep: | Cook: | Ready in:

Ingredients

- 1 cup fat free mayonnaise (I am not a big fan of the fat free, so I used Hellman's light version-feel free to use the full- fat variety)
- 2 tbsp. sugar
- 1 teaspoon vinegar (I used apple cider vinegar)
- 1/4 tsp. salt
- 1/4 tsp. black pepper (I used 1/2 tsp. of freshly ground)

- 8 oz. of Publix coleslaw (I used the full 16 oz. bag because I don't like a soupy or overly sweet coleslaw)
- 1 (11 oz.) can mandarin oranges, drained
- ****
- I added:
- 1/2 cup chopped red bell pepper
- 1 jalapeno pepper, seeded and chopped (if your pepper's not that hot like mine, could add two)
- 2 tbsp. of Italian parsley, chopped

Direction

- Combine mayonnaise, sugar, vinegar, salt and pepper.
- Place coleslaw in salad bowl with bell pepper, jalapeno and parsley.
- Toss with dressing until thoroughly blended.
- Gently fold in oranges.
- Place in refrigerator to marry flavors for at least one hour.
- Toss well; serve.

272.　　Maple Glazed Baby Carrots Recipe

Serving: 12 | Prep: | Cook: 15mins | Ready in:

Ingredients

- 3 pounds baby carrots
- 1/2 cup unsalted butter
- 3/4 cup maple syrup
- 4 tablespoons orange juice
- 1-1/2 teaspoon ground cinnamon
- 1 teaspoon ground allspice
- 1 teaspoon salt

Direction

- Place all ingredients in a saucepan.
- Bring to a boil over medium-high heat, stirring occasionally until the carrots are tender and

the sauce becomes a shiny glaze, about 15 minutes.

273. Maple Glazed Carrots Recipe

Serving: 6 | Prep: | Cook: 20mins | Ready in:

Ingredients

- 1 pound baby carrots
- 1 teaspoon butter
- 1/2 teaspoon lemon juice
- 1/3 cup maple syrup
- 1/2 teaspoon salt
- 1/2 teaspoon freshly ground black pepper

Direction

- Place carrots in a saucepan then add enough water to barely cover them.
- Bring to a boil then reduce heat, cover and simmer until tender.
- Melt butter in a saucepan then stir in lemon juice and maple syrup.
- Simmer for 3 minutes then add carrots and simmer 3 minutes more.
- Add salt and pepper just before serving.

274. Marinaded Roasted Asparagus With Garlic Recipe

Serving: 8 | Prep: | Cook: 20mins | Ready in:

Ingredients

- 1 pound asparagus, cut of woody end of stalks, then cut into 2 inch pieces
- 3 T extra virgin olive oil
- 8 large cloves fresh garlic, each sliced into 3-4 pieces
- salt and fresh ground black pepper to taste

Direction

- Break off the woody end of one piece of asparagus; use that as a guide to tell where to trim the other pieces.
- Cut off woody ends, then cut asparagus into 2 inch pieces.
- Cut each large garlic clove into 3-4 slices.
- ** Put asparagus, garlic, and olive oil into large Ziploc bag and let garlic marinate 1-2 hours. **
- Preheat oven to 450 F.
- Place asparagus on large cookie sheet and season with fresh ground black pepper and salt.
- Roast until asparagus is slightly softened and edges are starting to brown slightly, about 20 minutes.
- Serve hot with your favorite meal.

275. Marinated Grilled Corn With Chili Avocado Butter Recipe

Serving: 8 | Prep: | Cook: 5mins | Ready in:

Ingredients

- Marinate: 20 minutes
- Chill: 1 hour
- Grill: 5 minutes
- -----------------------------
- 8 ears fresh corn
- 4 small tomatoes, quartered
- 1/2 of an 8-ounce bottle light Italian salad dressing
- 1 small avocado, seeded, peeled, and chopped
- 1/2 cup butter, softened (no substitutes)
- 1 teaspoon chili powder or 1/4 teaspoon ground red pepper
- 1/4 teaspoon salt
- chili powder (optional)

Direction

- Remove husks and silks from corn. Snap each ear of corn crosswise into 2 or 3 pieces. Set a 1-gallon sealable plastic bag in a large, shallow bowl; place corn and tomato pieces in bag. Pour in salad dressing. Seal bag and let vegetables stand for 20 minutes or refrigerate for 4 to 24 hours, turning bag once or twice.
- Meanwhile, slightly mash the avocado with a fork in a cup or small bowl. Stir in the butter, the 1 teaspoon chili powder or ground red pepper, and the salt. Cover and chill for at least 1 hour.
- Using a slotted spoon, remove corn from marinade. Insert skewer into cut end of each piece of corn by pressing each piece firmly against the preparation surface. Use a turning motion to carefully twist the skewers down the center of the corn cob. Sprinkle each corn skewer with additional chili powder, if desired.
- Place corn on the rack of the grill directly over medium-high heat. Grill for 5 to 10 minutes, turning once.
- Serve corn with chili-avocado butter and the marinated tomatoes on the side.

276.   Mexican Coleslaw Recipe

Serving: 6 | Prep: | Cook: | Ready in:

Ingredients

- 2 cups very thinly sliced green cabbage
- 1-1/2 cups peeled and grated carrots
- 1/3 cup chopped cilantro
- 1/4 cup rice vinegar
- 2 tablespoons extra-virgin olive oil
- 1/4 teaspoon salt

Direction

- Place cabbage and carrots in a colander then rinse thoroughly with cold water to crisp.
- Let drain for 5 minutes.

- Meanwhile whisk cilantro, vinegar, oil and salt in a large bowl.
- Add cabbage and carrots and toss well to coat.

277.   Mushroom Asparagus And Artichoke Salad Recipe

Serving: 6 | Prep: | Cook: | Ready in:

Ingredients

- * 8 ounces small mushrooms (baby bella, crimini, or white)
- * 8 to 10 ounces slender asparagus
- * 10-ounce package frozen artichoke hearts, thawed and cut in half
- * 1 small zucchini, quartered lengthwise and sliced
- * 1 large half-sour dill pickle, chopped
- * 1/4 cup minced fresh dill
- * 1/ 4 cup minced fresh parsley
- * 1/3 cup regular or vegan mayonnaise
- * juice of 1/2 lemon
- * salt and freshly ground pepper to taste

Direction

- Wipe the mushrooms clean and trim away the stems.
- If the mushrooms are larger than button size, cut them in half.
- Place in a skillet with just enough water to keep moist; cover and steam over medium heat for two minutes, then drain and let cool.
- Trim the bottoms of the asparagus, then cut the stalks into 1-inch pieces.
- Using the same skillet, add just enough water to keep the bottom moist, cover, and steam until the asparagus is bright green and tender-crisp.
- Drain and rinse with cool water.
- Combine the mushrooms and asparagus in a serving container. Add the artichoke hearts, zucchini, pickle, and herbs.

- Add the mayonnaise and juice and stir together gently.
- Add salt and pepper to taste and toss again, then serve.

---

278. Mushroom Pancakes In Cheese Sauce Recipe

Serving: 8 | Prep: | Cook: 20mins | Ready in:

Ingredients

- 1 sm. packge fresh white mushrooms (about 250 gr.)
- 2 tbsp. flour
- 1 egg, beaten
- 1 handful basil leaves, chopped
- 1/2 tsp. of salt, or to taste
- 1/4 tsp. pepper
- oil for frying
- For the cheese sauce:
- 1 tbsp. butter
- 1 tbsp. flour
- 1/2 cup milk
- 1/4 cup grated cheese (like cheddar, or colby)
- 1/4 tsp. dried thyme
- salt and pepper to taste

Direction

- Wash and pat dry the mushrooms. Cut in half, drizzle with oil and bake in a 375F oven on a lightly greased cookie sheet for about 10 min., or until lightly browned.
- Chop the mushrooms in a food processor, until chopped finely.
- Add flour, beaten egg, chopped basil leaves, salt and pepper to the mushrooms. Stir to combine.
- Drop spoonfuls on a preheated skillet and fry in batches in about 3 tbsp. of oil on both sides until lightly golden. Add more oil if necessary during cooking. Remove to the plate and pour the cheese sauce on top.
- For the cheese sauce:
- Melt 1 tbsp. of butter in a skillet. Stir in the flour and cook 1 min. Whisk in the warm milk. Add thyme, salt and pepper. Whisk and cook until slightly thickened. Stir in the cheese. You can adjust the sauce consistency by adding more milk for the thinner sauce, or adding more cheese for the thicker version.

---

279. My Famous Green Beans Recipe

Serving: 10 | Prep: | Cook: 45mins | Ready in:

Ingredients

- 2 Large Bags of Whole frozen green beans
- 6 Large red potatoes
- 1 Pound of Meaty Hickory smoked bacon Chopped (2 Inch Pieces)
- 1 Large red onion Chopped
- 1 Medium yellow sweet onion Chopped
- 2 Large cloves of garlic Crushed
- 2 Tablespoons of parsley
- 2 Tablespoons of Chopped chives
- 1 Tablespoon of red pepper flakes
- 1 Tablespoon of sea salt
- 1 Tablespoon of cracked pepper
- Dressing:
- 1 Tablespoon sugar
- 1 Teaspoon of thyme
- 1 Teaspoon of apple cider vinegar
- 1 Teaspoon of Grey Poupon Country Dijon mustard
- 1 Teaspoon olive oil

Direction

- Meats and Onions and Spices:
- Combine Bacon, Red Onion, Yellow Onion, Garlic, Parsley, Chives, Red Pepper Flakes, Sea Salt and Cracked Pepper in A Large Skillet and Fry Until Bacon Starts to Turn Brown and Onions Become Transparent and Lightly Browned! Dump Into Medium Roaster Pan...
- Green Beans:

- In Another Large Pot Add Your 2 Large Bags of Green Beans and 2 Cups of Water and Enough Salt and Pepper to Taste, Boil Until Tender But Not Mush! Dump Into Same Roaster Pan...
- Potatoes:
- Wash Your Potatoes and Cut Off The Ends, Poke A Few Holes with A Knife and Put Into The Microwave On High for 15 Minutes, Make Sure to Check Them Sometimes They Cook Faster...They Are Done When The Are Easy To Push The Knife Through But Not Done to A Mush, Still A little Firm You Don't Want Them to Break!
- Then Thick Slice The Potatoes and Pan Fry Them In The Bacon Grease Left In The Pan Until Lightly Browned On Both Sides...When Done Add Them to The Roaster Pan As Well!
- Mix Together the...
- Dressing:
- 1 Tablespoon Sugar
- 1 Teaspoon of Thyme
- 1 Teaspoon of Apple Cider Vinegar
- 1 Teaspoon of Grey Poupon Country Dijon Mustard
- 1 Teaspoon Olive Oil
- After Preparing All of These Ingredients Separately and Putting Into The Roaster Pan, Pour Over The Dressing and Lightly Tossing It Together Being Careful Not to Break The Potatoes or The Beans...You Are Ready to Serve!!!
- You May Salt and Pepper Them More If You Like...
- So Very good...These Are the Best Green Beans I've ever eaten...Enjoy and Let Me Know How You like Them!

---

280.   New Age Green Bean Cassarole Recipe

Serving: 12 | Prep: | Cook: 30mins |Ready in:

Ingredients

- 2 lbs green bean fresh or frozen
- 1 large onion, sliced
- 1 small red pepper, sliced and then chopped smaller.
- 6 oz. mushrooms - button or portobello, sliced
- 6 oz. cheese - goat and cream cheese.
- olive oil
- brown sugar
- plain bread crumbs
- balsamic vinegar
- flat leaf parsley fresh - for garnish

Direction

- Trim fresh whole green beans, or frozen green beans.
- Cover with water and cook for about 3 minutes.
- In a casserole dish, combine beans with button mushrooms and sliced red peppers.
- Toss with olive oil and balsamic vinegar to coat.
- Roast in oven for 15 minutes at 375.
- Sauté onion wedges in olive oil and brown sugar, just until tender.
- Toss cooked onions with bread crumbs to coat for classic onion ring crispiness.
- Blend softened cream cheese with goat cheese.
- Toss with warm vegetables and place back in baking dish, top with onions and Bake in oven at 400 for 5 to 8 minutes till heated through.
- Scatter fresh snipped parsley on top for a peppery flavor when done.
- Enjoy.

---

281.   ORANGE GLAZED CARROTS WITH CRANBERRYS Recipe

Serving: 6 | Prep: | Cook: 20mins |Ready in:

Ingredients

- 1 lb. baby carrots

- 1/4 cup orange juice
- 3 Tbsp. brown sugar
- 2 Tbsp. butter
- 1 pinch salt
- 1/4-1/2 cup dried cranberries

Direction

- Place carrots in a shallow saucepan, and cover with water.
- Boil until tender.
- Drain, and return carrots to pan.
- Pour orange juice over carrots, and mix well.
- Add the cranberries.
- Simmer over medium heat for about 5 minutes.
- Stir in brown sugar, butter, and salt.
- Heat until butter and sugar melt.
- Even kids like them...

282.   Oklahoma Joes Smoked Cabbage Recipe

Serving: 4 | Prep: | Cook: 240mins | Ready in:

Ingredients

- 1 Whole cabbage
- butter
- 2-3 chicken or beef bouillon cubes

Direction

- Cut out the cavity of the cabbage until a hole 2-3 inched is formed.
- Pack cavity with bouillon cubes and butter.
- Wrap Cabbage in heavy duty foil except for the top.
- Add butter as needed and cook for 4-5 hours at 225 degrees.

283.   Oven Fried Zucchini Sticks Recipe

Serving: 4 | Prep: | Cook: 10mins | Ready in:

Ingredients

- canola oil cooking spray
- 1/2 cup whole-wheat flour
- 1/2 cup all-purpose flour
- 2 tablespoons cornmeal
- 1 teaspoon salt
- 1/2 teaspoon freshly ground pepper
- 1 1/2 pounds zucchini (about 3 medium), cut into 1/2-by-3-inch sticks
- 2 egg whites, lightly beaten

Direction

- Preheat oven to 475°F.
- Coat a large baking sheet with cooking spray.
- Combine flours, cornmeal, salt and pepper in a large sealable plastic bag.
- Dip zucchini in egg white, shake in the bag to coat, and arrange, not touching, on the baking sheet. Coat all exposed sides with cooking spray.
- Bake on the centre rack for 7 minutes. Turn the zucchini and coat any floury spots with cooking spray. Continue to bake until golden and just tender, about 5 minutes more. Serve hot.

284.   Oven Fried Zucchini In A Crunchy Parmesan Crust Recipe

Serving: 4 | Prep: | Cook: 15mins | Ready in:

Ingredients

- 1 tablespoon extra-virgin 0live oil
- 1/4 cup fine dried bread crumbs
- 1/3 cup grated imported parmesan cheese
- 1/2 teaspoon dried rosemary, crumbled
- 2 to 3 dashed cayenne pepper

- 1/2 teaspoon salt
- 1/4 teaspoon freshly ground black pepper
- 1 large egg
- 4 small green or golden zucchini squash

Direction

- Preheat the oven to 400 degrees F. Lightly grease a heavy baking sheet with the oil and set aside.
- In a shallow dish, combine the bread crumbs, Parmesan cheese, rosemary, cayenne, salt and pepper, and mix well. In a second shallow dish, lightly beat the egg.
- Trim the ends of the squash. Cut each squash in half lengthwise. Lay the halves flat and cut in half lengthwise again. Then cut the strips in half crosswise. Dredge each piece first in the egg and then in the Parmesan mixture, coating evenly. Arrange well-spaced in a single layer on the prepared baking sheet.
- Bake in the oven for 5 to 7 minutes, then turn the squash over and bake 5 to 7 minutes longer, or until crisp and lightly browned. Serve hot or at room temperature.

285.   Pa Dutch Old Fashioned Green Beans And Bacon Recipe

Serving: 4 | Prep: | Cook: 30mins | Ready in:

Ingredients

- 3/4 lb. green beans
- 8 slices bacon
- 2 medium potatoes, pared and cut into 1/2 in. pieces
- 1 small onion, sliced
- 1/4 cup water
- 1/2 tsp salt

Direction

- Cook green beans in a small amount of boiling, salted water 10 to 15 min. or until just tender.
- Dice the bacon and fry until crisp. Add green beans and remaining ingredients to bacon and cook, covered, about 15 min. or until potatoes are tender.

286.   Pan Fried Cabbage Recipe

Serving: 6 | Prep: | Cook: 12mins | Ready in:

Ingredients

- 1 head cabbage(cut into slices)
- 1 large onion,sliced
- 1 cup celery, chopped
- 1 cup sliced smoked sausage(you can also use bacon or ham if you prefer!)
- 6 tablespoons butter
- 3 tablespoons(more if needed) olive oil(you could sub vegetable oil)]
- 1/4 cup soy sauce
- 1 teaspoon cracked black pepper
- salt to taste

Direction

- Heat oil in large skillet. Add sausage (or other meat), onions, and celery and cook until sausage is lightly browned.
- Add cabbage and stir well.
- Continue cooking on med/high heat for 3 to 4 minutes, stirring often to prevent sticking.
- Add butter, sour sauce, and black pepper, cover, lower heat to low/med.
- Cook for 2 to 3 minutes.
- Taste, add salt if needed.

287. Paneer Butter Masala Recipe

Serving: 3 | Prep: | Cook: 25mins | Ready in:

Ingredients

- 125 grams paneer (cottage cheese)
- 1 tomato (grind to a fine paste)
- 1 Tsp tomato puree
- 2 onions (grind to fine paste)
- 1 tsp cumin powder
- 1 tsp Dhania Powder (coriander powder)
- 1 tsp ginger garlic paste
- 3 cloves
- 1 tsp cashews
- 1 cinnamon stick
- 1/2 tsp garam masala powder (http://www.recipedelights.com/basics/GaramMasala.htm)
- 1/4 tsp chilli powder
- 3 Tsp yogurt
- coriander leaves
- 4-5 Tsp butter
- salt

Direction

- Grind cloves, cinnamon to fine powder
- Heat oil, fry few paneer cubes on medium heat until golden brown. Set the paneer pieces aside.
- Grate remaining paneer and keep it aside
- Heat oil or butter, fry onions, ginger garlic paste, for 3 minutes.
- Add tomato paste and puree and simmer for 5 minutes.
- Add cashews, Dhania powder, Cumin powder, garam masala powder, salt, chilli powder, extra butter and masala powder from step 1.
- Add yogurt and stir until gravy becomes thick. Add fried paneer cubes, grated paneer add 1/2 -1 cup water and simmer for 5 minutes, until all the flavour is absorbed into paneer.
- Serve hot garnished with coriander leaves.

288. Papas Potato Cabbage Casserole Recipe

Serving: 6 | Prep: | Cook: 45mins | Ready in:

Ingredients

- 3 med. potatoes scrubbed
- 8 oz. bacon chopped
- 1/2 cup sliced onion
- 2 TBSP all-purpose flour
- 1/2 tsp dried thyme
- 1/2 tsp salt
- 1 (12 Oz.) can of beer
- 1/2 cup milk
- 6 cups shredded green cabbage
- 1 cup shredded swiss cheese

Direction

- Combine potatoes with water cook until tender. About 30 min. Cut potatoes into slices.
- Fry bacon in skillet until crisp. Remove bacon with slotted spoon reserving 2 TBSP of pan drippings.
- Preheat oven to 375 degrees. Spray a 3 qt. round baking dish with cooking spray.
- Sauté onion in reserved drippings until tender. Stir in flour, thyme and salt. Add beer and milk and mix well. Cook over low heat. Stirring continually, until sauce has thickened.
- Layer cabbage, potatoes, bacon, Swiss and beer sauce one half at a time in baking dish. Bake, covered for 30 min. remove cover. Bake until cabbage is tender, about 20 min.

289. Pinto Beans Recipe

Serving: 12 | Prep: | Cook: 180mins | Ready in:

Ingredients

- 1 lb. package dried pinto beans, soaked, rinsed and drained
- Approx 4 quarts water
- 1/2 yellow onion, chopped
- 3 garlic cloves, minced
- 4 chicken bouillon cubes
- 1 large palmful of chili powder (approx 2 tbs)
- 1 large palmful of cumin (approx 1 1/2 tbs)
- 1 Tbs garlic powder
- 1 bay leaf
- 1 Tbs dried parsley
- kosher salt and pepper to taste
- (1-2 Tbs pickled or fresh jalapenos, chopped - optional)

Direction

- Put beans in large pot, and add about 4 quarts of water over high heat.
- Add bouillon cubes, onion and garlic and bring to a boil.
- Reduce to low heat and add chili powder, cumin, garlic powder and bay leaf. (You can add jalapenos, if you like it spicy.)
- Simmer over low heat (you want a very slight bubbling), with lid partially over pot, for 2 hours.
- Add parsley, salt and pepper to taste (I use a couple of Tbsp. of salt and a couple of Tsps. of pepper)
- If it becomes too salty, add hot water to pot.
- Great served with Mexican food, or over rice. Awesome with cornbread, as its own meal!
- Enjoy!

---

290. Poached Eggs With Roasted Asparagus And Truffle Oil Recipe

Serving: 8 | Prep: | Cook: 20mins | Ready in:

Ingredients

- 1 LB asparagus

- 3 Tbsp Good olive oil
- salt and pepper to taste
- 6 Tbsp Natural rice vinegar, divided
- 8 eggs
- 1/2 cup parmigiano-reggiano cheese, grated
- 3 Tbsp chopped fresh chives
- 3 Tbsp Black Truffle extra-virgin olive oil

Direction

- Preheat oven to 450 degrees.
- Arrange asparagus evenly on baking sheet in single layer. Drizzle with 3 Tbsp. pure olive oil. Season to taste with salt and pepper. Roast on center rack of oven 8-10 min. Arrange in 8 bundles on large serving platter. Set aside.
- Heat 1 inch of water in each skillet on MEDIUM to simmer. Adjust to slow simmer. Add 3 Tbsp. rice vinegar to each skillet.
- Crack eggs carefully, one at a time, into ramekin. Gently slide each egg, one at a time, into simmering water (4 eggs per skillet). Cook until whites are set, about 3 min. Using a slotted spoon, remove one egg at a time and place on top of each asparagus bundle.
- Sprinkle each egg with grated cheese and chives, drizzle with truffle oil and season with pepper.

---

291. Pumpkin Fritters With Caramel Sauce Recipe

Serving: 8 | Prep: | Cook: 30mins | Ready in:

Ingredients

- 375 ml self raising flour (1 + 1/2 cup)
- 1 ml salt (1/4 teaspoon)
- 10 ml baking powder (1 tablespoon)
- 625 ml cooked, minced pumpkin (2 1/2 cups)
- 2 eggs, beaten
- oil for deep frying
- Sauce:
- 320 ml brown sugar (1 1/2 cups)
- 125 ml boiling water (1/2 cup)

- 250 ml milk (1 cup)
- 50 ml corn starch (4 heaped tablespoons)
- few cinnamon sticks

Direction

- Sift dry ingredients together for the dough.
- Stir in the pumpkin.
- Stir in the eggs.
- Deep-fry spoonful of the dough.
- Drain on brown paper.
- Place in a bowl.
- Sauce:
- Bring everything to the boil, except the maizena.
- Cook for 2 minutes.
- Take out the cinnamon sticks.
- Make a pasta with the maizena and a little bit of water.
- Stir into the sauce until thickened.
- Pour over fritters.

292. Quick N Tasty Carrot Casserole Recipe

Serving: 6 | Prep: | Cook: 35mins | Ready in:

Ingredients

- 1 med bunch carrots, peeled and chunked (I usually buy the peeled baby carrots for convenience, and you could do that, but, I wanted large chunks)
- 4-5 rigs celery, chunked
- 1 large yellow onion, large diced
- 1 tub fresh mushrooms, quartered (I actually bought the larger mushrooms that you indivdually bag, and eyeballed it to match the amount in the tubs)
- 1 red pepper, chopped large
- 1/2 stick margarine
- chicken or veg stock
- kosher salt
- fresh ground black pepper

- Veg-It seasoning (I think ms. dash would work, too)
- 1/2 t worcestershire
- 1/2 t lea & perrins chicken marinade
- Splash or two of dry white wine
- 1 can cream of selery soup
- 1 handful grated parmesan
- pepperidge Farm Stuffing Mix

Direction

- In a deep, 12 inch skillet, melt the butter
- Add in veggies
- Season with a couple if pinches of salt, 2 or 3 grinds of pepper, and a couple shakes of Veg-It
- Sauté about 5 minutes
- Add Worcestershire, marinade and wine
- Cook together about 8 minutes
- Remove from heat
- Stir in parmesan and soup
- Transfer to buttered casserole dish
- Lightly cover with stuffing mix
- Bake at 350 about 30 minutes, until bubbly around edges, and stuffing has browned slightly

293. Rapini With Garlic N Anchovies Recipe

Serving: 4 | Prep: | Cook: 15mins | Ready in:

Ingredients

- 2 pounds broccoli rabe, stem ends trimmed, chopped
- 3 tablespoons extra-virgin olive oil
- 6 cloves garlic, chopped
- 6 anchovy fillets, chopped
- 1/4 teaspoon crushed red pepper (optional)
- 1/4 teaspoon salt
- Freshly ground pepper to taste

Direction

- Bring a large pot or Dutch oven of water to a boil.
- Add broccoli rabe and cook until tender when pierced with a fork, 3 to 5 minutes.
- Drain well.
- Heat oil in a large skillet over medium heat.
- Add garlic, anchovies and crushed red pepper (if using); cook, stirring, until the garlic is very light brown, 1 to 2 minutes.
- Add the broccoli rabe, toss to coat, and cook, stirring occasionally, for 2 minutes more.
- Season with salt and pepper.

---

294. Ratatouille My Way Recipe

Serving: 8 | Prep: | Cook: 60mins | Ready in:

Ingredients

- 1 medium eggplant cut in medium sized cubes (don't bother to peel)
- 2 zucchini, scrubbed and cut in medium chunks
- 2 yellow squash, scrubbed and cut in chunks
- 1 full head of garlic, most of the outer peel pulled off
- 2 large yellow or red onions cut in coarse wedges, ends removed
- 1 8 oz. box of white button mushrooms or crimini, wiped down left whole (on the small side, don't aim for huge mushrooms here, you don't want to cut them; that is more work)
- 1 green pepper, seeded and cut in medium chunks
- 1 red pepper seeded and cut in medium chunks
- 1 yellow pepper seeded and cut in medium chunks
- 2 lbs. of roma tomatoes stem ends removed and halved
- extra virgin olive oil
- sea salt
- fresh ground black pepper
- fresh marjoram if available (I mysteriously kill mine each year)
- several sprigs of fresh thyme leaves
- a handful of parsley, stemmed and coarsely chopped
- two long pieces of lemon rind, juice of one lemon
- sprinkle of crushed red pepper flakes
- few shavings of parmesan if you must gild the lily

Direction

- Line a large sheet pan with foil.
- Preheat oven to 450 degrees while you prep the veggies.
- Toss the eggplants, zucchini, yellow squash in a scant amount of oil, you don't want them drenched.
- Put on sheet pan, don't crowd and sprinkle with sea salt and ground black pepper.
- Trim the end of the garlic bulb and rub generously with oil.
- Toss peppers and onion and mushrooms with scant oil and put on the other end of the sheet pan. Again, don't crowd.
- If there is too much for your sheet pan, fix up another sheet pan and plan to rotate the pans while cooking.
- DON"T ROAST THE TOMATOES.
- Roast the veggies in hot oven for about 20 minutes. You want each to maintain their shape but to get a tiny bit of char on the surface.
- Don't cook the garlic to mush, you want to be able to just squeeze it from the bulb.
- Finally dump all the veggies into a stock pot, including the prepped tomatoes, squeeze the garlic out of the bulb into the pot, the thyme leaves, the marjoram, the lemon rind and the lemon juice and a sprinkle of red pepper flakes.
- Cook over low heat until the tomatoes give up their juice and stir only enough to combine, you don't want to break down the veggies anymore if at all possible.

- At service, fish out lemon rind and thyme branches if you left them whole. Garnish with chopped fresh parsley and long shavings of parmesan.

---

295. Ratatouille Not The Movie Recipe

Serving: 6 | Prep: | Cook: 90mins |Ready in:

Ingredients

- 1 med. eggplant
- 2 lg. potatoes
- 2 lg. green peppers
- 1 lg. Spanish or red onion
- 2 med. size zucchini
- 3 lg. tomatoes, or a 28-oz. can plum tomatoes, well drained
- 8 garlic cloves, crushed, or 2 tbsp. minced garlic
- 2 tbsp. olive oil
- 2 tsp. dried basil
- 1 tsp. each of dried leaf oregano and salt
- 1/2 tsp. each of ground black pepper and cayenne
- 1 tbsp. sugar
- 2 tbsp. balsamic vinegar

Direction

- Peel eggplant and cut into 1-inch cubes.
- Put cubes in a large deep saucepan or casserole that will hold at least 16 cups.
- Cut unpeeled potatoes into 1/2-inch cubes, slice peppers into 1-inch pieces and finely chop onion.
- Add them to casserole.
- Slice zucchini lengthwise into quarters, then slice it into 1/2-inch pieces and add to other vegetables.
- Coarsely chop unpeeled tomatoes and add them along with any juices, or cut drained canned tomatoes into bite-size pieces and add.
- Preheat oven to 375 F.

- In a small bowl, stir garlic with oil and all seasonings.
- Add mixture to casserole and stir vigorously until vegetables are evenly coated.
- Place casserole in oven and bake, uncovered, for 1 1/2 hours.
- Stir at least every half hour.
- Vegetables at the top will appear to dry out but will actually take on a little roasted taste.
- Baking uncovered also allows some vegetables juices to evaporate, and concentrated vegetable juices will be soaked up by eggplant and zucchini.
- Remove hot casserole from oven.
- Sprinkle mixture with sugar. Drizzle in vinegar and stir until well mixed.
- Taste.
- You may want to add more salt, sugar or vinegar. It's wonderful sprinkled with lots of chopped fresh basil, coriander or parsley.
- GREAT ADDITION: Stir together 1/2 cup chopped parsley, 3 cloves minced fresh garlic and the finely grated peel of 1 lemon, then sprinkle over top of hot casserole just before serving.

---

296. Red Beans And Rice New Orleans Meat And Vegetarian Recipe

Serving: 12 | Prep: | Cook: 180mins |Ready in:

Ingredients

- 1 lb red kidney beans, dried (my suggestion: or eqivelent in canned drained and rinsed)
- 1 large onion chopped
- 1 bell pepper chopped
- 5 ribs celery chopped
- 4 cloves garlic chopped or as you like
- Meat:(omit if making vegetarian)
- 1 ring of smoked sausage sliced- I used turkey kilelbasa sausage
- 1 tsp dried thyme leaves

- 2 bay leaves
- dashes of Tabasco or hot sauce, and Worchestershire sauce
- Creole or Louisisina seasoning to taste
- liquid smoke as desired (esp for the vegetarian version if no smoked meat is used)
- salt and black pepper as needed
- Prepared hot cooked white rice

Direction

- Soak dried beans overnight if not using canned.
- If using canned, drain and rinse well
- Rinse, cover dry beans with water in pot and cook boiling till tender but not mushy about 45 minutes to an hour
- Meanwhile sauté the onion, pepper, celery and then garlic till veggies are softened and translucent in some oil and set aside
- Drain liquid from cooked beans, add sautéed veggies to the pot along with the sliced sausage (omit if vegetarian), bay leaf and cover all with fresh water
- Bring to a boil again and then cook and simmer at a low bubble several hours until beans get creamy, stirring often to avoid beans from burning on bottom
- If the beans are not getting creamy one may use a hand blender and blend the mixture creamy (remove the bay leave) which was I did for both the dried and the canned recipes
- Adjust seasoning as you cook: adding what you like such as hot sauce, Worcestershire sauce, liquid smoke etc.
- The beans are best if made ahead and reheated
- If needed, thin out cold beans if too thick with a bit of water
- Correct seasonings if needed
- Serve beans over hot cooked white rice
- Note: if using the canned beans, one does not need to cook as long as if using the dried beans

---

297.   Red Beans And Rice Recipe

Serving: 10 | Prep: | Cook: 150mins | Ready in:

Ingredients

- 2 pounds dried red beans
- 1 pound salt pork, cut into 1-inch cubes
- 1 cup onion, chopped
- 1/2 cup celery, chopped
- 1/2 cup carrot, chopped
- 2 tablespoon white vinegar
- 2 bay leaves
- 1 teaspoon salt
- 1/2 teaspoon pepper
- Hot cooked rice

Direction

- Sort and wash beans, place in large Dutch oven. Cover with water 2 inches above beans, let soak overnight.
- Drain beans, cover with more water and bring to a boil. Add next 6 ingredients, stir gently.
- Reduce heat, cover and simmer 2 to 2-1/2 hours or until beans are tender and a thick gravy is formed. Add water to prevent beans from sticking, if necessary.
- Stir in salt and pepper.
- Serve over hot cooked rice with hot sauce.

---

298.   Red Cabbage Recipe

Serving: 4 | Prep: | Cook: 120mins | Ready in:

Ingredients

- 1 red cabbage sliced finely
- 2 apples, chopped finely
- 1/4 cup vinegar
- 1/4 cup brown sugar
- 1/4 cup water
- 1 T. oil
- 1 1/2 tsp. salt

Direction

- Heat oil in a large skillet with a lid to medium. Add cabbage and apples and cook down slightly, stirring. DO NOT BROWN. Mix remaining ingredients together. After about 4 minutes of cooking down, add the liquid and turn the heat down to low. Simmer for two hours until the cabbage is very transparent and tender.

---

299. Red Lentil Patties Vegetarian Meatballs Recipe

Serving: 6 | Prep: | Cook: 5mins | Ready in:

Ingredients

- • 1 cup red lentils, uncooked
- • 2 and 1/2 cups water
- • 1/2 cup fine bulgur, uncooked
- • 2 tablespoons extra virgin olive oil, plus more for drizzling
- • 1 medium onion, finely diced
- • 1 tablespoon tomato paste
- • 1tbspoon red pepper paste
- • 2tbspoon pomegranade molasses
- • 2tbspoon lemon juice
- • 1 teaspoon salt or more, depending on taste
- • 1 tablespoon paprika, plus more for dusting
- • 1 tablespoon ground cumin (or up to 2 tablespoons if you prefer)
- • 1/2 cup flat leaf parsley, finely chopped
- • ¾ cup fresh mint ,finely chopped
- • 3 scallions, finely sliced

Direction

- Wash the lentils in a large bowl until water runs clear. In a medium saucepan, bring water to a boil. Add lentils, and simmer until soft (but not overly mushy), about 15 minutes while stirring occasionally. Mix in bulgur; turn off the heat, cover the pot, and let it rest until the residual liquid is absorbed by the bulgur, about 15 minutes or longer.
- While the lentils cook, bring a skillet to medium heat and with olive oil and sauté diced onions until tender and translucent, about 8-10 minutes. Add in tomato paste; red pepper paste stir and turn off heat.
- Use the resting time of the lentils mixture and onions cooking to chop scallions and parsley.
- Once the lentils and bulgur are cooked, it should be moderately moist and not completely dry, like cookie dough. Add salt, onions, paprika, cumin, fresh onions, lemon juice, pomegranate molasses and most of the parsley and scallions, fresh mints into the mixture and stir to combine.
- At this point, the lentil and bulgur mixture should resemble thick cookie dough when stirred. If it still seems too damp, add more bulgur and let the mixture rest longer. The bulgur should no longer be hard, but soft and melded in to the mix.
- When the lentil-and-grain mixture is cool enough to handle, use your hands to knead it together. With a bowl of water at your side, wet your hands and mold the lentil and bulgur mixture into mini golf-ball sized balls (or any shape you prefer) and place on a platter. A tablespoon is a good amount for each ball. Garnish with remaining scallions and parsley and drizzle with good extra virgin olive oil ,the lettuce leaves and onions, then drizzle over the dressing..
- Note Turkish red pepper paste is available from Turkish and Middle Eastern food stores.
- Red lentils and bulgur can be purchased in bulk food bins, which are probably the least expensive. Sometimes they are also available in the international food aisle.

---

300. Refrigerator Pickled Beets And Onions Recipe

Serving: 6 | Prep: | Cook: 7mins | Ready in:

Ingredients

- 1/2 cup apple cider vinegar
- 1/2 cup water
- 2/3 cup granulated sugar
- 1/4 teaspoon salt
- 1/2 teaspoon ground cinnamon
- 1 large sweet onion, peeled and thinly sliced
- 2 cans sliced beets, undrained

Direction

- In saucepan, combine vinegar, water, sugar, salt, cinnamon and juice from canned beets to a boil.
- Reduce heat and simmer 5 to 7 minutes.
- Pour over sliced beets and onion.
- Cover and chill overnight. (Stir occasionally if you think of it!)

---

301.   Remys Ratatouille Recipe

Serving: 6 | Prep: | Cook: 240mins | Ready in:

Ingredients

- Piperade (bottom layer):
- ½ red bell pepper, seeds and ribs removed
- ½ yellow bell pepper, seeds and ribs removed
- ½ orange bell pepper, seeds and ribs removed
- 2 tablespoons extra-virgin olive oil
- 1 teaspoon minced garlic
- ½ cup finely diced yellow onion
- 3 tomatoes (about 12 ounces total weight), peeled, seeded and finely diced, juices reserved
- 1 sprig fresh thyme
- 1 sprig flat-leaf parsley
- ½ bay leaf
- kosher salt
- For the vegetables:
- 1 medium zucchini (4 to 5 ounces) sliced in 1/16-inch-thick rounds
- 1 Japanese eggplant (4 to 5 ounces) sliced into 1/16-inch-thick rounds

- 1 yellow (summer) squash (4 to 5 ounces) sliced into 1/16-inch-thick rounds
- 4 roma tomatoes, sliced into 1/16-inch-thick rounds
- ½ teaspoon minced garlic
- 2 teaspoons extra-virgin olive oil
- ⅛ teaspoon fresh thyme leaves
- kosher salt and freshly ground black pepper
- For the vinaigrette:
- 1 tablespoon extra-virgin olive oil
- 1 teaspoon balsamic vinegar
- Assorted fresh herbs (such as thyme flowers, chervil, thyme)
- kosher salt and freshly ground black pepper

Direction

- Make the piperade, preheat oven to 450 F. Line a baking sheet with foil.
- Place pepper halves on the baking sheet, cut side down. Roast until the skins loosen, about 15 minutes. Remove the peppers from the oven and let rest until cool enough to handle. Reduce the oven temperature to 275 F.
- Peel the peppers and discard the skins. Finely chop the peppers, then set aside.
- In medium skillet over low heat, combine oil, garlic, and onion and sauté until very soft but not browned, about eight minutes.
- Add the tomatoes, their juices, thyme, parsley, and bay leaf. Bring to a simmer over low heat and cook until very soft and little liquid remains, about 10 minutes. Do not brown. (Note: I like to place the herbs in a metal tea infuser -- that way, when it's time to discard the herbs, I simply lift out the infuser and save myself the trouble of fishing around for a soggy bay leaf.)
- Add the peppers and simmer to soften them. Discard the herbs, then season to taste with salt. Reserve a tablespoon of the mixture, then spread the remainder over the bottom of an 8-inch oven-proof skillet.
- To prepare the vegetables, arrange the sliced zucchini, eggplant, squash, and tomatoes over the piperade in the skillet.

- Begin by arranging eight alternating slices of vegetables down the center, overlapping them so that ¼ inch of each slice is exposed. This will be the center of the spiral. Around the center strip, overlap the vegetables in a close spiral that lets slices mound slightly toward center. All vegetables may not be needed. Set aside.
- In a small bowl, mix the garlic, oil and thyme, then season with salt and pepper to taste. Sprinkle this over vegetables.
- Cover the skillet with foil and crimp edges to seal well. Bake until the vegetables are tender when tested with a paring knife, about two hours. Uncover and bake for another 30 minutes. (Lightly cover with foil if it starts to brown.)
- If there is excess liquid in pan, place it over medium heat on stove until reduced. (At this point it may be cooled, covered and refrigerated for up to two days. Serve cold or reheat in 350 F oven until warm.)
- To make the vinaigrette, in a small bowl whisk together the reserved piperade, oil, vinegar, herbs, and salt and pepper to taste.
- To serve, heat the broiler and place skillet under it until lightly browned. Slice in quarters and lift very carefully onto plate with an offset spatula. Turn spatula 90 degrees as you set the food down, gently fanning the food into fan shape. Drizzle the vinaigrette around plate.
- NOTE: Can also make individual servings in small skillets.

---

302. Roasted Asparagus Recipe

Serving: 4 | Prep: | Cook: 10mins | Ready in:

Ingredients

- 1 lb asparagus spears (thicker spears are best)
- 1-3 tbsp olive oil
- 2 clove garlic minces or 3 tbsp minced garlic in jar
- Kosher or sea salt
- Fresh grated black pepper
- lemon juice

Direction

- Preheat oven to 400
- Rinse asparagus and cut off tough ends only
- Lay asparagus spears in single layer on baking sheet lined with foil
- Drizzle oil, pepper, salt & garlic over asparagus
- Roll back and forth to evenly distribute seasonings
- Roast in oven approximately 10 minutes until lightly browned and tender when pierced with fork (return to cover for a few more minutes if still tough - watch not to overcook)
- Remove to plate and drizzle with lemon juice before serving
- WARNING: Make at least a double batch

---

303. Roasted Asparagus With Balsamic Browned Butter Recipe

Serving: 8 | Prep: | Cook: 12mins | Ready in:

Ingredients

- 40 asparagus spears, trimmed (about 2 lbs.)
- cooking spray
- ¼ tsp. kosher salt
- 1/8 tsp. black pepper
- 2 tbsp. butter
- 2 tsp. soy sauce
- 1 tsp. balsamic vinegar

Direction

- Preheat oven to 400 degrees F.
- Arrange asparagus in a single layer on a baking sheet.

- Coat asparagus with cooking spray.
- Sprinkle with salt and pepper.
- Bake at 400 degrees for 12 min. or until tender.
- Melt butter in skillet until lightly browned.
- Remove from heat and stir in soy sauce and vinegar.
- Add asparagus and toss. Makes 8 servings.
- Tip: When choosing asparagus, note that the fresh ones are firm not soft, at the tips. Bend a spear until it snaps and discard the bottom part. If asparagus is rather thick, use a vegetable peeler on the stems.

304.   Roasted Beets Recipe

Serving: 4 | Prep: | Cook: 60mins | Ready in:

Ingredients

- 3 medium beets
- 1 tablespoon olive oil

Direction

- Heat the oven to 375°F and arrange the rack in the middle.
- Rinse beets and trim off any leafy tops.
- Wrap beets in aluminum foil and place in oven.
- Roast until tender and easily pierced with a knife, about 1 hour. Remove from oven and let cool.
- When beets are cool enough to handle, peel using a paring knife or by pushing the skin with your fingers.
- Slice beets, drizzle with olive oil, and season with salt and freshly ground black pepper.

305.   Roasted Corn Salad Recipe

Serving: 8 | Prep: | Cook: 45mins | Ready in:

Ingredients

- 6 ears fresh corn
- ½ red pepper chopped small
- ½ green pepper chopped small
- ½ orange or yellow pepper chopped small
- ½ sweet or red onion diced small
- 1 can black beans drained
- *************************
- Dressing
- *************************
- juice of 4 lemons
- 4 cloves garlic minced
- salt and pepper to taste
- 1 tbls hot sauce
- ¾ - 1 cup chopped cilantro (fresh, washed and pressed dry.
- ½ cup olive oil
- 1 avocado sliced into small pieces
- ½ cucumber chopped small

Direction

- Husk and clean ears of corn.
- Place in heavy foil, fold closed.
- Roast in a 325 degree oven for 30 to 45 minutes.
- Cool and cut off cob.
- Mix with peppers, onion and beans.
- Dressing: blend together and add sugar to taste.
- Pour over veggies and let sit overnight.
- A few hours before serving add avocado and cucumber

306.   Roasted Green Beans Recipe

Serving: 4 | Prep: | Cook: 25mins | Ready in:

Ingredients

- 2 lbs green beans
- 1 tablespoon olive oil
- 1 teaspoon kosher salt

- 1/2 teaspoon fresh ground pepper

Direction

- Preheat oven to 400°F.
- Wash, dry well, and trim green beans.
- Put green beans on a baking sheet, and drizzle with olive oil (alternately, use an olive-oil spray).
- Sprinkle with salt and pepper to taste.
- Ensure all the beans are evenly coated, and spread them out into 1 layer.
- Roast for 20-25 minutes, stirring the beans after 15 minutes, until beans are fairly brown in spots and somewhat shrivelled.
- Serve hot or at room temperature.

307.   Roasted Herb Tomatoes Recipe

Serving: 12 | Prep: | Cook: 20mins | Ready in:

Ingredients

- 12 ripe tomatoes (large meaty type - beefsteak)
- 3 Tbsp. olive or canola oil
- 3 Tbsp. fresh parsley, chopped
- 3 Tbsp. fresh basil, chopped (or 3 tsp. dried)
- 6 cloves garlic, minced
- 1 tsp. freshly ground black pepper

Direction

- Preheat the oven to 375-F degrees. Remove the stem ends and cores from the tomatoes and cut each tomato in half, crosswise. Brush the halves all over with the olive or canola oil and arrange, cut side up, in a non-stick roasting pan.
- Roast for about 10 minutes or until slightly soft. Sprinkle evenly with the fresh herbs, garlic, and pepper, and roast an additional 5 to 10 minutes or until very soft. Serve warm.
- Tip: If you would like a little extra zing in you tomatoes, you may elect to add about half a

tablespoon of Romano or Parmesan cheese to each tomato half. Just remember, adding the cheese will add a few more calories to your light-hearted fare.

308.   Roasted Root Vegetables Recipe

Serving: 6 | Prep: | Cook: 30mins | Ready in:

Ingredients

- 2 sweet potatoes (about 1 pound), scrubbed and cut into wedges
- 1 (1-pound) bag baby carrots
- 1 bunch parsnips, peeled and cut into 1-inch pieces
- 1/3 cup extra-virgin olive oil
- kosher salt and freshly ground black pepper
- Preheat oven to 425 degrees F and position a rack in the center of the oven.

Direction

- On a baking sheet, toss the sweet potatoes, carrots, and parsnips with the olive oil and season with the salt and pepper. Roast stirring occasionally, until the vegetables are browned and tender, about 25 to 30 minutes.

309.   Roasted Shallots And Tomatoes Recipe

Serving: 6 | Prep: | Cook: 30mins | Ready in:

Ingredients

- 18 small shallots, peeled and halved
- 1/4 c. balsamic vinegar
- 1/4 c. olive oil
- 1-12 oz pkg. grape or cherry tomatoes
- 13/ c drained capers, plus 1 T brine from jar

- salt & pepper

Direction

- Preheat oven 450. Combine shallots, balsamic and olive oil in medium roasting pan, toss to coat. Sprinkle with salt and pepper. Roast about 15 minutes until shallots are browned and tender. Add tomatoes and roast until soft and browned, another 15 minutes. Remove from oven. Add capers and reserved brine and stir to blend.

---

310.   Roasted Vegetables Recipe

Serving: 12 | Prep: | Cook: | Ready in:

Ingredients

- 3 Yukon Gold (or baking) potatoes, cut into cubes
- 1 sweet potato, peeled and cut into cubes
- 1 small butternut squash, cut into cubes
- 2 red bell peppers, seeds removed and finely chopped
- 1 red onion, cut into quarters
- 1 tbsp fresh thyme, chopped
- 2 tbsp fresh rosemary, chopped
- 2 tbsp balsamic vinegar
- 1/4 cup olive oil
- salt and black pepper (freshly ground)

Direction

- Preheat oven to 475 degrees F.
- Mix together the Yukon Gold potatoes, sweet potato, squash, and red bell peppers, in a large sized bowl. Divide the onion quarters into pieces, then add to the mixture.
- In a small bowl, combine thyme, rosemary, vinegar, rosemary, salt and pepper then toss with vegetables until they are coated well. Arrange them evenly on a large roasting pan.

- Roast for 35-40 minutes, stirring every 10 minutes, (or until vegetables are cooked through and slightly browned.)

---

311.   Roasted Winter Vegetables Recipe

Serving: 16 | Prep: | Cook: 45mins | Ready in:

Ingredients

- 12 oz carrots peeled
- 12 oz celery root, peeled
- 8 oz turnips peeled
- 8 oz parsnips peeled
- 12 oz Waxy potatoes peeled
- 8 oz butternut squash peeled and seeded
- 12 shallots peeled
- 12 garlic cloves peeled
- 4 oz olive oil
- 1 1/2 tsp Dried thyme
- 1 1/2 tsp coarse salt
- 1 tsp Coarsely ground black pepper

Direction

- Cut the carrots, celery root, turnips, parsnips, potatoes, and squash into 1-in dice.
- Place these cut vegetables, plus the shallots and garlic cloves, in a baking pan.
- Pour the olive oil over the vegetables and sprinkle with the thyme, salt, and pepper.
- Toss or mix until the vegetables are well coated with oil.
- Add more oil if necessary.
- Bake at 375°F for about 45 minutes, until the vegetables are tender and lightly browned.
- Turn or stir the vegetables several times during baking so that they cook evenly.
- Do not allow them to become too browned, or they may be bitter.

312.   Romaine Grilled Avocado And Smoky Corn Salad With Chipotle Caesar Dressing Recipe

Serving: 6 | Prep: | Cook: 5mins | Ready in:

Ingredients

- • 1/4 cup grated parmesan
- • 1/2 cup extra-virgin olive oil
- • 1/4 cup fresh lime juice
- • 1 teaspoon minced garlic
- • 1 tablespoon minced canned chipotle chiles in adobo
- • 3 tablespoons vegetable oil
- • 2 ears of corn, shucked
- • 2 firm-ripe 6-to 8-ounces avocados, halved and pitted but not peeled
- • 1 head romaine (1 pound), tough outer leaves discarded and head quartered lengthwise, then cut crosswise into 1-inch strips

Direction

- Prepare grill for direct-heat cooking over hot charcoal (high heat for gas);
- Put parmesan in a medium bowl and add olive oil in a slow stream, whisking. Whisk in lime juice, garlic, chipotles, and 1/4 teaspoon each of salt and pepper.
- Rub vegetable oil on corn and cut sides of avocados, then season with 1/8 teaspoon each of salt and pepper. Grill avocados, cut sides down, and corn, covered only if using a gas grill, turning corn occasionally, until golden-brown, 3 to 4 minutes.
- Peel avocados and thinly slice. Cut corn kernels from cobs.
- Toss romaine with dressing and serve topped with avocado and corn.
- Cooks' note: Corn and avocados can be grilled, in batches if necessary, in a lightly oiled hot grill pan over medium-high heat.

313.   Root Vegetables Casserole Recipe

Serving: 8 | Prep: | Cook: 40mins | Ready in:

Ingredients

- 1 large rutabaga or a yellow turnip, about 2-1/4 pounds, trimmed, peeled, cut in chunks
- 2 medium purple-topped turnips, trimmed, peeled, cut in chunks
- 1 large sweet potato, peeled, cut in chunks
- 3 medium carrots, peeled, cut in chunks
- Sauce: (or use ready made béchamel)
- 1 tablespoon unsalted butter
- 2 big leeks (only the white part)
- 1 tablespoon flour
- 1/3 cup milk
- 1/3 cup apple cider
- 1/4 pound good melting cheese ,Cheddar or gruyere, cut in chunks
- Grated fresh Parmesan

Direction

- Bring water to a boil in a large pot or Dutch oven. Add the rutabaga chunks as they're prepped, even if water's not yet boiling. Once it comes to a boil, cook for about 10 minutes before adding the turnips, sweet potato and carrots. Drain.
- In a large skillet or Dutch oven, melt the butter on medium, add the leeks and cook, stirring often, till soft. Set aside.
- If making the sauce:
- In the skillet or Dutch oven used for the leeks, melt the butter on medium. Stir in the flour, removing all the lumps. A spoonful at a time at first, slowly stir in the milk, stirring all the time to remove all the lumps, not adding more till the lumps are stirred out. (Press with the back of a spoon if needed.) Add the apple cider. Stirring often, cook till the sauce thickens. Turn the heat off and stir in the cheese, the sautéed leeks and the cooked root vegetables.

- Transfer to a baking dish.
- Preheat oven to 375°F and bake for 30 minutes or until hot and bubbly throughout. Top with Parmesan and bake another 15 minutes.

314.   Rotkraut Red Cabbage Recipe

Serving: 6 | Prep: | Cook: 50mins | Ready in:

Ingredients

- 1 1/2 lb. red cabbage (shredded)
- 4 slices bacon (diced)
- 1 medium onion (diced)
- 2 tart apples (diced)
- 1 cup water
- 1 teaspoon salt
- 1 1/2 teaspoons sugar
- 1 1/2 teaspoons caraway seeds
- 1/2 cup red wine vinegar
- pepper

Direction

- In a large kettle fry bacon until crisp,
- Add onion and sauté until golden.
- Stir in sugar and cook until lightly brown.
- Add cabbage and apples. 1/2 cup water.
- Mix well, cover and cook approximately 30 minutes. On medium heat.
- Add caraway seeds, 1/2 cup water, and vinegar.
- Cover and cook another 20 minutes.
- Pepper to taste

315.   Ruths Chris Sweet Potato Casserole Recipe

Serving: 6 | Prep: | Cook: 30mins | Ready in:

Ingredients

- CRUST
- 1 cup brown sugar
- 1/3 cup flour
- 1 cup chopped nuts (pecans preferred)
- 1/3 stick butter -- melted (Do not omit or reduce this amount)
- SWEET POTATO MIXTURE
- 3 cups mashed sweet potatoes (Garnets looks best and I bake mine first)
- 1 cup sugar
- 1/2 teaspoon salt
- 1 teaspoon vanilla
- 2 eggs -- well beaten
- 1 stick butter -- (1/2 cup) melted (You can leave it out or reduce it, if you wish)

Direction

- Combine brown sugar, flour, nuts and butter in mixing bowl. Set aside.
- Preheat oven to 350 degrees.
- Combine sweet potatoes, sugar, salt, vanilla, eggs and butter in a mixing bowl in the order listed. Mix thoroughly.
- Pour mixture into buttered baking dish.
- Sprinkle the surface of the sweet potato mixture evenly with the crust mixture.
- Bake for 30 minutes. Allow to set at least 30 minutes before serving.
- Serves 6 Hint: Double the recipe. People will love the leftovers, which also freeze beautifully.

316.   SOUTHERN SPINACH Recipe

Serving: 6 | Prep: | Cook: 60mins | Ready in:

Ingredients

- 2 bunches of fresh spinach
- 1/2 tsp. salt
- 1 tsp. seasoning salt
- 1 chunk salt pork (3 oz.)

- water

Direction

- Remove stems and pick the yellow and brown leaves off the spinach.
- Wash spinach several times in kitchen sink.
- Wash until spinach is free of any residue and water runs clear.
- Cook all together on top of stove in large pot in about 3 cups water for 1 hour on medium high heat at a soft rolling boil.
- Add more water if necessary.

---

317.   Samhain Mushroom Casserole Recipe

Serving: 6 | Prep: | Cook: 45mins | Ready in:

Ingredients

- 1 8oz package mushrooms (if you want to be really creative, use a few different types of mushrooms)
- 1 small package frozen artichoke hearts (or canned packed in water, as long as they are NOT marinated)
- 1 can asparagus (fresh or frozen can also be used) (personally, I don't care for asparagus, so I leave them out)
- 1 can cream of mushroom soup
- ½ to 1 cup of sour cream
- salt, pepper & garlic to taste
- cooked rice

Direction

- Wash the mushrooms and cut into quarters. Place in casserole dish. Add artichoke hearts and asparagus on top of mushrooms.
- In a separate bowl, combine soup, sour cream, salt, pepper and garlic. Stir well then our over veggies.

- Cover casserole dish and bake at 350 for about 45 minutes, until hot & bubbly all the way through and the mushrooms are tender.
- When the casserole is almost done, cook up some rice.
- Spoon mushroom mixture over rice and enjoy!
- Variation:
- This recipe is also great with chicken. Just add 3 or 4 chicken pieces, such as split breasts. Pour veggies and soup over the top and bake until the chicken is done (about an hour). Serve over rice.

---

318.   Sauted Green Beans With Smoked Paprika And Almonds Recipe

Serving: 4 | Prep: | Cook: 15mins | Ready in:

Ingredients

- 1 tablespoon unsalted butter, softened
- 1/4 teaspoon smoked paprika
- 3 medium garlic cloves, thinly sliced
- 1 teaspoons olive oil
- 1 pound green beans, stem ends snapped off, beans cut into 2-inch pieces
- sea salt and ground black pepper to taste
- 1/4 cup water
- 1 - 2 teaspoons juice from 1 lemon
- 1/4 cup slivered almonds, toasted

Direction

- Combine butter, paprika, and garlic in small bowl; set aside.
- Heat oil in 12-inch non-stick skillet over medium heat until just smoking. Add beans, 1/4 teaspoon salt, and 1/8 teaspoon pepper; cook, stirring occasionally, until spotty brown, 5 to 6 minutes. Add water, cover, and cook until beans are bright green and still crisp, about 2 minutes.

- Remove cover, increase heat to high and cook until water evaporates, about 1 minute.
- Add butter mixture and continue to cook, stirring frequently, until beans are crisp-tender, lightly brown, and beginning to wrinkle, 2 to 3 minutes longer.
- Transfer green beans to serving bowl, toss with lemon juice and adjust seasoning with salt and pepper.
- Sprinkle with almonds and serve immediately.

319. Sauteed Asparagus And Mushrooms Recipe

Serving: 2 | Prep: | Cook: 5mins | Ready in:

Ingredients

- fresh asparagus cut into 1 inch pieces
- sliced mushrooms (white, baby portabello, etc.)
- butter
- tarragon
- minced garlic
- salt & pepper

Direction

- Wash and slice asparagus - removing hard ends
- Melt butter in sauté pan
- Add minced garlic
- Add sliced asparagus and mushrooms, tarragon, salt and pepper to taste
- Sauté on medium heat till tender but al dente

320. Sauteed Asparagus And Mushrooms In A Lemon Thyme Butter Recipe

Serving: 4 | Prep: | Cook: 10mins | Ready in:

Ingredients

- ½ tbsp olive oil
- 1 tbsp unsalted butter
- 6 oz asparagus spears, trimmed of woody ends and sliced on diagonal to 1" thick
- 2/3 lb button mushrooms, sliced
- ½ tbsp fresh thyme
- 1 tsp finely grated lemon zest
- ½ tsp lemon juice
- Salt and pepper, to taste

Direction

- Heat olive oil and butter together in a sauté pan until butter melts and is bubbling slightly.
- Add asparagus and cook 1 – 2 minutes, until bright green.
- Add mushrooms to the pan and toss lightly to mix.
- Continue to sauté 4 – 6 minutes, until mushrooms are browned and asparagus is tender.

321. Savory Cabbage Seasoning Recipe

Serving: 1 | Prep: | Cook: | Ready in:

Ingredients

- 1 part caraway seeds
- 1 part dill seeds
- 1 part celery seeds
- 1 part cracked black pepper
- 1 part crushed red pepper flakes
- 1 part cumin seeds
- 1 part nigella seeds
- 1 part yellow mustard seeds
- 1 part brown mustard seeds

Direction

- Mix all ingredients in a sealed jar.

- Use 1 to 2 teaspoons for seasoning braised cabbage or sauerkraut dishes.
- The most effective way to season braised cabbage is to melt the butter or oil and add the seasoning at that time; briefly heat the seeds and then add the cabbage. The oil will then distribute the flavors throughout the cabbage.

---

322. Savory Fresh Corn Fritters Recipe

Serving: 4 | Prep: | Cook: 8mins | Ready in:

Ingredients

- 2 large ears fresh corn, shucked and kernels removed
- 1 large egg, separated
- 1/2 cup all purpose flour
- 1/2 teaspoon baking powder
- 1/3 cup half & half
- kosher salt and freshly ground black pepper, to taste
- 2 tablespoons *peeled red bell pepper, finely diced
- 1 tablespoon chopped fresh parsley
- 1 tablespoon chopped fresh basil
- 1 tablespoon chopped fresh chives
- 2 tablespoons melted butter, divided
- About 1 tablespoon vegetable or olive oil

Direction

- Place the corn kernels in a large bowl. Add the egg yolk and half & half and mix well. Note: I like to briefly steam my corn cobs before cutting the kernels off.
- Whip the egg white to stiff peak stage, set aside.
- To the corn mixture, stir in the flour, baking powder, salt, pepper, bell pepper, parsley, basil, and chives. Add 1 tablespoon of the melted butter and beat well to create a somewhat smooth batter. The batter will be chunky but should be uniform in texture.

- Gently fold in the egg white. Note: This batter can be made ahead of time and kept in the fridge; just bring back up to room temp before cooking.
- Heat a large skillet or griddle over medium-high heat. Add the remaining tablespoon of melted butter and 1/2 tablespoon of the oil and let get hot, about 1 to 2 minutes. Add a heaping tablespoon of the corn batter and cook 2 minutes.
- Using a spatula, gently flip the fritter and cook another 2 to 3 minutes on the other side, or until golden brown.
- Repeat with the remaining batter, adding more butter and oil to the pan as needed.
- Note: to peel bell pepper, just use a sharp vegetable peeler

---

323. Scalloped Cauliflower Recipe

Serving: 4 | Prep: | Cook: 25mins | Ready in:

Ingredients

- 2 lbs. cauliflower, cut into small florets
- 2/3 c. grated cheese, such as gruyere, aged Cheddar, or parmigiano Reggiano (I suggest the Parm)
- 1/2 tsp. ground nutmeg or 1 TBSP. Dijon mustard (I use the nutmeg)
- Bechamel Sauce:
- 1 3/4 c. plus 2 TBSP milk
- 1/4 of a small onion
- 1 bay leaf
- 2 whole cloves
- 3 TBSP. butter
- 3 TBSP. all-purpose flour
- salt and ground white pepper, to taste
- Topping:
- 1/2 c. breadcrumbs, fresh or panko
- 2 TBSP butter, melted
- paprika

Direction

- Preheat oven to 350 degrees F. Butter a 2 quart baking dish.
- Prepare Béchamel Sauce: In a small saucepan over low heat, combine milk, onion, bay leaf, and cloves. Simmer gently for 15 minutes, uncovered, to infuse flavor into the milk. Discard the onion, bay leaf, and cloves.
- In a medium saucepan over low heat melt the 3 TBSP butter. Stir in the flour. Cook uncovered, stirring occasionally with a wooden spoon or spatula, over medium-low heat until the roux is just fragrant but not darkened, 2 to 3 minutes. Remove from the heat and let cool slightly.
- Slowly whisk in the warm milk and return the saucepan to the heat. Bring the sauce slowly to a simmer, whisking to prevent lumps, and cook, stirring often and skimming any skin that forms on the surface, over low heat, without boiling, until it reaches the consistency of thick cream soup, 8 to 10 minutes. Season with salt and pepper to taste.
- Stir in nutmeg or mustard (whichever you are using) into the finished sauce.
- For the cauliflower, while preparing the Béchamel Sauce, bring 4 quarts of water to a boil with 1 1/2 TBSP. salt and the juice of one lemon. Add the cauliflower and boil uncovered until the largest floret is tender, but still crisp, 3 to 5 minutes. Drain, and keep warm while finishing the Sauce.
- Spread cauliflower in prepared baking dish and top with half of the cheese. Spoon sauce over cauliflower and cheese. Sprinkle remaining cheese on top.
- For the topping, mix together the breadcrumbs and 2 TBSP melted butter. Sprinkle over the top of the cauliflower. Bake until bubbly and browned on the top, about 25 minutes. Sprinkle with paprika and serve.

324. Scalloped Eggplant Recipe

Serving: 5 | Prep: | Cook: 60mins | Ready in:

Ingredients

- 1 medium eggplant, cubed 1/2 inch pices
- 5 slices bread, cut in 1" cubes
- 3/4 cup cheddar cheese, grated
- 1 tablespoon onion flakes
- salt and pepper, to taste
- 2 tablespoons butter, melted
- 2 large eggs
- 1 cup milk

Direction

- Peel and clean eggplant. Cut into 1/2 inch pieces. Place in water and boil for 3 minutes. Drain and set aside.
- Grease 1-1/2 quart casserole dish. Alternate layers of bread cubes, eggplant, grated cheese and onion flakes. Salt and pepper each layer. The last layer should be bread cubes.
- Drizzle melted butter over the top layer.
- Beat eggs lightly, combine them with the milk and pour this mixture over the casserole. Sprinkle a little more cheese on top.
- Bake in preheated 350 degree oven for 45 minutes to an hour until moderately browned.

325. Sensational Asparagus Roll Ups With Herb Cheese And Sun Dried Tomatoes Recipe

Serving: 12 | Prep: | Cook: | Ready in:

Ingredients

- 24 fresh asparagus spears
- 2 red peppers roasted
- 6 tablespoons herb cheese spread at room temperature

- 4 sun dried tomatoes soaked in boiling water for 10 minutes finely chopped
- 10 flour tortillas

Direction

- Trim asparagus tips to 5 inch lengths.
- In boiling salted water cook asparagus for 7 minutes then rinse under cold water.
- Cut peppers into 1/2-inch wide strips then rinse and dry asparagus tips and pepper strips thoroughly.
- Mix herb cheese spread and sun dried tomatoes together then spread each tortilla with 1 tablespoon of the spread.
- Cut tortillas into 1 inch wide strips.
- Place one asparagus tip and one pepper strip together at one end of a tortilla strip and tightly roll up in spiral fashion.
- Repeat with remaining asparagus and peppers.
- Refrigerate covered until serving time.

326. Skinny Potatoes Recipe

Serving: 6 | Prep: | Cook: 40mins | Ready in:

Ingredients

- 4 Large potatoes - washed, peeled and sliced paper thin.
- 4 oz. Low Fat cream cheese.
- 8 oz. Fat Free Half n' Half
- 3/4 cup Low Fat/low sodium chicken broth.
- 1/2 cup Fresh Grated parmesan cheese.
- 2 green onions (white and green parts) - chopped fine.
- 2 tsp. kosher salt.
- 1 tsp. bacon salt

Direction

- Pre-heat oven to 400*
- Thoroughly butter a 13"x9" casserole dish.

- Layer the potatoes evenly in the bottom of the casserole dish.
- In a separate microwave safe bowl, mix together the remaining ingredients.
- Microwave on high for 60 seconds. Stir well and pour evenly over the potatoes.
- Bake uncovered on the middle rack for 40 minutes. Remove from oven, cover and let sit for 15 minutes. Serve warm.

327. Smoked Bbq Beans Recipe

Serving: 8 | Prep: | Cook: 120mins | Ready in:

Ingredients

- 2- 28oz cans Bush's baked beans (I use the vegetarian flavor)
- 1 1/2 cups Bar B Que sauce
- 1/2 cup chopped onion (I like Videlia)
- 1/2 cup chopped green bell pepper
- 3 cloves garlic chopped
- 1 1/2 cups diced smoked turkey ham (you could use any smoked ham)
- 2 Tbls. honey
- 1 Tbls. mustard
- 1 Teaspoon liquid smoke
- 1 teaspoon paprika
- salt/pepper to taste

Direction

- Add all ingredients into a heavy pot and mix well.
- Put on smoker and smoke for 1 1/2 to 2 hours stirring every once in a while, I usually smoke at around the 225-250 range.

328. Some Of The Best Green Beans Recipe

Serving: 6 | Prep: | Cook: 45mins | Ready in:

Ingredients

- 2-16 ounce cans green beans, drained. I like to use the Del-Monte Blue Lake Whole green beans (can use fresh cooked green beans)
- 10 strips of bacon
- 6 tablespoons sugar
- 6 tablespoons vinegar
- 1/4 cup slivered almonds

Direction

- Cook bacon, reserving drippings
- Crumble bacon
- Add sugar and vinegar to bacon drippings
- Layer *half* of the drained green beans in casserole dish
- Add *half* the crumbled bacon
- Add *half* the almonds
- Repeat layers
- Pour prepared drippings over all
- Bake in a 350 degree oven for about 45 minutes or until heated through
- Okay, nothing else will make this recipe taste like this and give it the flavor, except the "drippings" mixture. Sorry.

329. Southern Asparagus Casserole Recipe

Serving: 8 | Prep: | Cook: 30mins | Ready in:

Ingredients

- 2 cans (14.5 oz)asparagus, drain and reserve one cup juice (buy the cheap cans of cut spears)
- 1 cup asparagus juice from can
- 2 cups grated cheddar
- 6 eggs boiled, sliced
- 1/3 cup flour
- 1/2 tsp black pepper
- 1/2 sleeve Ritz crackers
- butter to top

Direction

- Drain asparagus and reserve one cup liquid
- Layer one can asparagus in square baking pan
- Add three boiled eggs, sliced
- Add one cup grated cheddar
- Repeat layers
- Mix flour with juice and pepper
- Pour over asparagus, eggs
- Top with crumbled Ritz crackers and dot with butter.
- Bake uncovered at 350 for about 30 minutes
- Serve as side with a variety of main dishes.

330. Southern Collard Greens Theyre Not Just For New Years Anymore Recipe

Serving: 6 | Prep: | Cook: 180mins | Ready in:

Ingredients

- 1-1/2 quarts water
- 1-1/2 pounds ham hocks
- 4 pounds collard greens, rinsed and trimmed
- 1/2 teaspoon crushed red pepper flakes (optional)
- 1/4 cup vegetable oil
- salt and pepper to taste
- Optional: 4 to 6 garlic cloves, crushed and chopped

Direction

- Optional: In the large pot, sweat the garlic before adding the water and ham hock.
- Place the water and the ham hock in a large pot with a tight-fitting lid. Bring to a boil. Lower the heat to very low and simmer covered for 30 minutes.

- Add the collards and the hot pepper flakes the pot. Simmer covered for about 2 hours, stirring occasionally.
- Add the vegetable oil and simmer covered for 30 minutes.

331. Southern Collards Recipe

Serving: 8 | Prep: | Cook: 150mins | Ready in:

Ingredients

- 1 1/2 quarts water possibly a little more
- 1 1/2 - 2 lbs pounds ham hocks
- 4 pounds collard greens, rinsed and trimmed
- 1/2 teaspoon crushed red pepper flakes (optional)
- 1/4 cup vegetable oil
- salt and pepper to taste
- dash of sugar
- MUST HAVE A GOOD pepper sauce!!!!!!!

Direction

- MAKE SURE TO WASH YOUR COLLARDS SEVERAL TIMES IN YOUR SINK BEFORE COOKING.....
- Place the water and the ham hock in a large pot with a tight-fitting lid. Bring to a boil. Lower the heat to very low and simmer covered for 30 minutes.
- Add the collards and the hot pepper flakes the pot. Simmer covered for about 2 hours, stirring occasionally.
- Add the vegetable oil and simmer covered for 30 minutes.
- EAT YOUR COLLARDS WITH PEPPER SAUCE (THIS IS PEPPERS BOTTLED IN VINEGAR, WHICH HAS SAT ON A SHELF FOR A FEW MONTHS) WITH CHOPPED ONION ON TOP OR BOTH!

332. Southern Corn Pudding Recipe

Serving: 4 | Prep: | Cook: 45mins | Ready in:

Ingredients

- 3 cups fresh corn, (can use frozen niblets, but fresh is best)
- 3 eggs
- 1 cup heavy cream
- 2 tablespoons sugar
- 1 tablespoon flour
- 1 teaspoon salt
- 1 teaspoon baking powder
- 1/4 pound melted butter

Direction

- Beat eggs, add heavy cream and slowly add the dry ingredients. Add corn and stir in melted butter.
- Pour the mixture into a small greased casserole dish and bake at 350 degrees for 45 minutes.
- Serves 4.

333. Southern Fried Cream And Butter Corn Recipe

Serving: 6 | Prep: | Cook: 7mins | Ready in:

Ingredients

- 3 cups fresh corn niblets removed from the cob (6-8 ears)
- 1 stick unsalted butter
- 1 tablespoon minced bell pepper (green) Optional
- salt and freshly ground pepper to taste
- 16 ounces half-and-half

Direction

- Melt butter in a 12-inch skillet

- Add corn, bell pepper (if using), salt, and pepper
- Stir and cook for 5 minutes
- Do not overcook
- Add half-and-half and reduce heat to simmer
- When cream has cooked away, about 7-10 minutes, serve hot

334.   Southern Fried Okra Recipe

Serving: 6 | Prep: | Cook: 20mins | Ready in:

Ingredients

- 1 pound fresh okra
- 2 eggs, beaten
- 1/4 cup buttermilk
- 1 cup flour
- 1 cup cornmeal
- 2 teaspoons baking powder
- salt and ground black pepper to taste
- vegetable oil for frying

Direction

- Wash and slice okra; pat dry with paper towels.
- Combine eggs and buttermilk; add okra, and let stand for 15 minutes.
- Combine flour, cornmeal, baking powder, salt and pepper.
- Drain okra, small portions at a time, using a slotted spoon.
- Dredge okra, small portions at a time, in flour mixture.
- Pour oil to depth of 2 to 3-inches in a Dutch oven or deep-fat fryer and heat to 375.
- Fry okra until golden brown. Drain on paper towels and serve immediately.

335.   Southern Scalloped Tomatoes Recipe

Serving: 6 | Prep: | Cook: 30mins | Ready in:

Ingredients

- 6 to 8 (approximate) tomatoes, unpeeled
- or 2 cups canned, drained
- 2 cups thinly sliced onions
- 4 tbs butter, divided
- 2 tsp salt
- 1/4 tsp black pepper
- 2 tbs brown sugar
- 2 tsp dried basil or 1`/3 cup fresh (preferred)
- 1 tsp minced fresh garlic
- 1 tsp oregano (optional)
- 2 cups bread cubed

Direction

- Sauté onion in 2 tbsp. butter until wilted, set aside
- Sauté bread cubes in 2 tbsp. butter in same pan used for onion, you only want to coat the cubes and this should only take a minute or two, set aside
- In greased casserole, place tomatoes and all seasonings, sugar and onion and mix to distribute ingredients evenly. Do not stir.
- Top with bread cubes
- Bake at 350 uncovered for 35 to 40 minutes.
- Note: You could add some bacon bits
- Note: You could add the oregano

336.   Southern Smothered Green Beans Recipe

Serving: 8 | Prep: | Cook: 45mins | Ready in:

Ingredients

- FRESH SNAP green beans OR 2 CANS OF green beans
- seasoning (I USE NATURES seasoning)

- black pepper
- 1 LARGE yellow onion DICED (OR YOU CAN USE green onions)
- water
- SMOKED pork (YOU CAN ALSO YOU ham, ham hocks OR A pork chop)
- I COOKED THESE FOR SUPPER TONIGHT AND TOOK A PICTURE TO SHARE WITH YOU.

Direction

- SAUTEE THE ONION WITH YOUR MEAT AND ABOUT ONE TABLESPOON OF OIL.
- ADD THE GREEN BEANS (IF YOU ARE USING CAN GREEN BEANS, DRAIN THE WATER OFF AND ADD WATER TO THE CAN WHILE BEANS ARE STILL IN CAN, POUR THIS WATER OFF AND ADD MORE WATER, THIS GETS RID OF THE CANNED TASTE)
- ADD 2 CUPS OF WATER
- COOK ON A MEDIUM HEAT UNTIL TENDER FOR ABOUT 45 MINUTES TO AN HOUR, BRING TO A BOIL THEN BACK DOWN TO A MEDIUM HEAT
- YOU CAN ALSO, ADD NEW POTATOES OR SMALL RED POTATOES

337. Southern Squash Casserole Recipe

Serving: 6 | Prep: | Cook: 30mins | Ready in:

Ingredients

- 2 lbs yellow squash, sliced
- 1/4 cup butter + extra for topping
- 1 large onion, chopped
- 1 egg, beaten
- 1/2 tsp salt
- 1/2 tsp black pepper
- 1 cup grated sharp chedder cheese
- 3/4 cup crackers, crushed (regular, not whole weat)

- Extra crackers for topping. Ritz works great

Direction

- Boil squash and onions until tender; drain well
- Add butter, cheese, cracker crumbs, egg and salt.
- Pour in well-greased baking or casserole dish
- Top with Ritz or regular cracker crumbs and dot with butter.
- Bake at 375 for about 20-25 minutes, or until crackers start to brown.

338. Spicy Eggplant Recipe

Serving: 2 | Prep: | Cook: 40mins | Ready in:

Ingredients

- eggplant diced - 1 large
- cumin seeds - 1/2 tsp
- fennel seeds - 1 tsp
- Nigella/Kalonji seeds - 1/2 tsp
- tomatoes chopped - 3 medium sized
- ginger-garlic paste - 1 tsp
- turmeric powder - 1/4 tsp
- Red Chilly Powder - 1 tsp
- coriander powder - 1 tbsp
- salt - to taste
- oil - as needed

Direction

- Put the eggplant in a bowl of cold water, wash them and drain the water. Then pat dry them with a towel.
- Heat oil in a pan and deep fry them in medium heat until they turn reddish brown. Drain them in a tissue paper.
- Heat another pan and add little oil into it. When hot, add cumin seeds and allow it to splutter.
- Now add nigella seeds and fennel seeds and fry for a while.

- Then add chopped tomato and ginger-garlic paste and sauté for a minute.
- Add coriander powder, turmeric powder, chili powder and salt and stir well. Cook it until gravy thickens.
- Add the fried eggplant into the gravy and mix gently.
- Simmer for 1 more minute, garnish with coriander leaves and serve hot with rotis.

339. Spiffy Spiced Roasted Carrots Recipe

Serving: 6 | Prep: | Cook: 35mins | Ready in:

Ingredients

- 2 pounds very fresh baby carrots
- 1 1/2 teaspoons sweet paprika
- 1 teaspoon ground cumin
- 1/2 teaspoon salt
- 1/2 teaspoon ground ginger
- 1/4 teaspoon ground cinnamon
- 1/4 teaspoon garlic powder
- 1/8 teaspoon cayenne pepper
- 1/4 teaspoon black pepper
- 1 tablespoon olive oil, plus more for drizzling
- 2 tablespoons lemon juice
- 1 tablespoon honey

Direction

- Preheat oven to 400°F.
- Put carrots, paprika, cumin, salt, ginger, cinnamon, garlic powder, cayenne, black pepper and 1 tablespoon of the oil into a large bowl and toss to coat.
- Transfer carrots to a large rimmed baking sheet and spread out in a single layer.
- Roast, tossing halfway through, until just tender, 30 to 40 minutes.
- Remove carrots from oven and transfer to a large bowl.
- Add lemon juice and honey and toss well.

- Drizzle with a bit more oil, if you like, then serve.

340. Spinach Artichoke Gratin Recipe

Serving: 6 | Prep: | Cook: 25mins | Ready in:

Ingredients

- vegetable oil spray
- 16 ounces fat free cottage cheese
- egg substitute equivalent to 2 eggs
- 3 tablespoons shredded or grated parmesan cheese
- 1 tablespoon fresh lemon juice
- 1/8 teaspoon white pepper
- 1/8 teaspoon nutmeg
- 2 10 ounce packages frozen chopped spinach, thawed and drained
- 3 medium green onions, thinly sliced (green part only)
- 10 ounce package frozen artichoke hearts, thawed and drained
- 2 tablespoons shredded or grated parmesan cheese

Direction

- Preheat the oven to 375*.
- Lightly spray a 1 1/2 quart baking dish with vegetable oil spray.
- In a food processor or blender, process the cottage cheese, egg substitute, 3 tablespoons Parmesan, lemon juice, pepper, and nutmeg until smooth.
- Squeeze the moisture from the spinach. Put the spinach in a large bowl.
- Stir in the cottage cheese mixture and green onions.
- Spread half the mixture in the baking dish.
- Cut the artichoke hearts in half. Pat dry with paper towels. Place in single layer on the spinach mixture. Sprinkle with 2 tablespoons Parmesan.

- Cover with the remaining spinach mixture.
- Bake, covered for 25 minutes.

341.   Spinach And Artichoke Au Gratin Recipe

Serving: 7 | Prep: | Cook: 30mins | Ready in:

Ingredients

- 26.5 oz.) jars marinated artichoke hearts,drained
- 3(3oz.) pkgs. cream cheese
- 4Tbs. butter,softened
- 6Tbs. milk
- 3(10oz) pkg. frozen chopped spinach-thawed,drained and squeezed dry
- 1/3c grated parmesan cheese
- salt and ground black pepper to taste

Direction

- Place artichokes in the bottom of an 11/2qt. baking dish
- In a mixing bowl, beat together the cream cheese and butter until smooth. Blend in milk and stir in spinach. Mix together until smooth.
- Pour into baking dish and sprinkle top with cheese, salt and pepper; refrigerate for 24 hours.
- Preheat oven to 350, bake for 30 mins. or until heated through. Place under the broiler to brown the cheese topping.

342.   Spinach With Chickpeas And Peppers Recipe

Serving: 46 | Prep: | Cook: 15mins | Ready in:

Ingredients

- 2 tbsp olive OR vegetable oil
- 2 lg garlic cloves, chopped
- 1 onion, chopped
- 1 sweet bell pepper, seeded and sliced in strips
- 1 tsp. cumin
- pinch cayenne pepper
- 1/2 tsp turmeric
- 14 oz canned chickpeas, drained
- 18 0z spinach leaves OR 1 package frozen spinach, defrosted
- salt and pepper to taste

Direction

- Heat the oil in a heavy skillet over med.-high heat. Add onions and garlic and sauté until golden and caramelised.
- Add the pepper strips and sauté for 3 more min. Add more oil if needed.
- Add cumin, cayenne and turmeric and cook, stirring for another minute.
- Add the chickpeas and stir until coated with spices.
- Stir in the spinach. You can add a little liquid like water or chicken broth at this point (about 2-3 tbsp.). Cover and cook until wilted for 4-5 min. (If using frozen spinach, cook until warmed through, but still retains green color).
- Uncover, season with salt and pepper and serve.

343.   Squash Casserole Country Style Recipe

Serving: 4 | Prep: | Cook: 30mins | Ready in:

Ingredients

- 2 Large yellow squash, sliced 1/4" thick
- 1/4 Cup milk
- 2 Tablespoons butter
- 1/2 Cup bread Crumbs
- 1/4 Cup cheddar cheese, shredded
- 1 Large egg
- 1/4 Cup onions, chopped medium size

Direction

- Sauté squash and onions in a medium skillet over medium high heat with a little oil until tender. Add salt and pepper to taste.
- Melt the butter (microwave works fine). Beat the egg and mix with milk, bread crumbs, cheese and butter in a medium mixing bowl. Add the squash and onions, fold together.
- Place in a small greased baking dish and bake at 325 degrees for 25-30 minutes.

---

344.   Squash With Dill Tejfeles Tokfozelek Recipe

Serving: 6 | Prep: | Cook: 20mins | Ready in:

Ingredients

- 2 1/2 lb yellow squash (green squash can be used but peel it)
- 1 tsp. salt
- 2 T butter
- 1 onion, minced
- 1/4 tsp paprika
- 1/4 tsp sugar
- 1 tsp vinegar or lemon juice
- Sprig fresh or dried dill
- 2 tsp flour
- 1/4 C hot water
- 3 T sour cream
- 1 bay leaf (optional)

Direction

- Pare squash, cut in half lengthwise, and remove seeds, then half crosswise into pieces about 3" long.
- Place pieces flat on board and cut into thin strips, place in bowl and sprinkle with salt. Let stand about 1 hour.
- Lift out of bowl and dry with paper towels.
- Melt butter in skillet, add onion and cook until tender, add squash, paprika, sugar, vinegar

and snipped dill, cover and cook 10 -12 min. Or until tender.

- Sprinkle flour over top of squash, gently stir, then cook 2-3 min.
- Pour in water and cook about 1 min.
- Gently stir in sour cream.
- Serve at once.

---

345.   Stir Fried Asparagus With Ginger Garlic And Basil Recipe

Serving: 4 | Prep: | Cook: 5mins | Ready in:

Ingredients

- 2 tablespoons soy sauce
- 1 tablespoon dry sherry
- 1 tablespoon chicken stock
- 1 tablespoon canola oil
- 1-1/2 pounds fresh asparagus ends snapped and cut into small pieces
- 2 teaspoons minced garlic
- 2 teaspoons minced fresh ginger
- 1/2 cup minced fresh basil
- 1 tablespoon chopped scallions
- 1/2 teaspoon granulated sugar

Direction

- Combine soy sauce, sherry and broth then set aside.
- Place a large skillet over high heat for 4 minutes.
- Add 2 teaspoons canola oil and heat for 1 minute then add the asparagus and stir-fry for 2 minutes.
- Clear the center of the pan then add the garlic, ginger and remaining oil then sauté for 10 seconds.
- Remove pan from heat and stir the ingredients to combine.
- Place pan back on heat then stir in the soy sauce mixture and cook for 30 seconds.
- Add basil, scallions and sugar.
- Cook and stir 30 seconds longer.

346.   Stir Fried Cabbage Recipe

Serving: 4 | Prep: | Cook: 15mins | Ready in:

Ingredients

- 1 tablespoon vegetable oil
- 2 cloves garlic, minced
- 3 cups sliced green cabbage (1/2 small head)
- 3 cups sliced red cabbage (1/2 small head)
- 2 small carrots, sliced (about 1 cup)
- 1 medium yellow onion, sliced (about 1 cup)
- 2 medium red or yellow bell peppers, julienned (about 2 cups)
- 1/4 cup reduced-sodium soy sauce
- 2 teaspoons ground ginger
- 1/4 cup water
- 2 tablespoons cornstarch

Direction

- In a wok or large nonstick skillet, heat oil over medium heat.
- Add garlic and cook, stirring constantly, for I minute.
- Stir in green cabbage, red cabbage, carrots, onion, bell peppers, soy sauce, and ginger. Cover and cook, stirring occasionally, until vegetables are crisp-tender, about 10 minutes.
- In a small bowl, combine water and cornstarch. Mix well. Add cornstarch mixture to wok, stirring until sauce thickens, about I minute. Serve immediately.
- VARIATION
- Use leftover cooked chicken to make a tasty main dish. Add I cup chicken to the wok in Step 3. Proceed as recipe directs.

347.   Stir Fried Eggplant Recipe

Serving: 2 | Prep: | Cook: 10mins | Ready in:

Ingredients

- 6 cloves garlic, minced
- 1-3 red chillies (including seeds), depending on how spicy you like it
- 1 Chinese (large, with dark purple skin) eggplant, or 2 (thinner, with light purple skin) Japanese eggplants
- 1/4 cup water
- 2-3 Tbsp. oil
- roughly 1/2 cup (or more) fresh basil
- SAUCE:
- 1 Tbsp. fish sauce
- 2 Tbsp. soy sauce
- 2 Tbsp. oyster sauce (or vegetarian oyster sauce)
- 1 tsp. brown sugar
- 1 tsp. cornstarch mixed with 2 Tbsp. water (mix until cornstarch is dissolved)
- 1 tablespoon of sasemi seed (optional)

Direction

- Mix cornstarch and water in a separate cup or bowl. Set both aside.
- Chop the eggplant up into bite-size pieces (be sure to leave the peel on - this is where most of the nutrients are).
- In a large frying pan or wok, over medium-high heat. Add the garlic, chili, and eggplant. Stir-fry for 5 minutes. When the wok or frying pan becomes dry, add a little of the water (a few Tbsp. at a time).
- Add all sauces and continue stir-frying for 5 more minutes, or until the eggplant is soft. Add the cornstarch/water mixture. Stir well so that the sauce thickens uniformly.
- In a serving platter, sprinkle basil leaves and sesame seed over top. Serve over rice.

348. Stuffed Artichokes Recipe

Serving: 4 | Prep: | Cook: 30mins | Ready in:

Ingredients

- 1 cup panko bread crumbs
- fresh basil and cilantro chopped
- ½ cup grated Pecorino-romano cheese
- 1 tablespoon parsley,
- 5 cloves chopped galic
- salt & freshly ground pepper to taste
- 6 tablespoons olive oil
- 4 artichokes

Direction

- Combine bread crumbs, Pecorino-Romano Cheese, parsley, basil, cilantro, salt, pepper, and 2 tablespoons of the olive oil in a medium bowl. Mix together well.
- Cut stems off artichokes, flush with bottom.
- Cut pointy leaves off the top of the artichokes.
- Take out fuzzy center in artichoke
- Spread leaves of each artichoke out and push stuffing in between them.
- In a pot just large enough to fit the artichokes, add the sliced garlic cloves, 2 tablespoons of the olive oil and the artichokes. Drizzle the remaining 2 tablespoons of olive oil over the top of the artichokes.
- Turn heat on to medium and cook until sizzling about 1-2 minutes. Add water to reach half way up the sides of the artichokes.
- Cover and cook until the artichokes are tender and a leaf is easily pulled out, about 45 minutes. If liquid is evaporating too quickly add a little more water.
- Transfer to a serving platter, drizzle a little of the liquid from the pot over the artichokes and serve. Surround with roasted red peppers aioli.

349. Summer Eggplant Gratin Recipe

Serving: 6 | Prep: | Cook: 45mins | Ready in:

Ingredients

- 2 + 1 + 1 T olive oil
- 1 T garlic, chopped
- ½ t red pepper flakes
- 2 – 14 ½ oz Del Monte diced tomatoes
- 1 t sugar
- salt to taste
- pepper to taste
- 1 T fresh basil, chopped
- 2 lb small slender eggplants, sliced 1/2" thick
- ½ c swiss cheese, shredded

Direction

- Preheat the oven to 375 degree.
- Butter a shallow oval gratin dish that is about 12 inches long, or a 2 quart baking dish (I use a round cooking stone).
- Sauce:
- Heat 1 tablespoon of the olive oil in a large, heavy, nonstick sauté pan over medium-high heat and add the garlic and red pepper flakes.
- Sauté until glossy, 20-30 seconds.
- Add the tomatoes, sugar, salt and pepper.
- Stir often, until the tomatoes cook down to a chunky sauce (about 15 minutes).
- Taste and correct seasonings.
- Stir in the basil.
- Eggplant:
- Rinse the eggplant.
- Instead of peeling the entire eggplant, slice off the stem and flower ends and peel off the skin lengthwise in alternating stripes about ½" wide.
- Add 2 tablespoons of the olive oil to a large nonstick skillet or an electric grill (I use a grill).
- Heat the skillet to medium-high.
- When the olive oil is hot, add the eggplant slices in an even layer.
- Cook on both sides until browned and tender, 3-5 minutes per side.

- Drain on paper towels.
- On the bottom of the dish, arrange half the eggplant slices, over- lapping each other slightly in concentric rings to form a single layer.
- Sprinkle evenly with salt and pepper.
- Top with half the tomatoes.
- Repeat the layer and sprinkle the top with the shredded cheese.
- Drizzle on the remaining table spoon of olive oil.
- Bake for 25 minutes, and then turn the oven heat down to 350 degrees.
- Bake another 20 minutes, or until the eggplant slices are completely tender when pierced with the tip of a sharp knife and the top is lightly browned.
- If the cheese begins to brown too much before the eggplant is done, cover the baking dish with foil.
- A perfect side dish for grilled or roasted meat or poultry. The gratin tastes wonderful if made a day ahead and reheated. Or try it cold with a splash of vinegar and a sprinkling of chopped fresh basil

---

350. Super Spinach Casserole With Bleu Cheese Recipe

Serving: 10 | Prep: | Cook: 35mins | Ready in:

Ingredients

- 4 boxes chopped spinach, defrosted and drained
- 2 t margarine
- drizzle olive oil
- 3/4 white onion, chopped
- 2 T chopped garlic
- 1-2 T worcestershire sauce
- 1 small can sliced mushrooms, drained
- 8 oz can artichoke hearts, drained and chopped
- 1/8 t capers
- dash red pepper flakes (adjust to your liking)
- 3/4 of a 16 oz container sour cream
- 1 can cream of mushroom soup
- 8 oz cream cheese
- 2 c bag of mozzerella, divided into 1.5 c and .5 c
- 1/2 c parmesan
- garlic pepper
- seasoned salt
- cayenne pepper
- 4 oz crumbled bleu cheese
- Perpperidge Farm seasoned stuffing mix
- 1/3 c chopped fresh tomatoes

Direction

- Preheat oven to 350
- Defrost spinach in microwave and drain all liquid
- While spinach is defrosting, add margarine and EVOO to large skillet
- When hot, add onion, garlic and Worcestershire
- Cook until onion is translucent
- Add mushrooms, capers and chopped artichoke hearts
- When spinach is thawed and drained, add to pan
- Add Garlic Pepper, red pepper flakes, seasoned salt (very little salt needed)
- Meanwhile, in large bowl, cream together the sour cream, cream cheese and mushroom soup
- Stir in 1.5 c mozzarella and parmesan
- Stir in spinach mixture
- Stir in bleu cheese and dash or two of cayenne pepper
- Transfer to buttered casserole dish
- Top with remaining mozzarella cheese and stuffing mix
- Bake until bubbly
- Top with chopped fresh tomatoes

351.   Thai Coleslaw Claim Jumper Recipe

Serving: 4 | Prep: | Cook: | Ready in:

Ingredients

- 1/2 head napa cabbage, thinly sliced
- 1/2 zucchini, julienned
- 2 jumbo carrots, julienned
- 2 green onions, sliced
- 1 tablespoon toasted sesame seeds
- 3 tablespoons shaved coconut
- 3 tablespoons roasted unsalted peanuts
- 2 tablespoons toasted almonds
- --THAI COLESLAW DRESSING--
- 8 ounces Thai sweet chili sauce (Lingham's brand is good)
- 8 ounces orange juice
- 1/2 ounce honey
- 1/2 teaspoon fresh ginger, chopped fine
- 1/2 teaspoon light brown sugar
- 1 teaspoon cilantro, chopped fine
- 1 tablespoon sesame oil

Direction

- For salad: Combine cabbage, zucchini, carrots, onions, sesame seeds, coconut, peanuts and almonds in large bowl. Chill until ready to use.
- For dressing: Place ingredients in a mixing bowl and whisk together. Slowly add sesame oil while whisking. Pour desired amount, about 1/4 cup, over chilled salad vegetables. Serve.

352.   Tomato Fritters Recipe

Serving: 4 | Prep: | Cook: 20mins | Ready in:

Ingredients

- 1 c. flour
- 1 tsp. baking powder
- 1 tsp. granulated sugar
- 3/4 tsp. salt
- 1/4 tsp. dried basil
- 1 (28oz) can tomatoes, drained
- 1 TB. finely minced onion
- 1/2 tsp. worcestershire sauce
- 2 eggs
- canola oil for frying

Direction

- In a large bowl combine flour, baking powder, sugar, salt and basil.
- Cut tomatoes into 1/2" pieces and drain. Add them along with onion, parsley and Worcestershire sauce to flour mixture, but DO NOT mix.
- In a small bowl beat eggs and add to flour-tomato mixture. Blend lightly with a fork.
- Heat 1/4" of canola oil in skillet over medium heat. Drop batter by Tablespoon, patting down with the back of the spoon. Fry until golden brown on one side, then turn and fry the other side. Keep fritters warm until serving time.

353.   Vegetable Fried Rice Recipe

Serving: 6 | Prep: | Cook: 15mins | Ready in:

Ingredients

- vegetable Fried rice
- 1-tbspn sesame oil
- 2-tspn bottled minced garlic
- 2-tspn fresh minced ginger
- 1-cup jarred red peppers, chopped
- 1 green bell pepper, chopped
- 1-onion chopped
- 1 small can sliced mushrooms, drained
- 1-cup baby carrots, sliced lengthwise three times each carrot
- 1 head of bok choy coarsely chopped
- 3=cups cooked brown rice, cooled

- 1 green onion, snipped tops and bottom

Direction

- Cook garlic and ginger in oil for 1 ½-minutes.
- Add mixed vegetables and bok choy and cook for 8 minutes.
- Stir occasionally.
- Add rice and soy sauce and cook and stir for about 5 minutes. Sprinkle with green onions and serve.

354.   Veggie Jack Salad Recipe

Serving: 6 | Prep: | Cook: 60mins |Ready in:

Ingredients

- 2 medium cucumbers(or zucchini) sliced
- 2 medium tomatoes, wedged or cubed(or 1 pint cherry or grape tomatoes)
- 2 green onions, sliced
- 6oz monterey jack cheese, cubed
- 2T dressing quality olive oil
- 2t balsamic vinegar
- dash of sugar
- 1-2T fresh herbs(basil, cilantro,oregano, thyme, chives, parsley, etc(any combination you like)
- salt and pepper

Direction

- Combine veggies and cheese in large bowl and set aside.
- Whisk together oil and vinegar, add sugar, salt and pepper and whisk well.
- Add herbs and mix to "break" herbs and combine.
- Pour dressing over veggies and toss to coat.
- Refrigerate at least 1 hour.

355.   Way Good Pinto Beans With Sausage Recipe

Serving: 8 | Prep: | Cook: 360mins |Ready in:

Ingredients

- 2 pounds dried pinto beans
- 1 tablespoons baking soda
- 1 pounds dark brown sugar
- 8 ounces molasses
- 2 tablespoons prepared mustard
- 1 pound kielbasa sausage sliced
- 1 white onion quartered
- 1 can tomatoes with green chilies
- 2 teaspoons freshly ground black pepper
- 1/4 cup worcestershire sauce

Direction

- Wash beans and soak overnight.
- When ready to cook combine all ingredients in large pot and fill with water.
- Cook in 300 degree oven for 6 hours.

356.   Wild N Wonderful Wine Poached Beets Recipe

Serving: 4 | Prep: | Cook: 45mins |Ready in:

Ingredients

- 3/4 cup dry red wine such as merlot or shiraz, or apple juice
- 1/2 cup water
- 1 Tbsp. packed brown sugar
- 2-1/2 lb. beets, peeled, and cut into bite-size pieces
- salt and ground black pepper
- honey (optional)
- 1 Tbsp. snipped fresh parsley
- lemon wedges (optional)

Direction

- In a large saucepan combine 1/2 cup of the wine, the water, and brown sugar.
- Bring to boiling, stirring to dissolve sugar. Add beets.
- Return to boiling; reduce heat. Simmer, covered, for 45 minutes until beets are tender and can be pierced with a fork, stirring occasionally. Drain.
- Transfer beets to serving bowl. Season to taste with salt and pepper.
- Splash with remaining 1/4 cup wine.
- Drizzle with honey.
- Sprinkle with parsley.
- Serve with lemon wedges.
- You can avoid staining your hands with beet juice if you wear plastic gloves while peeling and cutting the beets. Trim beet tops or leave tops on.
- That's it! Enjoy!

357.   Zucchini Boats With Corn Stuffing Recipe

Serving: 23 | Prep: | Cook: 15mins | Ready in:

Ingredients

- 6 very small zucchini
- 1 ear of fresh corn (boiled 10 minutes, cut the kernels off and coarsely chopped)
- 1/2 red bell pepper diced,
- about 1/2 cup bread crumb
- 6 or more shallots finely sliced
- 1/4 cup ground almond
- salt & pepper to taste
- toasted almond flakes for garnish

Direction

- Heat oil (an inch deep) in a small skillet, fry the shallot slices over high heat until they're slightly firm and brown. Drain and save the oil
- Pre-heat the oven to 350F/180C

- Cut 1/3 of the zucchini from the top, hollow out leaving 1/2 cm-thick shell (boat). Save all the scrap for other cooking
- Brush the boats allover with shallot oil, and sprinkle with salt
- In a mixing bowl, combine spoonfuls of shallot oil, corn kernels, red pepper, ground almond and bread crumb (the latter adjustable according to how wet the content is). Salt and pepper to taste.
- Scoop the stuffing into the boats, place them on tray and bake for about 20 minutes or until the zucchini slight soft and the top golden brown
- Garnish with toasted almond flakes and fried shallot to serve

358.   Zucchini Fritters 1 Recipe

Serving: 6 | Prep: | Cook: 10mins | Ready in:

Ingredients

- 1 lb of zucchini (about 2 medium sized), coarsely grated
- kosher salt
- ground black pepper
- 1 large egg
- 2 scallions, finely chopped
- 1/2 cup all-purpose flour
- 1/2 cup grape seed oil or olive oil
- sour cream or plain yoghurt

Direction

- 1 Salt the zucchini with about 1 teaspoon of salt. Try to remove the excess moisture from the zucchini by either squeezing the liquid out with a potato ricer, or by squeezing with paper towels. (The original recipe calls for putting the zucchini in a colander set in the sink to let it drain for 10 minutes after salting it. I think it works much better to use a potato ricer.)

- 2 Whisk egg in a large bowl; add the zucchini, flour, scallions, and 1/4 teaspoon of pepper. Mix to combine well.
- 3 Heat oil in a large skillet over medium heat. Cook fritters in two batches. Drop six mounds of batter (2 Tbsp. each) into the skillet. Flatten slightly. Cook, turning once, until browned, 4-6 minutes on each side. Transfer to a paper towel-lined plate. Sprinkle with salt. Repeat with remaining batter.
- Serve immediately, with sour cream or plain yoghurt on the side.

---

359.   Zucchini Lace Fritters Recipe

Serving: 8 | Prep: | Cook: 4mins | Ready in:

Ingredients

- 1 egg
- 2 tablespoons milk
- 1/2 cup flour
- 1 teaspoon baking powder
- Tabasco to taste
- salt and freshly ground black pepper to taste
- 2 pounds small green zucchini, coarsely grated, OR can use food processor and make into julienne strips
- 1/2 coarsely grated onion

Direction

- In bowl, lightly beat egg
- Stir in milk, flour, baking powder until mixed well
- Add Tabasco, salt, pepper
- Stir in zucchini and onion
- Let mixture rest for about 15 minutes
- Place 1/4 inch of vegetable oil in a large heavy skillet (iron is best)
- Heat until hot over medium heat
- Drop by teaspoons of batter into oil, without overcrowding

- If making as an appetizer, use teaspoons, if using for a side, make them larger
- Cook until brown on both sides, about 2 minutes per side
- Drain fritters on paper towels
- Repeat until all have been cooked
- Serve warm with pesto, cilantro mayonnaise, or your favorite dipping sauce

---

360.   Zucchini Parmesan Recipe

Serving: 4 | Prep: | Cook: 25mins | Ready in:

Ingredients

- 1/3 cup Italian-style seasoned bread crumbs
- 1 tablespoon grated parmesan cheese
- 2 medium zucchini cut into 3-inch long,1/2-inch thick slices
- 2 egg whites, lightly beaten
- 1 can (18 ounces) crushed tomatoes
- 1 teaspoon dried Italian seasoning
- 1 cup shredded mozzarella cheese

Direction

- Preheat oven to 400.F. Spray a baking sheet with vegetable cooking spray.
- In a small bowl, combine bread crumbs and parmesan. Mix well.
- Dip zucchini in egg whites. Dredge zucchini in some bread crumb mixture, patting so crumbs adhere. Place on prepared baking sheet. Reserve remaining crumb mixture.
- Bake, turning once, until golden, about 15 minutes.
- Meanwhile, spray a 2-quart baking dish with vegetable cooking spray. Combine tomatoes and Italian seasoning in prepared dish. Mix well.
- Arrange baked zucchini over tomatoes. Sprinkle with mozzarella and remaining crumb mixture. Bake until casserole is heated

through and cheese melts, about 10 minutes. Serve immediately.

361. Zucchini Patties Recipe

Serving: 4 | Prep: | Cook: 20mins | Ready in:

Ingredients

- 2 cups grated zucchini, squeezed in towel to get excess liquid out
- 2 eggs, beaten
- 1/4 cup chopped onion
- 1/2 cup all-purpose flour 1/2 cup grated parmesan cheese
- 1/2 cup shredded mozzarella cheese
- 1/2 t. garlic powder
- salt to taste
- 2 tablespoons vegetable oil

Direction

- In a medium bowl, combine the zucchini, eggs, onion, flour, Parmesan cheese, mozzarella cheese, garlic and salt. Stir well enough to distribute ingredients evenly.
- 2. Heat a small amount of oil in a skillet over medium-high heat. Drop zucchini mixture by heaping tablespoonfuls, flatten heap out a little with back of spoon and cook for a few minutes on each side until golden.

362. Zucchini Rice Casserole Recipe

Serving: 1012 | Prep: | Cook: 60mins | Ready in:

Ingredients

- 1 1/2 cups long-grain brown rice
- 3 cups reduced-sodium chicken broth
- 4 cups diced zucchini and/or summer squash (about 1 pound)

- 2 red or green bell peppers, chopped
- 1 large onion, diced
- 3/4 teaspoon salt
- 1 1/2 cups low-fat milk
- 3 tablespoons all-purpose flour
- 2 cups shredded pepper Jack cheese, divided
- 1 cup fresh or frozen (thawed) corn kernels
- 2 teaspoons extra-virgin olive oil
- 8 ounces chicken or turkey sausage, casings removed
- 4 ounces reduced-fat cream cheese (Neufchâtel)
- 1/4 cup chopped pickled jalapeños

Direction

- Preheat oven to 375°F. Pour rice into a 9-by-13-inch baking dish. Bring broth to a simmer in a small saucepan. Stir hot broth into the rice along with zucchini (and/or squash), bell peppers, onion and salt. Cover with foil. Bake for 45 minutes. Remove foil and continue baking until the rice is tender and most of the liquid is absorbed, 35 to 45 minutes more. Meanwhile, whisk milk and flour in a small saucepan. Cook over medium heat until bubbling and thickened, 3 to 4 minutes. Reduce heat to low. Add 1 1/2 cups Jack cheese and corn and cook, stirring, until the cheese is melted. Set aside.
- Heat oil in a large skillet over medium heat and add sausage. Cook, stirring and breaking the sausage into small pieces with a spoon, until lightly browned and no longer pink, about 4 minutes.5. When the rice is done, stir in the sausage and cheese sauce. Sprinkle the remaining 1/2 cup Jack cheese on top and dollop cream cheese by the teaspoonful over the casserole. Top with jalapeños.
- Return the casserole to the oven and bake until the cheese is melted, about 10 minutes. Let stand for about 10 minutes before serving.

363. Zucchni Patties Recipe

Serving: 6 | Prep: | Cook: 2mins | Ready in:

Ingredients

- 2 cups grated zucchini
- 2 eggs, beaten
- 1/4 cup chopped onion
- 1/2 cup all-purpose flour
- 1/2 cup grated parmesan cheese
- salt to taste
- 2 tablespoons olive oil

Direction

- In a medium bowl, combine the zucchini, eggs, onion, flour, parmesan cheese, mozzarella cheese, and salt. Stir well enough to distribute ingredients evenly.
- Heat a small amount of oil in a skillet over medium-high heat. Drop zucchini mixture by heaping tablespoonfuls, and cook for a few minutes on each side until golden.

364. Pan Fried Green Beans Recipe

Serving: 4 | Prep: | Cook: 10mins | Ready in:

Ingredients

- 1 pound fresh greenbeans
- 3tablespoons light soy sauce
- 1 tablespoon balsamic vinegar
- 1 teaspoon white sugar
- 2 tablespoons sesame oil
- 2 teaspoons minced garlic

Direction

- Place beans in pot and bring to boil
- Cover and cook 5 minutes
- In small bowl mix soy sauce, vinegar, and sugar
- Heat oil in skillet

- Add garlic and cook until brown
- Add beans and stir to coat with the oil and garlic
- Stir in soy sauce mixture and simmer for about 2-3 minutes uncovered to reduce the sauce
- Transfer to serving dish
- ENJOY!!!

365. South Of The Border Baked Cous Cous Recipe

Serving: 4 | Prep: | Cook: 30mins | Ready in:

Ingredients

- whole grain cous cous
- salsa of your choice
- mexican cheese grated in package
- onions
- corn
- parsley
- olive oil
- black olives
- after baking add put some sour cream and avocado on the top and this one is good...

Direction

- Make the couscous per package, chop up the onions and add a can of your favorite south of the border salsa. Add some chopped up corn and black olives. Drizzle olive oil over the top before putting in the oven.... Put this in a baking dish and top with grated Mexican cheese and sprinkle with parsley....let this bake in the oven for about 40 minutes medium heat...
- This is a south of the border delight.

Index

A

Almond 4,5,7,35,42,77,137

Anchovies 5,7,74,125

Apple 5,38,74,76,120

Apricot 3,21

Artichoke 5,7,8,58,61,67,118,146,147,150

Asparagus
5,6,7,8,59,60,61,62,63,64,65,66,99,117,118,124,131,138,140,142,148

Avocado 5,6,7,65,67,69,105,110,117,135

B

Bacon
3,4,5,6,7,9,10,11,14,19,21,22,23,27,31,33,35,44,52,66,78,82,87,89,119,120,122

Baking 127

Barley 5,70

Basil 5,6,8,83,105,148

Bay leaf 61

Beans
5,6,7,8,73,74,84,91,95,99,104,119,120,122,123,127,128,132,137,141,142,144,153,157

Beer 3,5,7,21,71,90,115

Brazil nut 69

Bread 3,4,5,15,33,34,67

Broccoli 5,6,76,77,78,90,109

Broth 11

Brussels sprouts
9,10,11,12,13,14,15,16,17,18,19,20,21,22,23,24,25,26,27,28,29,30,31,32,33,34,35,36,37,38,39,40,41,42,43,44,45,46,47,48,49,50,51,52,53,54,55,56,57

Butter
3,5,6,7,22,25,26,27,34,62,65,78,90,99,105,113,117,123,131,138,140,143,150

C

Cabbage
5,6,7,8,71,76,80,81,89,101,104,121,122,123,128,136,138,149

Cake 6,15,96,100

Capers 4,56

Caramel 3,7,24,33,41,124

Carrot
4,5,6,7,8,33,35,58,68,81,82,101,111,115,116,117,125,146

Cauliflower 3,4,5,6,7,12,33,74,82,92,139

Cheddar 3,20,31,91,103,104,135,139

Cheese
3,4,5,6,7,8,22,27,31,34,64,65,76,82,83,87,119,140,150,151

Cherry 5,83

Chestnut 3,14,20

Chicken 11

Chickpea 8,147

Chipotle 3,5,6,7,27,84,85,106,135

Chives 119

Chorizo 3,19

Cider 4,6,35,85,120

Cinnamon 6,85

Cocktail 15

Coleslaw 6,7,8,87,116,118,152

Collar 6,7,86,142,143

Couscous 5,73

Cranberry 3,6,24,87

Cream
3,4,5,6,7,19,22,23,24,25,35,37,40,48,68,76,87,88,89,99,102,103,105,143

Crumble 32,142

Cumin 123

D

Dijon mustard 32,34,35,36,37,39,41,44,48,50,64,103,111

Dill 4,8,38,148

E

Egg 5,6,7,8,67,75,92,93,94,124,140,145,149,150

Elderflower 82

F

Fat 9,102,108,109,141

Fontina cheese 96

French bread 17,92

G

Garlic 3,4,5,6,7,8,18,21,25,39,48,68,74,75,77,99,100,104,117,119, 125,148,151

Gin 6,7,8,101,114,148

Grapes 4,46

Gratin 3,4,5,6,8,16,29,33,34,62,64,99,146,147,150

Guacamole 6,106

H

Heart 6,109

Honey 6,110,111

Horseradish 3,19,22

J

Jus 7,46,90,108,133,137,142

K

Kale 5,6,76,100

L

Lemon 3,4,5,6,7,25,26,42,50,53,60,65,99,115,138

Lettuce 6,105

Lime 4,38

Ling 152

M

Mandarin 3,7,32,116

Marjoram 3,30

Mayonnaise 6,105

Meat 7,119,127,129

Milk 80

Mince 104,112

Miso 4,43

Mushroom 5,6,7,70,72,102,103,118,119,137,138

Mustard 3,4,30,44,120

N

Nut 3,4,5,30,33,36,60,83,109

O

Oil 7,11,94,101,120,124

Okra 7,144

Olive 11,15,120

Onion 3,4,5,6,7,11,24,31,32,33,41,44,50,69,76,78,83,89,92,94,100 ,107,115,119,129

Orange 3,4,5,32,45,72

P

Pancakes 7,119

Pancetta 3,12,19,28,30

Paneer 7,123

Paprika 7,137

Parmesan 4,5,7,8,15,25,34,42,45,60,61,62,63,67,79,81,90,96,99,105,1 21,122,133,135,136,146,155,156

Parsley 15,119

Pasta 4,6,46,99

Pear 3,11,33

Peas 6,88

Pecan 3,22

Pecorino 9,150

Peel 47,53,57,69,71,83,89,93,101,111,127,130,135,140

Pepper 6,8,11,94,104,119,120,136,147,151

Pesto 6,92

Pheasant 15

Pickle 5,7,82,129

Pie 111,119

Pistachio 3,21

Port 6,87,103

Potato 3,4,5,7,11,40,47,69,120,123,136,141

Pumpkin 6,7,109,124

Q

Quinoa 6,90,114

R

Ratatouille 7,126,127,130

Red lentil 129

Rice 5,7,8,73,76,127,128,152,156

Risotto 5,61

Rosemary 3,19

S

Salad 3,5,6,7,8,9,73,78,103,109,114,116,118,132,135,153

Salsa 5,65

Salt 11,22,24,35,40,44,49,65,70,105,119,120,138,140,154

Sausage 8,153

Savory 7,138,139

Scallop 4,7,8,51,139,140,144

Seasoning 7,86,138

Shallot 3,4,7,15,16,33,56,133

Sherry 3,23

Soup 6,102,103,109

Spices 119

Spinach 5,8,57,68,81,146,147,151

Squash 6,8,110,145,147,148

Stew 6,88

Stuffing 8,125,154

Sugar 9,108,120

Syrup 5,72

T

Tabasco 86,128,155

Tea 119,120,141

Thyme 7,11,120,138

Tomato
3,5,6,7,8,20,67,69,78,83,88,89,102,104,109,133,140,144,152

Truffle 7,124

V

Vegan 7,114

Vegetables 5,6,7,70,90,108,127,133,134,135

Vegetarian 7,127,129

Vinegar 3,5,11,24,29,70,120

W

Walnut 3,4,6,22,28,31,32,49,85

Waxy potato 134

Wine 5,8,72,74,153

Worcestershire sauce 39,79,113,152

Z

Zest 4,50,114

Conclusion

Thank you again for downloading this book!

I hope you enjoyed reading about my book!

If you enjoyed this book, please take the time to share your thoughts and post a review on Amazon. It'd be greatly appreciated!

Write me an honest review about the book – I truly value your opinion and thoughts and I will incorporate them into my next book, which is already underway.

Thank you!

If you have any questions, **feel free to contact at:** _author@limerecipes.com_

Nina Petty

limerecipes.com

Printed in Great Britain
by Amazon